The Ethics of
Accounting and Finance

The Ethics of Accounting and Finance

Trust, Responsibility, and Control

Edited by W. Michael Hoffman,
Judith Brown Kamm, Robert E. Frederick,
and Edward S. Petry

From the Tenth National Conference on Business Ethics
Sponsored by the Center for Business Ethics at Bentley College

QUORUM BOOKS
Westport, Connecticut • London

Library of Congress Cataloging-in-Publication Data

National Conference on Business Ethics (10th : 1994 : Bentley College)
    The ethics of accounting and finance : trust, responsibility, and
control / edited by W. Michael Hoffman . . . [et al.].
        p.   cm.
    Held Oct. 17 and 18, 1994.
    "From the Tenth National Conference on Business Ethics sponsored
by the Center for Business Ethics at Bentley College."
    "This volume contains the best of the conference papers"—Introd.
    Includes bibliographical references and index.
    ISBN 0-89930-997-6 (alk. paper)
    1. Business ethics—Congresses.   2. Accounting—Moral and ethical
aspects—Congresses.   3. Finance—Moral and ethical aspects—
Congresses.   I. Hoffman, W. Michael.   II. Title.
HF5387.N37   1996
174'.4—dc20   95-50746

British Library Cataloguing in Publication Data is available.

Library of Congress Catalog Card Number: 95-50746
ISBN: 0-89930-997-6

First published in 1996

Quorum Books, 88 Post Road West, Westport, CT 06881
An imprint of Greenwood Publishing Group, Inc.

Printed in the United States of America

The paper used in this book complies with the
Permanent Paper Standard issued by the National
Information Standards Organization (Z39.48–1984).

10 9 8 7 6 5 4 3 2

3 2280 00760 0059

Contents

Figures and Tables

Acknowledgments

"Trust, Responsibility, and Control: The Ethics of Accounting and Finance," the Tenth National Conference on Business Ethics, was hosted with the assistance of the Bentley College Department of Accountancy. The conference was supported in part by generous donations from the Bath Iron Works Company and the Dun & Bradstreet Corporation. Conferences and other activities of the Center for Business Ethics are also supported by grants from the following: Arvin Industries, Stephen Baker, Harold P. Brown, Robert W. Brown, M.D., Champion International, Chase Manhattan Foundation, Bruce Coles, The Council for Philosophical Studies (sponsored by the National Endowment for the Humanities), Keith Darcy, Dawn-Marie Driscoll, Exxon Education Foundation, The General Electric Corporation, The General Mills Foundation, The General Motors Corporation, Goodyear Tire and Rubber Company, Liberty Mutual Group, Midland-Ross, Inc., Monsanto Company, The Motorola Foundation, Robert K. Mueller, Norton Company, NYNEX Corporation, Northrop-Grumman Corporation, Polaroid Corporation, Primerica Corporation, The Raytheon Charitable Foundation, Raytheon Company, Rexnord, Inc., Richardson-Merrill, Inc., The Rockefeller Foundation, Semline, Inc., Mark Skaletsky, Stone & Webster, Inc., Stop and Shop Manufacturing Companies, The Whitehead Foundation, and F. W. Woolworth and Company. On behalf of the Center, we wish to thank these contributors and all of the participants of the Tenth Conference for sharing their support and ideas with us. We also wish to thank Kerrin Carter, Peter Doherty, Vickie Iwasa, Kimberly Smith, Katherine Sullivan, and especially Sheryl Morrissette for all their help with the conference and this book. As always, Mary Chiasson, the

Administrative Coordinator for the Center for Business Ethics, deserves special recognition for her outstanding efforts in support of the many activities of the Center.

Introduction

Robert E. Frederick and Judith Brown Kamm

"Trust, Responsibility, and Control: The Ethics of Accounting and Finance," the Tenth National Conference on Business Ethics, was held on the campus of Bentley College on October 17–18, 1994. The conference, which was sponsored by the Center for Business Ethics with the advice and assistance of members of the Bentley Department of Accountancy, covered a variety of issues that are of central importance for contemporary businesses. These included fiduciary responsibility and conflicts of interest in the financial services industry; ethical issues in financial reporting; the ethical implications of new financial instruments, such as derivatives; and the expanding ethical role of auditors and audit committees.

This volume contains the best of the conference papers, organized as chapters, submitted on these and related topics. The volume is divided into four parts. To assist the reader in exploring the chapters in more depth, in the remainder of this introduction each of the chapters will be briefly discussed, and common themes running through them will be identified.

Part I, "Ethics, Fiduciary Responsibilities, and Conflicts of Interest," examines the ethics of the fiduciary relationship between principals and agents. Chapter 1, Richard N. Ottaway's "Defining Trust in Fiduciary Responsibilities," characterizes fiduciary relationships as founded on trust. A fiduciary is an agent who acts on behalf of a principal, and who has specific duties to the principal. These include: skillful and diligent performance of contracted services; prompt communication of all relevant information; loyal commitment to act solely on behalf of the principal; obedience to the principal's instructions; and a complete and accurate account of all funds. In addition, the principal has duties to the agent: compensation for services;

reimbursement for expenses and indemnification of liability; cooperation with the agent; and safe working conditions.

Ottaway notes that the strength of the duties between agents and principals varies according to both the specifics of the contract and the nature of the services contracted. He also points out that in recent years the concept of a fiduciary relationship has been applied outside its traditional boundaries. For example, the relationships between doctors and patients, social workers and clients, and clergy and church members have all been seen as fiduciary relationships. This attempt to expand the application of fiduciary relationships, he suspects, will continue in the future, perhaps even extending to the relationship between individuals and the communities in which they live and work.

Chapter 2 is Elaine Sternberg's "In Defense of Finance: Understanding Fiduciary Responsibility and Conflicts of Interest." Sternberg argues that consumers often misunderstand or incompletely understand the nature of financial markets and services. Thus, in certain situations (e.g., when they suffer losses), they may believe that there has been a breach of fiduciary duty when none has in fact occurred. A fiduciary relationship arises, Sternberg says, when a client entrusts assets to an adviser. In the absence of specific instructions, the adviser is duty bound to act on behalf of the client as a reasonable person would, were he or she to have the adviser's financial expertise. Assuming the adviser is competent, as long as he or she acts with the client's best interests in mind there is no breach of fiduciary duty, even when the outcome is disappointing. Incompetence or failure to act in the client's best interests are failures of duty, but financial losses need not be. In addition, Sternberg points out that when an agent has no discretion to act, there can be no fiduciary responsibility other than accurately carrying out the principal's instructions. For example, if, against all advice, a client instructs a broker to buy a stock that subsequently falls in value, there is no breach of duty.

Another result of misunderstanding finance and fiduciary responsibility, Sternberg continues, is that financial conflicts of interest are commonly thought to be more frequent and serious than they actually are. Many of these alleged conflicts arise not because of some special moral failing on the part of the adviser, but because of the presumed financial incompetence of the customer. Since the customer is thought to be incapable of protecting his or her own interests, unnecessarily restrictive rules are promulgated. But the real issue, Sternberg argues, is the fiduciary relationship between client and adviser. If business success is measured, as it should be, by long-term owner value, then there is no conflict between the interests of the client and adviser. The client's success is a precondition for the success of the adviser. Consequently, their interests are complementary rather than conflicting.

In Chapter 3, "Should Mutual Fund Managers Be Banned from Personal Trading?", Ronald F. Duska investigates the potential conflict of interest that arises when mutual fund managers trade for their own account. Duska analyzes in detail portions of a report issued by the mutual fund industry's Advisory Group on Personal Investing. The report, which was presented to the Securities and Exchange Commission (SEC) in May 1994, recommended a number of rules intended to prevent possible conflicts of interest. However, personal investing was not banned, although the authors of the report noted that personal investing "merits special discussion."

Duska contends that the report's discussion of reasons for banning personal investing consists largely of a series of straw man arguments; that is, arguments that are easily refuted. For example, one argument considered in the report is that personal investing should be banned so that portfolio managers can devote more time to managing fund assets. But this argument, which Duska describes as "silly," makes the completely unwarranted assumption that it is not possible to both manage a fund competently and have private interests. Thus, it is not surprising that the authors of the report do not find it compelling.

Another problem with the report, Duska says, is that it creates false dichotomies. For instance, the report concludes that a complete ban on personal trading would be unwise. But it does not discuss partial bans, such as prohibiting trading on certain specific types of financial instruments.

After considering arguments for a complete ban on personal trading, the advisory group report goes on to develop a positive defense of personal trading. Duska finds these arguments (e.g., that banning personal investing would create a talent drain) no more persuasive than the previous ones. He concludes that the report did not scrutinize the arguments for and against personal trading thoroughly enough, and thereby missed an opportunity to examine genuinely substantive issues and prevent possible future problems in the industry.

Chapter 4, "Fiduciary Responsibility and the Duty to Account for Clients' Funds," by Franklyn P. Salimbene and Gerald R. Ferrera, probes the legal and ethical implications of fiduciary relations from the perspective of accounting as it applies to the duties of an attorney handling money for a client. They argue that ethical requirements imposed by the bar on an attorney's handling of a client's funds can provide useful insights for all professionals charged with managing other people's money. For example, attorneys are required to maintain separate accounts of a client's funds, and avoid commingling of funds. They are also required to provide a complete and accurate accounting of the funds. Unfortunately, as Salimbene and Ferrera demonstrate, these apparently commonsense rules are violated more often than might be expected. As one might anticipate, the consequences are seldom favorable for either client or attorney.

At the conclusion of Chapter 4, the authors note that over the last few decades the public has become much more aware of illegal and unethical behavior on the part of legal and financial representatives. Since the public's fear and wariness are not likely to be assuaged by the argument that "most fiduciaries are honest," Salimbene and Ferrera recommend continuing education in ethics for professionals involved in managing money. It is not enough, they argue, to cite codes of professional responsibility if practitioners are not convinced they are relevant. The challenge to the profession is to make fiduciary responsibility consonant with its roots in ethical theory and moral behavior, and thus with the tradition of the competent and caring professional.

Chapter 5 is Patricia H. Werhane's "Some Ethical Issues in Financial Markets." Werhane argues that ethical dilemmas in finance often arise because of a "narrow perception of what is at issue, or because one has failed to see clearly how one's model or point of view concerning financial markets may be incomplete, narrow, or even erroneous." She uses two illustrations to support her argument. The first is activism by institutional investors, and the second is municipal bond trading. In both cases, she maintains, more inclusive moral frameworks better serve to resolve ethical dilemmas that sometimes arise.

For example, it was once common for investment bankers to make political contributions in return for or in expectation of underwriting fees for municipal bonds. Although this quid pro quo arrangement is not illegal, there is an obvious potential for favoritism on the part of politicians. One firm rather than another might get the contract, not because it offers the best terms, but because it makes the largest political donations. Clearly, this can be costly to taxpayers, who do not necessarily get the best price for underwriting fees. Furthermore, from the underwriter's perspective, the contributions are not always voluntary. Underwriters are "held hostage" to the system, and forced to participate in payoff schemes regardless of whether they approve of them or not. Once political contributions are made the precedent is set, and individual underwriting firms go against the precedent at their peril.

To break out of this cycle of corruption, Werhane argues, one must expand one's moral horizons and get another perspective on the problem. This provides a new model for understanding and dealing with the problem. And in October 1993, a number of Wall Street firms managed to do just this. They began a voluntary ban on campaign contributions and announced guidelines for putting the ban into effect. This move, Werhane says, took creativity and imagination. It required fresh thinking and a willingness to take risks. However, it is only through exercising such moral imagination and leadership that systematic moral problems can be dealt with effectively, and perhaps even eliminated.

Part II, "Ethics and Financial Disclosure," contains three chapters that address the ethics of presenting financial information. Accountants and financial service providers often face a dilemma that requires ethical reasoning to resolve: disclosure versus maintaining confidentiality. On one hand, investors and taxpayers need sufficient amounts of accurate information to protect their financial interests and to make good decisions. On the other hand, organizations (businesses, hospitals, schools) and individuals need confidentiality in order to protect themselves from competitors and from invasion of their privacy.

Chapter 6, "Ethical Issues in Financial Reporting for Nonprofit Healthcare Organizations," by Nancy M. Kane, addresses this dilemma from the viewpoint of the need for disclosure. Research funding agencies, donors, and the community have a right to accurate data about nonprofit hospitals' revenues, appropriate use of resources and, in the case of public hospitals, availability of resources for their communities, whose taxpayers' dollars support them. Financial statements should provide such data, Kane argues, but often do not because there is no equivalent to the SEC or other regulatory body overseeing this sector. Her chapter concludes with a call for federal legislation requiring hospitals to make publicly available timely, audited financial statements in a central location in each state. She also recommends the formation of visible, accounting-literate hospital watchdog groups representing the public interest at the state or municipal level.

Chapter 7, "The Ethical Implications of Financial Derivatives," by David Mosso, focuses on accountants' roles in the financial reporting of derivatives, another of the financial instruments innovations, such as junk bonds, to raise ethical problems. The author assumes that derivatives themselves are ethically neutral, but the way they are accounted for by the acquirer and the acquirer's purpose in buying derivatives do have ethical implications. The paper lists the purposes derivatives can serve from the least to the most potentially harmful to investors, and discusses the difficulties of accounting for them that need to be addressed before they can appear in financial statements. According to the Financial Standards Accounting Board (FASB), the "ethical imperative for financial reporting of derivatives is the fair presentation of neutral information for economic decision-making." FASB, therefore, issued Statement 119 in October 1994 requiring more footnote information to help gauge the risks of derivatives, as well as that they be recorded at current market value on balance sheets. Mosso concludes, however, that FASB has an ongoing problem: Its standards lag behind the introduction of new instruments created by financial engineers. He implies that despite regulations and standards, *caveat emptor* is still the way of the financial marketplace.

Chapter 8, "Confidentiality in a Professional Context with Especial Reference to the Accounting Profession in Australia," by P. B. Jubb, represents the other side of the ethical dilemma: the need to withhold information. The author's thesis is that in the public accounting context, the normal relationship of trust and disclosure between an informer and a confidant does not hold, despite a code of confidentiality maintained in the accounting profession. In interpersonal, nonprofessional relationships, one person trusts another to keep disclosed information confidential, and therefore voluntarily discloses it. The confidant receiving the information trusts that the information is accurate and not being disclosed to manipulate or harm the confidant. Jubb's chapter explores the reasons why this trust does not, and in some instances legally *cannot* exist, in public accounting, thereby making it unreasonable to expect professionals to maintain confidentiality. His conclusion is that the accounting profession must stress the primacy of independence over confidentiality as a value for its members to uphold.

Part III, "Trust, Responsibility, and Control: Cases and Analyses," contains six chapters about such disparate organizations as Bank of Credit and Commerce International (BCCI), Praise the Lord (PTL), the Dutch accounting profession, and the U.S. defense industry. Chapter 9, "Accounting for Fraud: Auditors' Ethical Dilemmas in the BCCI Affair," continues to explore the ethical ramifications when public accountants maintain confidentiality. In this chapter, Nikos Passas attempts to answer the same question Third World investor and depositor victims and government regulators asked. That is, how was it possible for fraud of the magnitude perpetrated by BCCI's top management to continue undetected for more than ten years?

The first answer provided by the author is that there was a professional concern to preserve client confidentiality. Other explanations presented in Passas's analysis include: incomplete audit responsibility (Ernst and Whinney shared it with Price Waterhouse); the perception that the problems detected were solving themselves; discrepancies among different nations' accounting standards; the auditors were duped; the government of Abu Dhabi assured the auditors that BCCI's problems were being taken care of; and fear that writing a "qualified" audit would cause a run on the bank. Among the author's recommendations is that

External auditors should look for fraud with the help of internal auditors and should not be prevented by confidentiality requirements from reporting fraud to the authorities. This responsibility has remained outside the scope of the auditors chiefly because of the profession's wishes. Public pressure and demand by clients of accounting firms could make it an explicit objective of the audit function.

Chapter 10, "Was Maintaining the Executive Payroll at PTL an Example of Auditor Independence?", by Gary L. Tidwell, also examines the ethics of auditing, but focuses on independence rather than on confidentiality. PTL was a religious organization created and led by Jim Bakker. The author suggests that having responsibility for PTL's executive payroll compromised both Deloitte Haskins and Sells's and Levanthol and Horwath's ability to "avoid a situation that may lead outsiders to doubt their independence." First, the concept of independence is defined and its importance is explicated. A thumbnail sketch of PTL and its problems follows. The auditor companies prepared payroll, some bonus, and other types of compensation checks to more than twenty PTL executives as directed by PTL top management. The auditors did not determine the amount of or sign the checks, and hence believed they maintained professional independence as required.

Tidwell concludes that because the auditors never questioned the *entire* Board of Directors about the inordinate sums of money expended on payroll given what the auditors knew to be PTL's precarious financial condition, they gave the appearance of not being independent from management. The board contended it did not know the actual size of the payroll checks, implying that it was duped by Bakker. The author implies that had the auditors been more proactive and less mechanical in their administration of the payroll, PTL would not have gone bankrupt and victimized as many contributors as it did.

Dutch public accountants are now required by their own internal standards to be more proactive than their counterparts in other countries, according to Chapter 11. In "From Monitor to Master? Ethical Comments on the Regulation of Fraud Notification by Accountants," H. J. L. van Luijk analyzes Dutch accountants' 1994 decision to tighten their self-regulation. They are now required to notify government authorities about clients' fraud, thereby breaching their confidentiality standard under certain conditions. After describing the new regulation, which was in direct response to a government-initiated move to impose such a law, the author presents the arguments for and against it. He then elaborates on three ethical considerations that he later applies to the arguments in order to make judgments about their moral value: whistle-blowing; confidentiality and trust; and civil virtues.

Van Luijk first critiques the most common argument against notification. It is that it endangers confidentiality and hence trust in the accountant-client relationship. He contends that "first and foremost professional confidentiality and trust do not apply without restriction . . . a legal obligation and harm to third parties . . . expressed as a monetary value." He refers to tax fraud as such harm because "it curtails the political and social policy space of the government." He also attacks the argument against requiring accountants to de facto act as government investigators. He argues that the government should fight crime itself, not require that accountants do it for no compensation by turning in their clients, who do compensate them. As part of his argument, he refers to a previous discussion of civic virtue: "criminality and unlawful behavior are too important to leave their definition and prevention purely to the government; society must take up such matters." Thus, he concludes that there is moral quality in the new regulation, Directive 3.03, saying "as monitors of social traffic, accountants are preeminently active in a position which embodies our joint concern for a sound, reliable financial sector."

Shifting from public to managerial accounting, the audit function in the defense industry is the subject of Chapter 12, "Unique Ethics Challenges in

Defense Industry Auditing," by Harry W. Britt. An internal auditor for Bath Iron Works, he describes how his industry responded to its primary stakeholder's demand for more ethical conduct. That primary stakeholder is the U.S. government, especially the Department of Defense (DOD). The federal government taken as a whole has a complex relationship with any firm that sells defense products to it. Not only is it a customer, but it may also be a vendor, and it is also a regulator over any number of company operations. Furthermore, the federal government is even more powerful in relationships with firms like Bath Iron Works, whose business is entirely defense-related.

Britt cites some of the defense contractors' unethical practices, then describes the Packard Commission that was appointed in 1985 by President Ronald Reagan. The commission's report called for "significant improvements in contractor self-governance," and specified requirements for such self-policing. In 1986, eighteen defense contractors drew up the Defense Industry Initiative (DII) on Business Ethics and Conduct. A company that becomes a DII signatory pledges to implement certain policies, procedures, and programs, which the author briefly describes. As of 1994, almost half of the firms winning federal defense contracts were DII signatories.

In DII firms the role of internal auditor is expanded in two main ways: investigating allegations of wrongdoing reported on hotlines and auditing the ethics office and operations on a regular basis. Britt elaborates on these functions and identifies one other unique responsibility: sitting on the audit committee that oversees the ethics program. He notes that never before has the internal audit function had such a strategically vital part to play in a company's success. If the DOD finds a contractor guilty of violations it can suspend or debar it from contracting with the government. Given some firms' dependence on this one customer, such an event could have severe financial implications, including bankruptcy.

The chapter concludes by observing that the 1991 Federal Sentencing Guidelines for all organizations share many similar requirements to the ones self-imposed by defense contractors in 1986, including an active internal audit function. Thus, it is likely that, regardless of their industry, corporate auditors will find themselves increasingly involved with issues in business ethics.

Chapter 13 follows logically from the preceding one because it elaborates on the history of audit committees. "The Critical Oversight Role of the Audit Committee," by Curtis C. Verschoor, begins with a brief definition and statement of why boards of directors' audit committees are essential for insuring ethical corporate conduct. The chapter carefully cites the major governmental and self-regulatory professional organizations, such as the Securities and Exchange Commission, the New York Stock Exchange (NYSE), and the American Institute of Certified Public Accountants (AICPA), that were instrumental in bringing about the audit committees that large corporations have today. The final report of the Treadway Commission on Fraudulent Financial Reporting is also summarized as a mile-stone event, as is the Packard Commission's.

The chapter also presents an overview of the extent to which and how corporations have responded to external demands for audit committees on their boards. Results from studies conducted in 1988 and 1989 are sum-marized. And in a later section of the chapter, Verschoor presents his own research findings on the functions that audit committees typically perform. The notes should therefore be useful to practitioners and academics wanting to know what U.S. corporations are doing about audit committees. Despite all the pressure for corporations to have audit committees, however, the only state to require them is Connecticut. And the only federal-level law requiring audit committees is found in the 1991 FDIC Improvement Act that followed the savings and loan crisis of the 1980s. This Act is described in useful detail in the paper.

How audit committee members' legal responsibilities are to be deter-mined and evaluated is evolving in the courts. Verschoor predicts these duties will be similar to those of other members of boards, but more ex-tensive, and he summarizes them. He notes, however, that the legal profes-sion is reassessing corporate governance structures in general and is recommending changes that would further insure that all large, publicly held corporations have audit committees. The audit committees' responsi-bilities would include insuring the independence of external auditors, in part by serving as the communication conduit to corporate management. Thus, public accounting firms' methods of relating to their clients may be affected in the future. The author concludes that "audit committee members must be selected with great care and provided the information and support they need to accomplish their very important functions."

Chapter 14, "Why Banks Fail," by Mark Cheffers, returns to ethics prob-lems in the case of the banking industry. However, the focus is on the U.S. savings and loan industry. The author analyzes the situation that resulted in the FDIC Improvement Act of 1991 described in the previous chapter. He argues against most of the reasons analysts have cited to explain the savings and loan failures of the 1980s and 1990s that resulted in the di-version of taxpayer dollars into cleaning up the mess left behind. He cites and shows the weaknesses in many commonly stated factors. He then ar-gues that bank managers' lack of ethics was the root cause of what hap-pened, and that even the existence of internal control systems to identify and curb unethical behavior did not prevent the disasters.

Based upon his personal experience as an investigator of several bank failures, the author presents and defends an alternative list of what caused their demise. The list includes tardiness of external controls being applied; profit motives dominating external auditors' desire to uphold professional standards of independence from management; audit committees' overly close relationships with management; and bank management culture that condones manipulating internal controls for management's advantage. The weaknesses of internal controls are then explored.

Cheffers elaborates on the concept of internal control, dividing it into three types: organizational behavior, attitude, and accountability. Attitudinal controls pertain to hiring, training, and developing a climate that values ethical behavior and compliance with controls and the standards and laws these controls protect. He asserts that attitudinal controls can be the most effective in preventing a recurrence of banking failure because they most directly pertain to individual bank managers, who, he believes, are most to blame when banks fail. In particular, he points to individual managers' lack of competence and/or honesty as root causes. Because so many key decisions are made by a small group of managers in banks, if they choose to ignore internal and external controls, disasters will happen.

Thus, increasing control mechanisms is not the way to prevent recurring bank failures, the author concludes. Instead, he recommends that "an objective, comprehensive and effective program of certification and ethics training" should be required of all key bank officers. In Cheffers's view, a key bank officer is accountable to society as "a fiduciary of the public trust." Furthermore, lending and investing should be viewed as highly skilled professions and should be conducted and regulated as such. Therefore, members of the banking industry should create the same types of codes of ethics and certification programs that the legal, accounting, medical, and education professions use.

Part IV, "Lessons from the Past and a Look toward the Future," comprises four chapters that examine a diversity of topics. Chapter 15, Jay C. Lacke's "The Ethics of Financial Derivatives in the History of Economic Thought," shows that contemporary concerns about the danger of financial derivatives is not new, but is firmly rooted in discussions of financial speculation that go all the way back to Aristotle. The basic argument is between those who, like Adam Smith, believe that the production of physical commodities is the ultimate source of social wealth, and those who allow that financial services, and even financial speculation, are not necessarily economic drains. For example, Alfred Marshall regarded some forms of financial speculation as no more than gambling. However, he also argued that there are beneficial forms of speculation which tend to dampen price fluctuations and thus mitigate uncertainty associated with the inherent variability of the economy as a whole. Moreover, when used astutely, speculation can be a useful hedge against unanticipated changes in the prices producers must pay for materials. Thus, under certain conditions speculation provides benefits for both consumers and producers. Still, Marshall was quite aware that excesses and exploitation could occur. However, he believed that the competitive nature of markets, and not ill-conceived efforts to regulate it, would prove the most effective method of control.

Lacke concludes that the history of economic thought provides little support for those who believe that regulation is the best way to manage financial derivatives. The best protection for the public, he argues, is full disclosure of all relevant information combined with the recognition by financial managers that they have ethical duties not only to their principals, but to the public at large. Financial markets cannot operate without trust, and financial managers bear a major portion of the burden of creating and maintaining that trust.

Chapter 16 is "Accounting Ethics and the Traditional Jewish Perspective," by Rabbi Gordon M. Cohn. As Patricia H. Werhane advocates in Chapter 5 of this book, Rabbi Cohn proposes a framework for analyzing ethical issues that arise in the accounting profession from a perspective that may not be familiar to many practitioners. He uses Talmudic sources and legal analysis to discuss the ethical implications of accounting changes that artificially inflate earnings, thus leading to an increased stock price.

Cohn uses the Talmudic concept of overcharging as his basic analytic tool. Overcharging is a form of stealing since it extracts an unfair price; in this case, an unfair price for the stock in question. The examination probes four independent issues: corporate versus individual responsibility; indirect damages; the concept of a fair market price for stock; and whether a purchaser of the stock suffers financial harm. Each of these issues, Cohn argues, uncovers reasons for leniency; that is, reasons that protect one from the claim that one has overcharged by reporting inflated earnings that cause an increase in the stock price. The reasons for leniency include, for example, the lack of a standard market price for a share of stock and the problem of proving that investors are actually damaged. Cohn concludes by suggesting that the kind of Talmudic analysis he uses can be applied to a variety of business problems, and can be usefully compared to the analysis of theorists who use other secular and religious viewpoints. Such a comparison would no doubt be illuminating, and might well be one way to begin to discover and energize the kind of moral imagination Werhane believes businesspersons will need in the tumultuous years to come.

Chapter 17, "The Development of Moral Reasoning and Professional Judgment of Auditors in Public Practice," is an empirical study by Daniel Brugman and Marcelle E. W. Weisfelt. Using Kohlberg's theory of moral reasoning competence as a framework for analysis, the authors administered the Defining Issues Test (DIT) and the Defining Issues Test for Auditors (DITA) to 121 auditors in public practice in the Netherlands. Their aim was to investigate two questions: (1) Is moral reasoning as applied in hypothetical moral dilemmas related to moral reasoning applied in professional dilemmas among auditors?; (2) which personal, situational, and demographic characteristics influence professional moral reasoning?

One finding of the study was that there is a "gap" between principled moral reasoning as measured by the DIT and moral performance as measured by the DITA. The average score on the DIT was 36.5 (range of possible scores, 0–95), while the average score for the DITA was 22.2. Another finding was that auditors that worked for larger firms had lower average scores on the DITA. These scores, which, the authors point out, are rather lower than one might expect given the level of education of those taking the tests, bring up three questions that the authors discuss in some detail. They are: (1) How can we explain "backsliding" (the gap between DIT and DITA scores) within a theory about stage-by-stage development of moral reasoning?; (2) what are the consequences of relatively large backsliding in principled moral reasoning with regard to the confidence society places in the auditing profession?; (3) would an educational program to stimulate moral reasoning be the most effective method for decreasing this gap?

Concerning the last question, the authors recommend that education in ethics should not only be undertaken during auditors' college years, but should be an integral part of continuing professional education for auditors. In addition, they recommend that education aimed at developing moral reasoning should emphasize the use of cases based on professional moral dilemmas rather than general moral problems. Only in this way, they argue, can auditors gain the experience necessary to make moral judgments at the higher stages described in Kohlberg's theory.

Chapter 18 is Christopher S. Eklund's "Trust Is Good Business." Drawing on his years of experience in the financial services industry, Eklund argues that maximizing client welfare is the most reliable long-term source of profits on Wall Street. His argument is divided into three parts. In the first part, he maintains that it is a myth that cheating and self-dealing are the best source of profit. Instead, firms that help their customers achieve or surpass their financial goals are far more successful in the long term. He notes that for a financial firm, the trust of customers is an invaluable asset that only comes after customers have many positive experiences with both product and personnel. And trust can only be developed, he says, by focusing on serving customers rather than more traditional measures of performance, such as return on assets or stock price.

The second part of his argument is that customer-oriented firms are best governed by "principles," that is, broad guidelines for behavior, rather than detailed and inflexible rules. For example, in 1993, Merrill Lynch articulated five principles of business conduct. The first two are: (1) Client focus—our clients come first. They are the driving force behind everything we do; (2) respect for the individual—we believe in treating everyone with dignity, whether an employee, shareholder, client, or member of the general public.

The final part is that firms should recognize and address the problem of potential conflicts of interest. Eklund identifies several areas in which conflicts of interest may occur. These include illegal conflicts such as buying or selling stocks before executing customer orders, structural conflicts such as investment banks engaging in merchant banking, and compensation-related conflicts such as inadvertently encouraging churning by using commissions to compensate brokers. Eklund concedes that such conflicts raise difficult issues, but claims that in each case the first and most important step in resolving them is to insure that the firm is oriented primarily toward the financial success of its clients. This does not, of course, protect against all misdeeds, but it does go a long way toward protecting the firm and its clients against the sorts of problems and scandals that have been so evident in recent years.

I

Ethics, Fiduciary Responsibilities, and Conflicts of Interest

1

Defining Trust in Fiduciary Responsibilities

Richard N. Ottaway

INTRODUCTION

The purpose of this chapter is to lay some parameters around the definition and concept of trust in fiduciary roles.

DEFINITIONS

In some ways, there is no role in fiduciary relationships other than trust. At the most basic level, fiduciary is both an adjective and a noun deriving its meaning from the Latin *fiducia*, based on or related to faith or trust. One can use the word to describe "fiduciary responsibility" or to name persons or actions: "the fiduciary changed the account."

Clarkson, Miller, and Jentz (1986) say that fiduciary relationship is "a duty to act for someone else's benefit, coupled with a relationship of trust." They base their definition on agency law:

The Reinstatement, Second, Agency, defines *agency* as "the fiduciary relation which results from the manifestation of consent by one person to another that the other shall act in his behalf and subject to his control, and consent by the other so to act." In general, the law of agency is based on the maxim that "one acting by another is acting for himself." (p. 553)

The most common form of agency is the corporate officer. Corporate officers are agents for principals who are the owners of the enterprise. They can bind the principals in contract, incumber the principals' assets, and carry out their business aims and objectives. Without agency law, there

would be no business as we know it. Owners of business enterprises enhance their assets and carry out their missions in the world through their
agents.

Clarkson, Miller, and Jentz (1986: 559–562) describe five duties the
agent owes the principal: performance, notification, loyalty, obedience, and
accounting. Performance is the requirement of the agent to deliver the contracted services with the purported skills and diligence. Notification basically means that the agent cannot keep any information from the principal
which bears on the contract. This is often expressed as "all the agent knows,
the principal knows."

Whereas each duty is a vast field of ethical actions, loyalty is the most
discussed. Loyalty dictates that the agent act in the sole interest of the
principal, not in the interest of the agent nor a third party. This precludes
the agent from selling personal assets to the principal as well as buying
assets from the principal. This gets very sticky in terms of working for
competitors when one is an agent for several principals. As discussed later,
there are shades of loyalty such as the difference between a trustee and an
investor in stocks sold on an exchange.

Obedience requires an unbroken line of support of the interest of the
principal. This is often required by law and further intensified by institutional codes of behavior. Conflict often arises as a result of the agent's
obedience to both the principal and the good of society, when the agent
thinks the principal's actions are not in the best interest of society. This is
the basis of whistle-blowing activities and laws.

Accounting of funds is critical. Agents must keep accurate records and
make them available to the principal. This includes gifts received by the
agent for work done for the principal and appreciated by a third party.

Clarkson, Miller, and Jentz (1986: 562) also describe four duties of principals to the agents: compensation, reimbursement and indemnification, cooperation, and safe working conditions. The principal's duty is to pay the
agent the agreed value (or customary value, if not articulated) for services
in a timely manner. The principal also has a duty to reimburse the agent
for any expenses incurred in performing the services. The principal in an
agency contract also assumes the agent's losses from liability. This would
constitute a main difference between agency contracts and contractor agreements, where the contractor assumes liability.

The principal has a duty to cooperate with the agent. The principal can
do nothing to prevent agent performance by way of withholding assets or
information. The principal has a duty to provide safe working conditions.
This is seen most often in the work sites of subagents or the employees of
the corporations, which have been created by owners to carry out their
wishes.

All of these duties are most clearly seen in the simple agency contract of
one principal hiring one agent to carry out simple actions such as being the

sole representative of an investor in a foreign port. It becomes less clear and more open to ethical and legal discussions when many principals form a corporation, elect directors, and empower them to hire officers to act on their behalf. Most principals (stockholders) in modern American corporations are actually other corporations, such as pension funds. This diffusion of definition can be clarified by discussing the degrees of fiduciary duty required of various fiduciaries.

DEGREES OF DUTY

Some think that the presence of fiduciary trust is sought in too many settings. McLennan (1993: 40) quotes the Canadian Justice Southin as saying:

The word "fiduciary" is flung around now as if it applied to all breaches of duty by solicitors, directors of companies and so forth. But "fiduciary" comes from the Latin "fiducia" meaning "trust." Thus, the adjective fiduciary means of or pertaining to a trustee or trusteeship.

Not many would agree with the Justice. He does restrict the term to the most duty-bound form of fiduciary action. The trustee is bound by law and custom to act solely in the interest of the principal. The signature of a trustee is the "strict ban on self-interest transactions," the foregoing of clearly present economic or social opportunity for the benefit of agent, which is often called the "prudent man" standard. (Easterbrook and Fischel, 1993: 437)

Whereas the trustee highlights the essence of trust in all fiduciary relationships, the wide range of application of the term needs discussing. For instance, corporation officers can both exercise their fiduciary duties to the principals of the corporation and invest in competing corporations if it is through a national stock exchange. For instance, an AT&T officer could buy stock in MCI, but would probably be criticized for it. But an investment by the same officer in a mutual fund which owns MCI stock would be less likely to be criticized. This would change immediately if the officer accepted a directorship in the competing company. Yet officers are regularly directors of other corporations. Some may see that as lack of loyalty to the first principal while others see it as enhancing the officer's value to the first corporation. Of course, directors cannot and would not be asked, in an ethical situation, to serve on boards of competing companies.

Financial brokers are a case where duty to client (principal) varies according to the investment instrument. The pattern of loyalty duty to clients seems to be:

Stocks traded on national stock exchange	no duty except avoiding churning, leading, etc.
Stocks traded OTC	some duty
Limited partnerships traded	strong duty

As was seen in the Prudential Securities scandal of selling limited partnerships, the strong loyalty duty to client was the breach of fiduciary duty. Eichenwald (1993) cities a number of actions by brokers that illustrate the strong duty that was not followed: unsuitable trading in institutional accounts, selling unsuitable investments, unlicensed employees improperly receiving commissions, and others. In order for Prudential Securities to correct these breaches of fiduciary duty it will have to train brokers more thoroughly in the technicalities of various instruments, and exercise more management control at the policy level as well as in the brokerage offices in the various states. The increased fiduciary duty requires increased management action.

Investors have little if any duty to the firms they now own if they have purchased shares on a national exchange. This is particulary true of mutual fund investments. Investing in partnerships is different. Easterbrook and Fischel (1993: 437) hold that "partners owe each other greater duties because of the incomplete separation of management and risk bearing."

There are examples of fiduciary duty being stretched to extreme lengths. Baxter (1993: 7) points out that "When Congress substantially strengthened the enforcement powers of banking agencies in 1989, it instructed the agencies 'to aggressively utilize this new authority.' " These agencies soon

espoused a very contentious version of the fiduciary duty doctrine as one of the grounds for implementing their new enforcement powers. They argued that federally insured depository institutions, their officers and directors, and persons who contract with them, are under a direct fiduciary duty to act in the interests of the federal regulators.

This is a departure from the traditional, tightly focused definition of the principal who has assets and agents who act on the principal's behalf. Baxter argues that "By attaching an additional, 'fiduciary' label to the statutory/soundness duty, the regulators have—whether intentionally or unintentionally—created an *in terrorem* effect, causing unneccesary debate and acrimony between the legal profession and the regulators" (p. 8).

In the case of Gibson Greetings Inc. suing Bankers Trust, "a central point of the suit is that Bankers Trust had a special obligation to look after Gibson's interests and prevent it from doing things that were too risky." At issue here is whether Bankers had a fiduciary responsibility to Gibson "to see that investments are 'suitable' " (Hansell, 1994: D4). This is the first time fiduciary responsibility for suitability of investments has been tested between institutions.

FURTHER STRETCHING THE DEFINITION

One cannot for long use terms like agent, trust, and even faith, as is often associated with fiduciary action, without investigating the use of the same terms in other settings. Kutchins (1991: 107) develops the notion that social workers have fiduciary relationships with their clients. He sees three aspects of this definition:

(1) special duties arise because of the trust or confidence reposed in the fiduciary; (2) the fiduciary has special powers to dominate and influence the client because of the nature of the relationship; and (3) as a consequence, the fiduciary must act in the best interest of the client and cannot take advantage of the client to promote the fiduciary's own interest.

This language does not sound much different from that used in describing professionals in the financial services industry.

Kutchins points out that the H. Maine essay, published in 1861, "argued that the basic principle governing the relationships between members of society has evolved over time from status to contract" (p. 107). This stretching of the definition of fiduciary to include other professions can be seen as a current manifestation of that evolution. The current definition includes a wide range of contracts with fiduciary aspects.

In 1982, the New York State Appellate Court declared in *MacDonald v. Clinger* that "a patient could sue a psychiatrist who divulged personal information to the patient's wife that the therapist learned during psychotherapy. The court held that this was a breach of the fiduciary duty of confidentiality." (Kutchins, 1991: 109) Helping professions of all kinds are becoming aware of the trust nature of helping relationships, and policies are being put into place mandating training to insure that all know the limits of trust and the corrective measures of those found abusing that trust. Clergy are receiving training heighten their awareness of the problems of sexual harassment and exploitation. Sometimes this is to enable the church to have liability insurance against sexual misconduct charges (Niese, 1994). University faculty are likewise receiving documents from deans announcing training sessions and defining sexual harassment: "Sexual harassment is believed to be an exploitation of a power relationship, and not exclusively a sexual issue" (Fairleigh Dickinson University, 1994).

What is next? I look to the work being done on communitarianism as a possible next step. Etzioni (1988), Bellah et al. (1991), and others are forwarding this concept which basically looks to the highest social unit as the source of values in the most significant social interactions. Etzioni is ex-

ploring the myth, in his eyes, that all economic decisions are made by individuals. He feels strongly that they are made by social groups like families
and social sets. Bellah is exploring what makes the good society and he
concludes that it is not pure, individualistic, market-driven behavior, but
rather a focus on the community as an entity.

Bellah and his colleagues are using phrases like "Responsibility, Trust,
and the Good Society." He likes ideas like "institutions are defined as those
patterns which human agents create to regulate action in a 'continuing community of agents.' " When he explores trust he uses the work of Richard
Niebuhr, *The Responsible Self* (1978): "Trust—and here Niebuhr is being
both sociologically realistic and religiously perceptive—is never to be taken
for granted" (Bellah et al, 1991: 284). This sounds like the kind of trust
we have always seen in the legal literature.

Business ethicists are beginning to put communitarian ideas into their
work. Donaldson and Dunfee (1994a, 1994b) are probably in the lead on
this application. They have made a significant step toward a unified concept
of business ethics in social contracts theory, which may be where linkages
are made.

Fiduciary relationships have to move beyond the closed loop of principals
and agents. They have already moved beyond the legal and financial world
to helping professions. It appears that they will move to relationships between contractors on the broad scope of international, social contracts. The
next challenge is to conceptualize fiduciary relationships between corporations and the environment, between professions and society, and between
business people and the economy.

REFERENCES

Baxter, L. G. (1993). "Fiduciary Issues in Federal Banking Regulation." *Law and
    Contemporary Problems 56* (1): 7–44.
Bellah, R. N., R. Madsen, W. M. Sullivan, A. Swidler, and S. M. Tipton. (1991).
    The Good Society. New York: Alfred A. Knopf.
Clarkson, K. W., R. L., Miller, and G. A., Jentz. (1986). *West's Business Law Text
    & Cases* (3d ed.). St. Paul, MN: West Publishing Company.
Donaldson, T., and T. Dunfee. (1994a). "Integrative Social Contracts Theory: A
    Communitarian Conception of Economic Ethics." Working paper 93-2-170.
    Philadelphia: Wharton School of the University of Pennsylvania (forthcom-
    ing: *Economics and Philosophy*).
———. (1994b). "Towards a Unified Conception of Business Ethics: Integrative
    Social Contracts Theory." *Academy of Management Review 19* (2): 252–
    284.
Easterbrook, F. H, and D. R. Fischel. (1993). "Contract and Fiduciary Duty." *Jour-
    nal of Law & Economics 36* (April): 425–446.
Eichenwald, K. (1993). "New Cloud Over Prudential Branches." *New York Times*,
    December 17, pp. D1, D4.

Etzioni, A. (1988). *The Moral Dimension: Toward a New Economics*. New York: The Free Press.

Fairleigh Dickinson University. (1994). FDU sexual harassment policy and complaint procedures.

Hansell, S. (1994). "Challenged Bank Defends Its Derivatives Actions." *New York Times*, October 13, p. 4.

Kutchins, H. (1991). "The Fiduciary Relationship: The Legal Basis for Social Workers' Responsibilities to Clients." *Social Work* 36 (2): 106–113.

McLennan, G. (1993). "Trust Not: The Notion of Fiduciary Duty Has Proven Eerily Expansible in Recent Court Cases." *CA Magazine* (June/July): 40–43.

Niese, A. N. (1994). Personal letter.

2

In Defense of Finance: Understanding Fiduciary Responsibility and Conflicts of Interest

Elaine Sternberg

Nothing stimulates claims of sharp practice more quickly than losing money.[1]

Ivan Boesky . . . Mike Milken . . . Robert Maxwell . . . BCCI. . . . On both sides of the Atlantic, the finance function and financiers have been the subjects of major scandals. As a result, finance has often been imagined to be the source of particularly grave problems of business ethics. But that perception is based on fundamental confusions. When fiduciary responsibility and financial conflicts of interest are properly understood, many supposedly intractable problems of business ethics can be resolved quite straightforwardly.

THE PROMINENCE OF ETHICAL PROBLEMS IN FINANCE

A major source of the undeniably bad reputation of finance is the nature of finance itself: Its "products" are typically abstract services, which are often not properly understood, either by consumers[2] or by commentators. Unable to evaluate these services directly, customers characteristically cry foul when their hopes are not fulfilled, and thereby give finance its bad name.

Complexity and consumer incompetence are, of course, not exclusive to financial services: Consider the staggering 80 percent of British adults who reputedly cannot program their home video recorders.[3] Electronics manufacturers are not castigated the way financiers are, however, because most VCR owners nevertheless have reasonably realistic expectations of what their machines can do: They typically do not accuse the vendors of fraud when their VCRs do not make the tea or walk the dog.

Those disappointed in finance, however, frequently make complaints which are almost as absurd. And that is because they regularly fail to understand concepts as basic to finance as "market risk" . . . or even "market." Although inured to losing in the pools or on the ponies, too many punters have been encouraged, in part by government privatization programs, to believe that the financial markets offer a sure thing. When, therefore, the inevitable losses occur, the financially naïve are surprised, and convinced that someone (else) must be at fault. Furthermore, they believe that someone, usually in the financial services industry, should be blamed . . . and punished.

ADVISERS AND FIDUCIARY RESPONSIBILITY

This mistake is typically exacerbated by fundamental confusions concerning the role of advisers and the nature of fiduciary responsibility.[4] Both are prominent in finance precisely because the opacity of financial matters increases clients' felt need for guidance. Advisers are normally employed because they are presumed to be more capable of achieving the clients' objectives than the clients can themselves; the client seeks to harness the adviser's superior knowledge or experience or access to technical facilities.

Fiduciary responsibility ordinarily arises when a client entrusts his assets or his affairs to the care of an adviser. In the absence of more specific instructions, a fiduciary is expected to pursue his client's best interests in the way a reasonable man would, had he the fiduciary's specific expertise. For financial advisers,[5] this normally means maximizing the client's asset value, within the terms of reference agreed upon. Those terms might stipulate the degree of risk acceptable to the client, the period over which returns are to be maximized, the types of investments to be made, or the instruments to be avoided. Whatever the particular constraints, however, the essence of the fiduciary relationship is that the client expects, indeed relies upon, the adviser's taking the client's best interests as his objective and criterion of action. Accordingly, what determines whether the fiduciary responsibility has been fulfilled is simply whether that criterion of client interest has actually been employed.

This basic fact has several important consequences. First, it shows that the adviser's personal motivation is largely irrelevant to whether fiduciary responsibility has been discharged.[6] Unless his decisions are affected, it does not matter whether an adviser's actions are prompted by a sense of duty or by professional pride, by financial self-interest or a wish to spite his rivals. So long as the client's best interest is the operative decision criterion determining the adviser's actions, so long as those actions are directed at achieving the client's best interests, the fiduciary responsibility has been duly fulfilled. Wholly correct decisions may result from thoroughly disagreeable motives.

Second, fiduciary responsibility is not necessarily violated when objectives other than the client's best interest are also served by the adviser's actions. There is no reason why, for example, an adviser may not benefit financially from a transaction that he recommends. Trustees often receive some compensation for fulfilling their fiduciary responsibilities, and performance-related incentives are both legitimate and sensible. What must be exclusive for satisfying fiduciary responsibility is the criterion used in generating a recommendation, not the effects that it causes.

The most important consequence of understanding that it is the decision criterion which determines whether fiduciary responsibility has been fulfilled, however, is that it shows why not all disappointing outcomes represent failures of fiduciary responsibility. It is possible for a financial transaction to be unsatisfactory, even to generate significant losses, without the adviser responsible having violated his fiduciary responsibility.

To understand why, it is useful to examine three distinct cases. In the first, the correct criterion of client best interest is employed, but the outcome is nevertheless disappointing. In the second case, the correct criterion also seems to be employed, but the adviser is less than expert. In the third case, the wrong criterion of action is used. Although a disappointing outcome is equally disappointing whether caused by an honest bungler or a clever crook, the degree to which the adviser is morally culpable nevertheless differs from case to case.

The first case is the simplest, from the point of view of business ethics: It involves no violation of fiduciary responsibility and no unethical conduct. Markets are so complex and unpredictable that even genuine experts can misjudge them on occasion; however scrupulous and sophisticated an adviser may be in employing the correct criterion, things can still go wrong. When that happens, there will have been no violation of fiduciary responsibility, and no one will have acted unethically. Unfortunate though the outcomes may be for the client, the adviser in such cases will deserve no blame.

The adviser is to blame, however, if he is incompetent. There is a significant difference between making the odd misjudgment or mistake and being culpably ignorant or inexperienced. If the adviser does not know how to apply the criterion of client best interest[7]—if he is not properly equipped, mentally or otherwise,[8] to deliver what he has offered—then the adviser is indeed acting unethically: it is as immoral for him to misrepresent his abilities as it is to lie about the objectives employed. In putting himself forward as an expert, the honest adviser must portray his capabilities accurately. He must therefore have a realistic view as to what they actually are; self-deception may permit sincerity, but it is no excuse for lacking the appropriate, necessary skill. When the "expert" adviser is incompetent, he is morally at fault.

And so, possibly, is the client. For it is the client's responsibility to choose his expert: There is a sense in which *caveat emptor* applies even here. Although the client typically lacks the adviser's specific expertise, he will often be capable of judging his probity and general competence. The client can, for example, investigate the expert's qualifications and reputation and track record; he can also seek a second opinion. A client need not be a motor mechanic to realize that an offer to transform a beat-up truck into a brand new limousine is unrealistic; so, too, should he be capable of suspecting that a promise of enormous, risk-free financial returns is probably too good to be true. If the client fails to take adequate precautions in vetting and selecting his expert, then he is contributorily negligent, and shares some of the moral blame when things go wrong.

The most striking cases of business immorality are those of the third sort, in which the adviser employs the wrong criterion in pursuit of the wrong objective. Such cases are what most critics of financial practice take as standard. Even when this is an accurate diagnosis, however, the real immorality is seldom properly identified.

Consider, for example, an adviser who, though purporting to be seeking the best interests of his clients, instead seeks his own interests at their expense. What makes this sort of action unethical is not that the adviser has been greedy, or that he has served his own interests. His motives are irrelevant, and it is not inappropriate for his interests to be furthered. What is immoral is not that the adviser's interests have been served, but that they have served as the criterion of action. In misrepresenting the objectives, the adviser has lied; he has betrayed the trust essential to a fiduciary relationship. And by using anything but the client's best interests as his criterion of action, the adviser has violated the key condition of fiduciary responsibility.

Violations of fiduciary responsibility account for much of what is genuinely unethical in business. In finance, however, they are considerably rarer than is commonly imagined. And that is because, contrary to popular belief, most financial arrangements, like most contracts generally, involve no fiduciary responsibility. Financial transactions often occur without a client entrusting either his assets or his affairs to the care of an adviser.

Fiduciary responsibility arises most obviously when advisers are given discretionary authority to invest a client's funds. In such cases, there can be no question as to where the adviser's obligation lies. The adviser's clear duty is to invest the funds so as best to achieve the objectives agreed with the client, regardless of the effect that any implementing transaction may have on his own interests. Such full discretionary authority is, however, the exception rather than the rule.

Consider a nonfinancial parallel: repairing a car. If one entrusts the vehicle to a mechanic, the mechanic has both discretionary authority and a fiduciary responsibility to make the car work properly. There are, however, other methods of effecting repairs which involve no fiduciary responsibility.

One might give him precise instructions: "Replace the battery with a model 123.45 from Bloggs Ltd." In that case, the mechanic's responsibility is limited to obtaining the specified part and installing it correctly; if he does that, he is not to blame if the car still doesn't work. Or one might repair the car oneself, with a part bought from an automotive parts outlet. The only moral responsibility the vendor has is the basic one of accurately identifying the item sold. He typically will not even have seen the vehicle, much less have made any representations about what ails it, or about the part's ability to effect a cure.

In the same way, "execution-only" brokers make no representations about a security's performance or suitability for any investment strategy or given investor. Execution-only brokers assume no fiduciary responsibility; nor do most securities salesmen. Significantly, new issue prospectuses tell prospective investors about the size and timetable and risks of a public offering; they make no promises about the securities' likely future performance. Equally, commercial lenders normally have no fiduciary responsibility to their borrowers: That funds are provided for a project is no guarantee that the project will prove successful.

Even when a fiduciary responsibility does exist, it may be significantly different than commonly supposed. Auditors' fiduciary responsibility, for example, is normally limited to assessing whether financial statements have been drawn up in accordance with Generally Accepted Accounting Principles. Financial auditors do not determine which of the many variants allowed by those principles should be employed; far less do they certify the general health or viability of the underlying business.[9] Moreover, their fiduciary responsibility is not to the client: Although it is typically a corporation's managers who hire the firm's accountants, their duty as auditors is not to those managers, but to the company's shareholders as a whole.[10]

FINANCIAL CONFLICTS OF INTEREST

It is because finance and fiduciary responsibility are so widely misunderstood that financial conflicts of interest seem to pose exceptional moral difficulties. Given the pervasiveness of finance, the international spread of integrated investment banks, and the extent to which professionals are increasingly acting as business consultants, the potential for financial conflicts of interest is indeed significant.

Substantial conflicts can arise between various kinds of financial advisers and their clients, and between the managers and owners of financial businesses. Conflicts are possible between accountants in their different roles as auditors and proprietors of consulting businesses. Within investment banks, conflicts often exist between agency brokers and principal market markers, between corporate financiers and everyone else. But although comparable conflicts of interest are resolved routinely and unproblematically in other business sectors, without raising any particular problems of business ethics, those in finance are commonly thought to present serious ethical quandaries. This is usually a mistake.

Consider the various sorts of conflicts of interest which might arise between investment banks and their clients. The potential for one type exists when investment bankers' fees are contingent on the success of a transaction: Advisers may be tempted to complete, for example, an acquisition, regardless of the cost to the client. Or a conflict may arise within a securities business, insofar as the investment bank might seek to benefit its own trading position at the expense of a customer's. This latter possibility has been the subject of particular concern in Britain: One of the chief anxieties associated with the "Big Bang" rule changes was that they allowed the same financial firm to operate as both agent and principal, as broker and market maker. It was feared that such "dual capacity" would jeopardize the interests of clients, by giving firms an incentive to sell unsuitable securities.

In some ways, this is a strange fear. Although in the United States "front running" has long been disallowed for securities, accumulating stock for a business's own account and selling from it at a profit are standard practices for most nonfinancial wholesalers and retailers. Similarly, the fact that department stores act as both agents and principals is not ordinarily imagined to jeopardize their customers interests. Nor does combining specialist judgment with sales automatically present moral difficulties: Antique dealers do it regularly, and U.K. pharmacists routinely dispense both advice and medication.

Why, then, should acting as both agent and principal be thought to pose an ethical problem in finance? The reason is not any special moral failing of financiers; it is, rather, the presumed financial incompetence of the customers. Even though many are themselves extremely sophisticated financial institutions, financial clients are nevertheless believed to be unable to judge the quality of the advice they are given, and to be particularly vulnerable and in need of protection. The critical issue in these conflicts of interest is not the functional compatibility of agent and principal, but fiduciary responsibility.

As shown above, however, fiduciary responsibility is not necessarily impaired by a business's pursuing its own investment or other objectives. Even putting those objectives ahead of its clients' need not be unethical, so long as that is the basis on which the clients have agreed to do business. A principal trading operation, committed first and foremost to the profitability of its own trading position, could quite ethically[11] seek custom from investors prepared to invest in its wake. Its relationship to those clients would have no fiduciary component: Its only responsibility would be to put the investors' funds where it put its own, albeit on terms that would typically be less favorable. Would investors ever agree to such an arrangement? They might, if the trader's record of investment were so successful, thanks to its exceptional information or analysis or judgment, or its low management fees, that even its leavings provided returns superior to those available elsewhere. Such a business would be unusual, but it would involve no violation of fiduciary responsibility, no conflict of interest, and no violations of business ethics: The customers would know, and would have agreed, that they come last.

One of the most commonly cited conflicts of interest is that which is presumed to exist between the professional as an expert or adviser, and the professional as the owner of a business. This is the conflict which has been thought to pose ethical dilemmas for the accounting profession, as accountants supplement their traditional auditing role with diverse consulting activities. The worry is, presumably, that the auditor will allow his professional judgment to be distorted by the fear that an unfavorable report might lose him profitable consulting clients.

Common though the charge is, however, the nature of the supposed conflict is nevertheless obscure. For the success of a professional business should be directly related to the professionalism of the advice it offers; if the adviser or the advice is bad, its reputation and its clientele are unlikely to survive. If an auditing firm is known to overlook accounting irregularities so as to promote its related consulting business, responsible directors will not trust its reports or approve its appointment.[12] Nor should they trust the advice of the associated consultants, if the firm's probity is questionable. Similarly, a corporate financier who is known to recommend transactions solely for the fees they generate, without proper regard for their suitability for his corporate clients, will attract only gullible customers.[13]

When business success is correctly measured by *long-term owner value*, ethical conduct is normally a condition of its achievement. Current period accounting profits may sometimes be increased by sharp dealing, but the business's ability to operate successfully over the long term normally is not. Consequently, the central conflict which underlies most supposed financial conflicts of interest simply does not arise: Far from conflicting with ethical conduct, business success normally requires it.

When success and ethical conduct do conflict, it is often because a misunderstanding of the business objective has produced a moral hazard. Official incentives to do the wrong thing are all too common; they are a particularly dangerous consequence of improperly structured, performance-related pay. If staff are remunerated on the basis of anything other than their contributions to maximizing long-term owner value, immoral conduct is positively encouraged. When brokers are rewarded for the volume of transactions they undertake, or bankers for the numbers of new loans they book, it is not surprising that the result is churning and bad debts. In such circumstances, clients undoubtedly suffer. But so do the businesses involved. It is when the proper purpose of business is ignored that unethical behavior is most likely to arise.

NOTES

1. *The Economist*, February 22, 1992, pp. 92–99.

2. Or, one suspects, most providers . . . or regulators. A survey by KPMG Management Counseling of 120 middle and senior managers from top U.K. companies revealed that more than half did not understand basic financial concepts. See Paul Taylor, "Managers Lack Finance Skills, Says Survey," *Financial Times*, February 24, 1992, p. 8.

3. Compare "Sonic, Stamps and Sex," *Financial Times*, December 31, 1992, p. 11.

4. This section is an application of a more general analysis developed in Elaine Sternberg, *Just Business: Business Ethics in Action* (New York: Little, Brown & Company Limited, 1994), especially pp. 97–99.

5. Typically investment advisers, but also those providing corporate finance advice.

6. For a full discussion of the role of motives and mixed motives, see Sternberg, *Just Business*, especially pp. 94–97.

7. Compare the first audit regulation report submitted by the (U.K.) Association of Authorized Public Accountants to the Department of Trade and Industry, which revealed that almost two-thirds of the auditors monitored were judged unsatisfactory. Jack, Andrew, "Many Auditors Are 'Unsatisfactory,' " *Financial Times*, January 31, 1993, p. 6. Similarly, in a (U.K.) Management Information Centre survey of 492 small- and medium-sized accountancy firms, an alarming 28 percent admitted that they employed staff who were "not competent in the use of audit procedures." Andrew Jack, "Auditors 'Inhabited' by Client Pressure," *Financial Times*, November 9, 1992, p. 5.

8. In an academic study of 112 newly qualified accountants, 30 percent were tempted to take short cuts in audits because they found the work boring, and 41 percent because they thought it unimportant. Andrew Jack, " 'Bored' junior audits take short cuts,' " *Financial Times*, April 8, 1993, p. 8.

9. Pending the development of guidelines on going concerns and internal controls, the U.K. Accounting Practices Board (APB) has strongly advised auditors not to comment on these topics. APB, *Disclosures Relating to Corporate Governance*, Accountancy Books, P.O. Box 620, Central Milton Keynes MK9 2JX; reported in Andrew Jack, "Auditors Receive Cadbury Guidance," *Financial Times*, December 10, 1993, p. 8.

10. Compare the Caparo case in the United Kingdom.

11. Where it was legal.

12. Though admittedly, with all six of the Big Six accounting firms being sued for improper practice, good alternatives may be difficult to find.

13. Which is not, sadly, to guarantee that he will be unemployed. Too many clients choose their financial advisers for the imagined prestige that they confer rather than the quality of the advice that they actually give.

3

Should Mutual Fund Managers Be Banned from Personal Trading?

Ronald F. Duska

On May 9, 1994, the mutual funds industry's special Advisory Group on Personal Investing issued a report with a set of recommendations governing the personal investing activities of portfolio managers and other "access persons." The report was presented to the Securities and Exchange Commission (SEC) to forestall the possibility of new SEC regulations which would limit the personal trading of managers of mutual funds. Further regulation would be aimed at preventing potential conflicts of interest. The report involved specific recommendations which included:

- bans on purchasing securities in an initial public offering (IPO) and on profiteering from short-term trading activities;
- strict limits on acquiring securities in private placements and on accepting gifts;
- mandatory blackout periods for personal trading in securities a fund is trading;
- preapproval to serve as directors of publicly traded companies; and
- six specific compliance procedures.

The report also encouraged close regular oversight by funds' boards of directors, disclosure to investors about fund managers' personal investing, and continued vigorous oversight and enforcement by the SEC.[1]

The report was issued by a special advisory group set up by the Investment Company Institute (ICI) to examine the personal investing practices of mutual fund personnel. The advisory group was set up by the ICI in response to inquiries from Edward Markey, the chairman of the House Subcommittee on Telecommunications and Finance, addressed to Arthur Levitt of the SEC. Markey's concern was triggered by a story in the *Wash-*

ington Post which reported the activities that led to the firing of John Kaweske of Invesco Funds Group of Denver. Although Kaweske was fired for violating rules governing reporting of personal trade, his firing brought about a host of inquiries about other practices of "access" persons in the mutual funds industry from "front-running" to private trading.

In response to Markey's inquiries the Investment Company Institute reviewed Rule 17J-1 under the Investment Company Act and Section 204A of the Investment Advisers Act. Rule 17J-1 requires codes of ethics and compliance procedures. The inquiry was meant to determine whether current law and rules are strong enough to protect the investment public from the possible conflicts of interest that might arise if and when a fund manager gets involved in various private investment activities.

Rule 17J-1, among other things, "prohibits portfolio managers from engaging in deceitful, fraudulent or manipulative trading with respect to securities held or to be acquired by the fund." It also requires the adoption of codes of ethics by mutual fund companies, filing of reports of personal transactions, and maintaining extensive records of the implementation of procedures.[2] The rule was designed to forestall potential conflicts of interest and manipulation such as that in front-running, that is, privately buying stock one knows the fund is going to purchase prior to the fund's purchase, with the expectation that the fund's activity will raise the stock's value in the short run.

The advisory group issued its recommendations on May 9, 1994. In an executive summary the advisory group claimed further regulation was probably unnecessary because the SEC regularly inspects investment companies, their advisors, and principal underwriters in the light of their codes of ethics, and relatively few enforcement actions have been necessary because of the effectiveness of those codes of ethics. (Since the codes of ethics are not public, it is difficult for the outsider to assess the claim "that investment companies have crafted their codes carefully to address potential conflicts most effectively in light of their particular circumstances."[3])

The absence of much enforcement action against mutual fund managers led the advisory group to conclude that the industry is well enough regulated and to reject the suggestion of some, such as William Berger, that a ban on personal investing be instituted. The report argued against a complete ban on personal trading, but the advisory group did recommend a "series of additional measures to obviate conflicts, prevent and detect abusive practices, and preserve the confidence of investors."[4] The purpose of this chapter is to play devil's advocate and ask whether the advisory group's recommendations went far enough, especially with respect to banning personal trading.

The additional measures to obviate conflicts of interest that the advisory board recommended fell into six categories. We will examine each briefly.

- The first category issued a statement of general principles calling for investors to put the interest of shareholders first, follow the code of ethics, and avoid conflicts of interest and taking advantage of one's position.
- The second category of recommendation suggested that each individual code be tailored to the specific workings of each fund.
- The third category of recommendation asked that "codes include, at a minimum, substantive restrictions to guard against the most likely conflicts of interest, including: (1) prohibitions of investment personnel from acquiring any securities in an initial public offering (IPO); (2) requirements of prior approval, and disclosure of any acquisition of securities by investment personnel in a private placement as well as independent review of such securities if they are to be purchased by the fund; (3) blackout periods; (4) a ban on short-term trading profits in investments the fund is involved with; (5) a ban on substantial gifts; and (6) prohibition from serving on the boards of directors of publicly traded companies unless there is approval and initiation of "Chinese Wall" or other procedures.
- The fourth category of recommendation suggested that companies adopt certain compliance procedures; namely, preclearance, recording securities transactions, posttrade monitoring, disclosing personal holdings, and certifying compliance with codes of ethics. It was recommended that each company prepare an annual report that lists existing procedures, identifies past year violations and recommended changes in existing restrictions. The report also recommended that the National Association of Securities Dealers, Inc. adopt a rule requiring all broker-dealers to notify a registered investment advisor when any of its employees opens a brokerage account.
- The fifth category of recommendation suggested that investment company prospectuses disclose whether the company permits personnel to engage in personal trading.
- The sixth and final category of recommendation suggested that the SEC continue vigorous oversight and enforcement in this area.

What emerges from the report is a picture of a basically honest, well-regulated industry with little or no problems, whose members have integrity for the most part and which does not need further regulation because it is already regulated enough.

Do the recommendations go far enough? After all, up until now the industry seemed to be doing decently, but the stories of Kaweske and others raise the question of whether the present system is still working. One certainly does not want to challenge the maxim, "If it ain't broke don't fix it." But the Kaweske case might be the indicator that the system is beginning to break down. We might do well, then, to be a bit less sanguine about whether the system works as well as the report indicates.

Our critique begins by asking whether the reasons given for not banning personal trading are adequate. There are other questions to be asked of the report. For example, why are there no uniform, public codes, and why, for example, do only sixty-five of the ninety-six companies' codes specify restrictions for "access persons," or why do only sixty-three have blackout periods? Why do only fifteen companies expressly discourage or prohibit short-term trading, or why do only thirty-seven have restrictions on gifts? It seems that in some cases a large minority or even a majority of investment companies do not follow the guidelines for ethics codes set down by the institute. A further question could be asked about why the recommendations do not address the problem of conflicts which arise with the taking of payment for consulting, and why blackout periods apply to portfolio managers and not to other access persons? Each of these deserves thorough treatment. However, in this chapter we will limit our concerns to whether the report went far enough with its recommendations about personal trading by fund managers. But given the constraints of space, I will address only the issue of whether there should be an industrywide ban on personal investing. Such an analysis may be useful in showing the mind-set of the industry, a mind-set which may not be critical enough of the possible abuses that may arise from the conflicts of interest that can result from engaging in personal trading.

SHOULD PERSONAL INVESTING BE BANNED?

The reasons for not banning personal investing appear in Section III of the Report, under the title of "Consideration of a Ban on Personal Investing." As the report says, "The advisory group . . . carefully considered one option—a ban on personal investing by portfolio managers."[5] Although the ban was rejected by the advisory group, it "merits special discussion."

The discussion begins by examining the rationales of "some commentators" who have suggested a "complete" ban.

- First,"personal investing activities may give rise to the possibility of an impropriety, even when the transactions themselves are entirely appropriate and beyond reproach.
- Second, it has been argued that portfolio managers should be confined to participating personally in the markets in exactly the same manner as the fund shareholders whom they serve—in essence, by requiring them to "eat their own cooking."
- Finally, "a complete ban would eliminate the possibility of time and attention being devoted by portfolio managers to their personal investments, at the expense of time that should be devoted to management of fund assets."[6]

The fact that these are the only rationales addressed lead one to believe that the defenders of the status quo answered the objections of those in disagreement with them by adopting a technique known in logic as creating a straw man; that is, setting up arguments and rationales that are easily refuted. At least the last two rationales are straw man arguments. These last two arguments are so bad that they give no defense for a ban. If there are no other reasons for a ban, then a ban is indefensible.

Consider the last two reasons for a moment. The third reason, that personal investing would take away time from investing for one's clients, is just silly. It only works as an argument if one assumes that the investors *should* spend every waking hour on their jobs. While taking time from one's job to devote it to private affairs is clearly wrong, it is perfectly possible to do one's job conscientiously and still have time left over to engage in "extracurricular" activities.

As to the second argument, to ban personal investing because fund managers should "eat their own cooking" is simply a non sequitur. To the claim that one should eat one's own cooking, one answers, "one person's meat is another person's poison." A chef with a heart condition who makes rich heavy pastries is not precluded from making the pastries, only from eating them. Hence, someone working in a high risk fund who needs to be conservative should not "have to eat his own cooking." It may be perfectly good cooking, just not good for him.

Given that the second and third arguments for a ban on personal trading are admittedly bad, there is only one serious argument for a ban on personal investing examined in the report. That is the argument that claims that personal investing activities give rise to the possibility of an impropriety. This argument seems to have merit. Even if personal investing does not give rise to impropriety, it surely may lead to what Chairman Levitt calls "the perception of a conflict of interest," which can undermine consumer confidence; and it certainly can lead to a temptation, a consideration no one raises in the report.

How then does the report dispose of this argument that personal investing may lead to impropriety or the perception of a conflict of interest? As far as we can tell, the report does not address this argument directly. Rather, it shifts gears and asks "whether to bar altogether personal trading by fund insiders." It may address the question obliquely, for the report asks, "What purpose does it serve? How does it benefit shareholders?" But the answer to those questions depends on what you are banning. Should long-term personal investment be banned? Should short-term speculative trading be banned? If the purpose of the ban is to preclude conflicts of interest and appearance of impropriety, then banning long-term personal investment seems unnecessary. Indeed, one can ask the question the report asks, "How will that benefit shareholders?" If however, one talks of banning short-term speculative trading, the answer to how that will benefit shareholders is that it will keep the fund managers faithful to the interests of the shareholders, because the temptation to set aside the shareholders' interests which are in conflict with their own is not likely to arise, except in the context of short-term speculative trading. If long-term investment will not cause conflicts of interest or perceptions of impropriety, then there is probably no reason to ban it. But what of short-term speculative investment? Is there a reason to ban it?

The report, then, baits and switches. Having promised a careful analysis of the purpose of a ban and what benefit a ban would have for shareholders, the advisory group doesn't consider all the options. It considers only the option of a "complete" ban, or whether to "ban altogether," and brings up reasons why that would be unwise. By considering only a "complete" ban, the advisory group sets up a false dichotomy. For example, I can assert that you either love me or you hate me. Since you don't love me you must hate me. But there are clearly middle grounds here. It is relatively easy to show how unwise a complete ban would be, but this leaves unexamined the question of whether there should be some activity banned.

But there are in the business community ample examples of accounts of why there should be partial bans, or bans against specific kinds of personal investing. By way of a foil to the advisory group's report, I wish to present a section from a code of ethics of a prominent bank on the east coast of the United States. It does not have a complete ban on personal trading, but it does give reasons for not engaging in certain kinds of activities. By way of illustration, it has a guideline against accepting gifts, in its section covering the rule, "Carefully Avoid Conflicts of Interest." "Bank X's general rule against accepting gifts is to prevent corruption or breach of trust." Here the purpose is stated clearly. The purpose of this ban (not a complete ban) is to help keep its employees trustworthy and to keep them out of temptation. Could not the advisory board have said that defenders of a ban on personal trading see the purpose of the ban to "prevent corruption or breach of trust?" That is the reason that is usually operative in conflict of interest situations. It is why baseball has a rule against gambling, and banned Pete Rose for life. A hard question for the advisory group would be, why are mutual fund personnel less susceptible to corruption, than, say, baseball players?

Bank X's code covering Speculative Investments is equally straightforward and direct: Bank X encourages its employees to invest wisely. *However, employees' short-term speculative investments are risks to the employee and to Bank X.* Short-term investment transactions, especially those involving Bank X's or a customer's stock, invite insider trading questions. *The possibility of significant losses from speculative investments may give rise to unusual pressures, requiring management to give special attention to the employee and the problems.* For these reasons, Bank X discourages its employees from entering into speculative transactions such as short sales, purchases of securities on margin, and trading in options, futures and currency transactions—even when the employee has the skill to judge and the financial means to handle the risks. Bank X most strongly discourages flagrant speculation, such as excessive gambling. Any of the above activities may be considered when Bank X evaluates an employee's performance.[7]

Bank X has a straightforward answer to the question of the advisory committee, "What purpose would a (not a complete) ban on trading serve? It would avoid risks of conflicts of interest and risks of insider trading. It would avoid the possibility of significant losses that "may give rise to unusual pressures." In short, it avoids what medievalists would have called "occasions of sin."

So the purposes for a ban, not a complete one, seem relatively straightforward. But the advisory group does not deal with them straightforwardly. It does admit that "for some investment companies, a ban on personal investing indeed may recommend itself as a clear standard to follow."[8] But why would it recommend itself for one company and not another? What are the relevant differences? The only reason given in the report is that "such a ban may be relatively easy to implement and administer and less burdensome and costly than the alternatives." But that was not the reason for the ban given by Bank X. Could some investment company give Bank X's reasons? Furthermore, why would the alternatives to a ban be burdensome and costly, if not for the fact that short-term speculation leads to all sorts of possible conflicts of interest and temptations that need to be checked by complicated monitoring procedures such as those developed in the compliance areas of the codes of ethics.

The advisory group, then, condescendingly allows that "Any investment company is, and should be, at liberty to adopt such a standard if it sees fit." On what grounds? If such a standard is not reasonable, then why should a company be at liberty to adopt it, for its adoption would unfairly limit the freedom of its personnel. A company should have good reasons. What are they? "Nevertheless," the report continues, "it is unnecessary, and it would be unfair and contrary to the interests of shareholders, to impose such a ban on investment companies at large." (One wonders why it would be fair in the case of one company and not in another. The only way to decide that is to take the analysis of the reasons for the ban seriously, something the report does not do.)

It appears that the report has avoided analyzing the substantial reasons for a ban against short-term speculative trading. It makes the assertion that "It is unnecessary, unfair, and contrary to the interests of shareholders to impose such a ban (complete) on investment companies at large."

ARGUMENTS AGAINST A (COMPLETE) BAN

Still, the advisory group does develop a positive defense of its position. What sort of arguments does it generate in support of the claim that there should be no ban on personal trading?

The first reason is somewhat muddled. Lest it appear that I am caricaturing the argument, I will cite the entire passage.

First is the importance of one very stark truth about the industry: Investment managers compete fiercely in the marketplace, and their competition is waged first and foremost on the basis of proven performance. Today, there are over 5,200 investment companies registered with the Commission and thousands of other pooled investment vehicles. While there always has been a healthy level of competition in the industry, this is especially so today, when there are so many alternative funds whose performance is widely publicized. No investment management firm will succeed in this environment unless it consistently serves the interests of the customer first. No firm is likely to tolerate a portfolio manager becoming preoccupied with personal investments at the expense of a fund and its shareholders. Nor is a portfolio manager whose personal compensation frequently is linked to the performance of the fund, likely to be motivated to engage in trading activities that benefit him at the expense of fund performance.[9]

I take it that this is the defense of the "unnecessary" aspect of a "complete" ban on personal investing, unnecessary because the competitive nature of the marketplace is such that no firm will tolerate a portfolio manager preoccupied with personal investments. But, as a matter of fact, Invesco did just that with Kawaske. His performance was so good, there were two sets of rules in his company, one for him and one for the others. Further, the competitive nature of the industry is at best irrelevant. The issue isn't someone not doing his job; the issue is the temptation that arises because of conflicting interests which arise from the portfolio manager's outside trading. Further, this argument doesn't address the free rider problem of the manager who rests on the laurels of her fellow managers. Finally, a portfolio manager whose personal compensation is linked to the performance of the fund may very well be motivated to engage in trading at the expense of the fund when that trading will benefit him more than the compensation. A footnote that notes that "most managers don't trade that much" returns to that trivial consideration of banning trading because it eats up too much of the manager's time.

The second argument against a complete ban is that the advisory group is "convinced that the industry can continue to address these concerns in a decisive manner . . . through the imposition of various restrictions and the implementation of related compliance procedures short of a total ban."[10] In an appeal to authority, the report indicates that "those many Commission members and senior officials with whom the Advisory Group met in the course of its work concurred *unanimously* in this judgment." One of the issues addressed by an advisory group of which I was a member was the question of "How extensive should any ban on personal trading be?" There probably should be "unanimous" agreement against a total ban, since that would preclude owning any stock, long or short term, but one must ask whether the report does not trivialize the problem by its constant reference to a total ban? Where was the serious discussion, for example, of a ban on short-term speculative investment? Be that as it may, the second reason turns out not so much a reason in defense of the position, but a reiteration of the conviction that the position is correct.

The third argument claims that an outright prohibition on personal investing would heavily—and unfairly—penalize many portfolio managers. The heaviness would come from "completely foreclosing a trustee from entering into an entire category of personal transactions *unrelated* to the administration of the trust or to the trust assets." But whether and which personal transactions are related is exactly the question.

The unfairness comes from changing the contract, or "to those numerous professionals who entered the industry with one set of rules, only to find those rules radically changed." But there may be good reasons for changing the rules. That is what is at stake.

In this instance the group asks "what legitimate purpose would be served, for example, by precluding the young manager of a money market fund, whose professional activities are limited to markets in short-term, high-quality debt instruments, from investing in growth stocks for his retirement account or in blue-chip stocks as gifts to his minor children?" The answer, of course, is "probably none." But put a slightly different question to the group. "What purpose would be served by precluding the young manager of a fund from investing in short-term, highly speculative stocks?" Here we can recall the purpose given by the bank. It would lead to the avoidance of pressures. Speculations akin to gambling do not "vindicate the reasonable expectations" of the American public.

The fourth reason against a ban is that such a ban would be detrimental to the fund shareholders by driving the highly talented investment professionals away. It is claimed that there would be a talent drain. This might be an empirical question if one could definitively come up with the criteria that make one a highly talented investment professional. What are the criteria for determining who are the highly talented professionals? How much of success is hard work and how much is luck? If they are that talented why are they working for the fund in the first place? Was Kaweske that talented? Some claim his early successes began to fade. What image of the "best" is operating here? Are they not amply enough rewarded for their work? Dare we ask whether the "best" might not turn out to be the greediest? Do we need to keep them? Somewhere along the line, one wants to ask the question that Berger asks, "Don't fund managers make enough money at work?" Must they supplement an already substantial income with short-term speculation? I am put in mind of an accountant friend of mine who wanted the rules against being a broker loosened. Of course, accountants know a lot about certain securities. That's the nature of their job. But we expect them to keep that to themselves, as we expect doctors to keep privileged information they could use to acquire personal wealth to keep that to themselves. But enough. On to the next defense.

This brings us to the final argument against a ban, the argument that "investment company portfolio managers already are subject to more detailed accountability for their personal investing activities than are the employees of other investment companies. Foreclosing these experts from investing would establish significant and needless disincentives to their entering or continuing to serve in the investment company industry." One is always sympathetic to a claim of unfairness when one is asked to live by rules that don't apply to others playing the same or a similar game. Persons at Bank X would often bemoan the fact that their bank is harder on them than other banks are on their employees. But that does not make their bank wrong. It may be the other banks are not stringent enough. Perhaps what needs to come out of this entire investigation is a reexamination of the question, "Why is the mutual fund industry subject to more detailed accounting than employees of other investment companies?"

It is certainly true that one should not have one's liberties curtailed without good reasons, and in this case a personal ban would curtail liberties. The question, though, is whether the reasons are good enough. The main difficulty with the report is that it did not examine the reasons thoroughly enough, and thereby missed a golden opportunity to examine a number of substantial issues. The purpose of this paper is to prod the industry into a more careful analysis of possible future problems, so that its response can be proactive, rather than reactive.

NOTES

1. Investment Company Institute, news release, May 9, 1994.
2. "Report of the Advisory Group on Personal Investing," May 9, 1994, p. ii.
3. Ibid, pp. ii–iii.
4. Ibid, p. v.
5. Ibid., p. 19.
6. Ibid.
7. From p. 13 of a code of ethics of an unnamed bank.
8. "Report of the Advisory Group on Personal Investing," May 9, 1994, p. 20.
9. Ibid., pp 21–22.
10. Ibid., p. 22

4

Fiduciary Responsibility and the Duty to Account for Clients' Funds

Franklyn P. Salimbene and Gerald R. Ferrera

In the months since the Securities and Exchange Commission began asking mutual fund companies for information on the personal trading habits of their fund managers, many in the mutual funds industry have been forced to take a sobering look at the legal and ethical implications of managing other people's money. Actions by fund managers like personal trading, investing portfolios in unsuitably risky and speculative stock, and obtaining personal benefits through private deals with stock analysts are a constant threat to the foundation of trust, which supports the entire mutual funds industry. As lawyers looking at the professional implications of these activities for the investment manager, the authors are mindful of similar issues of trust and fiduciary responsibility that arise for attorneys who receive clients' funds during the various stages of legal representation. Here, as in investment management, the attorney is faced with the legal and ethical implications of accounting for other people's money.

This chapter will attempt to review the concept of accounting as it applies to the duties of an attorney in handling the money of a client. Specifically, it will discuss the legal and ethical requirements imposed by the bar on the attorney in the handling of clients' funds. It also will discuss the philosophical underpinning of these requirements and will offer useful insight into how the legal profession is dealing with breaches of the requirements. The objective is to provide information and guidance to investment managers and other professionals who grapple similarly with the dilemmas posed when dealing with other people's money.

INTRODUCTION

The duty of a trustee or agent to account to his client for funds held in the client's behalf is one of ancient pedigree. In common law, the action of account has been traced back to A.D. 1232, where it appears upon the register during the reign of Henry III.[1] As the action developed, it came to be used against accountants acting as manorial bailiffs and guardians in socage.[2] In each instance the agent was commanded to render to the client an account for the time during which he was in receipt of the client's money.[3] By the late 1600s, the common law action of account was superceded by other actions, but despite this development, the duty to account lost none of its legal force.[4]

Today, an accounting of money and other assets held by a trustee or agent must be rendered in a variety of legal situations. An executor or administrator of an estate must render an account in the probate court as part of settling the estate; partners must render an accounting to each other as part of the dissolution of the partnership; trustees in bankruptcy must account to the creditors for the assets of the business. The implication in all of these situations is that the trustee or agent holds assets for the benefit of another and must account to that other for the disposition of those assets. The duty of the fund manager is essentially the same.

The matter of an attorney's clients' funds also falls within this regime. The attorney must account to the client for funds that belong to the client, but that are held by the attorney for the purpose of supporting the client's legal representation.[5] Such funds may be advanced by the client for expenses to be incurred in pending litigation or as a retainer for legal services, or they may be paid by a third party to the attorney as a result of a real estate transaction or an insurance settlement on behalf of the client. As shall be shown, the legal and ethical obligations of the attorney with regard to these funds require that they be separated totally from the attorney's personal and business funds and that adequate records be kept so that an accounting to the client can be rendered upon request. Yet, regrettably, there exist continually recurring instances of attorneys misusing and even appropriating clients' funds.

THE SCOPE OF THE PROBLEM

The issue of attorney misappropriation of clients' funds was given national attention a few years ago by the well-publicized escapades of Timothy O'Leary. O'Leary, a Massachusetts attorney and state legislator, secretly fled Boston in the fall of 1991; he did so to commit suicide in Maine. In the course of his activities as a lawyer and politician, O'Leary had embezzled over $100,000, about $85,000 of which belonged to his clients.[6] Confronted by mortgage payments that he could not meet and college tuition bills for his children, he literally stole from his clients. When he determined that his theft was only compounding the problem, he decided to kill himself. His suicide odyssey took him from Boston to Maine, and then on to seven other states when he finally ended his flight unable to do himself in. Instead, under a barrage of media attention, he returned to Boston to face disbarment and prosecution.[7]

As bizarre as the O'Leary escapade seems, the statistics on attorney misappropriation of clients' funds sadly indicate that O'Leary's defalcation is not unique to the profession. The amount of clients' money verified as having been stolen by Massachusetts attorneys in 1990 was $759,000. In California, the amount was $2.1 million, and in New York, it reached the outrageous sum of $4.4 million.[8] Unfortunately, since 1990, the problem seems not to have lessened. Paul J. Liacos, the chief justice of the Massachusetts Supreme Judicial Court recently conceded that lawyer theft is and remains a "serious problem."[9]

The issue of lawyer abuse of clients' funds is squarely addressed in the American Bar Association's (ABA) Model Rules of Professional Conduct and in its Model Code. Model Rule 1.15 provides that the property of clients held by an attorney "shall be kept in a separate account." Such accounts are commonly referred to as "clients' funds accounts" or "trust accounts." Further, the Rule provides that "[c]omplete records of such account funds shall be kept by the lawyer," and that a full accounting be rendered to the client upon request.[10] The Model Code follows upon the Rules; it provides attorneys with practical disciplinary guidelines for implementing the principles enunciated in the Rules.[11] It should be noted, however, that because the ABA's Rules and Code are advisory, their enforceability against attorneys in any state depends upon their adoption by the appropriate state licensing authority. Commonly, that authority is the state's highest court. Further, because each state acts independently in these matters, it is usual to find variations in the rules from state to state.[12] This regime obviously differs from regulation of the mutual funds industry by the SEC, a federal agency with national jurisdiction.

Irrespective of any state variations in the regulation of attorneys, however, the essential elements of Rule 1.15 are universally accepted. An attorney will breach the fiduciary duty to the client whenever the attorney commingles personal or business funds with the clients' funds or whenever the attorney fails to maintain complete records of clients' funds accounts.[13] In its manual on professional conduct, the ABA cautions that "losing track through sloppy recordkeeping of a client's money or mixing the client's money with that of the lawyer so that its separate identity is lost, commonly—and logically enough—presages misappropriation."[14]

COMMINGLING AS A BREACH OF DUTY

Commingling results whenever a client's money is intermingled with his attorney's money so that its separate identity is lost.[15] Such an intermingling is a violation of duty because it enhances the possibility of misappropriation. As the Supreme Court of California stated in *Black v. State Bar of California,* "The rule against commingling 'was adopted to provide against the probability in some cases, the possibility in many cases, and the danger in all cases that such commingling will result in the loss of clients' money.' "[16] In effect, commingling always raises "the key question, Whose money is it?"[17] When the answer to this question is difficult to discern, the likelihood that the attorney will spend clients' money for personal purposes is enhanced.

The duty to keep funds separate can be violated in a variety of ways. The violation can occur even when there is no intention to steal. The situation of Massachusetts attorney H. Hoover Garabedian is a case in point.[18] Upon being retained by a widow in the probate of her husband's estate, Garabedian received a retainer of $6,000. He immediately deposited the retainer in his personal account and then issued a check to the Internal Revenue Service to pay his personal income tax. The Massachusetts Board of Bar Overseers ruled that such action constituted the misuse of client's funds, and the Supreme Judicial Court agreed.[19] The states generally hold that a retainer does not become the property of the attorney until it is "earned."[20] In Garabedian's case, since he had only just been retained, he could not have earned the fee. Not having yet earned it, he commingled it when he deposited it into his personal account.

A violation may also occur in the reverse. Thus, the attorney who, rather than depositing clients' money into the attorney's personal account, deposits his own money into the clients' funds account, or who leaves money which he has already earned in such an account, may likewise have commingled. Regarding personal deposits into clients' accounts, several states, although not all, allow for the deposit of small amounts of the attorney's personal funds into such accounts in order to cover bank charges which may be levied against those accounts.[21] No state, however, would likely have condoned the shocking behavior of Iowa attorney Robert Gross. In an attempt to avoid attachment of personal funds and hide them from his wife who was seeking to satisfy back child support payments, Gross deposited all his money into his clients' funds account.[22] The Iowa Supreme Court was quick to rule such behavior as violative of the rule against commingling. Those cases which involve money that the attorney has already earned, but which he has left in the clients' funds account, will also result in disciplinary action in several states. In the previous case cited, while Garabedian was wrong to place a retainer which he had not yet earned into his personal account, he likewise would have been wrong in many states if, after properly placing it in a clients' funds account, he had not withdrawn it within a reasonable period of time after having earned it.[23]

Further, a violation of the attorney's duty can occur even when no injury results to the client. In *Garabedian*, the Massachusetts court ordered him suspended from the practice of law in part because of his commingling of clients' funds. It did this even though it likewise found that the client was not harmed by the commingling. The facts in the case demonstrated that two years after being retained, Garabedian was discharged by his client, and that upon discharge, he refunded the full amount of the retainer.[24]

INCOMPLETE RECORDKEEPING AS A BREACH OF DUTY

Just as commingling presages misappropriation of clients' money, so does incomplete recordkeeping. In 1982, New Jersey attorney Ralph Fucetola was reported to the Division of Ethics and Professional Services in his state by a client who claimed that it had never received a check on account of collections made in its behalf by Fucetola.[25] An audit of the attorney's records was ordered by the Division. The auditor found that Fucetola "did not maintain a running balance of his cash receipts and disbursements in his trust account," nor did he record all deposits or keep any reconciliations regarding the account. Ruling that Fucetola violated the duty to keep complete records, the New Jersey Supreme Court, in publicly reprimanding the attorney, stated, "The purpose of discipline is to protect the public from the attorney who does not meet the standards of responsibility of every member of the profession."[26]

Fucetola does not stand alone in his failure to follow basic recordkeeping form. Thomas Hetzel, a Wisconsin attorney, was suspended from the practice of law by the Wisconsin Supreme Court in part because he answered a written request for a full accounting by offering an oral account in the form of a deposition. When informed that such an account was insufficient, Hetzel countered that his oral account did not violate the rule "requiring a lawyer to maintain complete records of all client funds coming into his possession, for the reason that the rule does not specify what form those records are to take."[27] Add to Hetzel's case the circumstances of a New Jersey law firm that fired its bookkeeper, combined all business funds and clients' funds into one account, kept no account balance, and then telephoned its bank once a week to find out what its account balance was.[28] When overdrafts inevitably resulted, the firm argued that due to its ignorance of proper accounting procedures, the misappropriation of clients' funds was innocent because it was inadvertent. The New Jersey Supreme Court, in disbarring the partners of the firm, countered that it is "no defense for lawyers to design an accounting system that prevents them from knowing whether they are using clients' trust funds."[29]

These rather blatant examples of the breach of the duty to keep complete records have led to several attempts by courts and bar associations to offer specific guidance to attorneys in meeting the duty. For instance, in a 1985 decision, the Court of Appeals of North Carolina indicated that attorneys were obligated to maintain a system that allowed them to know at any one time what amount in their trust account belonged to a particular client. This required the maintenance of "a running balance of the funds kept in a trust account for a particular person."[30] The court concluded that check stubs, cancelled checks, and bank statements, all of which the respondent in the case had presented to the court, were in themselves inadequate.

A further and much more detailed clarification of the duty to keep complete records was adopted by the American Bar Association in 1993. In its Model Recordkeeping Rule, the ABA offered a precise statement of the duties incumbent upon attorneys with regard to all bank accounts related in any way to their practice of law.[31] In its comment on this new rule, the standing committee which drafted it recognized that under ABA tenets, while lawyers are held to the fiduciary's standard of care regarding the maintenance of clients' fund accounts, nowhere did the ABA "provide lawyers or law firms with practical guidance . . . in establishing basic and essential accounting control systems for their law practices."[32] The proposed rule as offered was intended to address "these functional deficiencies." The new rule is adapted from existing rules already in effect in New York and New Jersey. In sum, the rule requires: (1) the maintenance of a journal record of all bank deposits and withdrawals, including monthly balance sheets; contracts for payment; check stubs, statements, cancelled checks, and duplicate deposit slips; and at least quarterly reconciliations; (2) regarding trust or clients' funds accounts, the maintenance of monthly reconciliations; (3) the permissible maintenance of bookkeeping records on computer capable of providing an account on demand; and (4) the retention of all records for a period of five years.

PREVENTING BREACHES OF DUTY

Penalties for breach of the fiduciary duties that disallow commingling and that require complete recordkeeping include private reprimand,[33] public reprimand,[34] censure,[35] suspension for a period of time,[36] and disbarment.[37] Each of these is punitive in nature; each is a reaction to an already committed breach.

Unfortunately, such reactive penalties have not prevented violations. Because of this, many jurisdictions are implementing additional, preventative measures. These preventative measures seek to avert a breach of duty before it happens. The types of preventative measures in use in various jurisdictions include annual lawyer disclosure to state agencies, random audits, notification by banks of overdrafts in attorney accounts, and insurer notification to claimants of payments being made.

Serving to promote complete recordkeeping and to insure against commingling, Delaware requires its attorneys to submit an annual certificate and questionnaire disclosing their compliance with the rules on recordkeeping.[38] Minnesota, having established a detailed recordkeeping requirement, compels attorneys to certify their compliance to the requirement at the time of the lawyer's annual registration.[39]

Auditing attorney bank accounts also works to prevent breaches in fiduciary duties. Sixteen states have a rule allowing some type of audit and eight of those allow for random audits.[40] Such random audits entitle the state's attorney-licensing authority to order attorneys selected at random to produce their bank records for review. In Massachusetts, in 1992, the Board of Bar Overseers (BBO) rejected a recommendation from the Massachusetts Bar Association for random audits. James R. DeGiacomo, chair of the BBO, argued that random audits would be very costly, would create great hardship for sole practitioners, and would not stem lawyer theft.[41]

Overdraft notification is another preventative measure. It would require a bank to inform either the attorney involved or the state's attorney-licensing authority that a check drawn on a clients' funds account has bounced. Thirteen states and the District of Columbia have overdraft notification regulations.[42] The details of these notification regulations vary. In Virginia, for instance, once a check has bounced, the bank notifies the attorney who then has three days within which to rectify the overdraft. If the overdraft is not rectified, the bank then notifies Virginia authorities.[43] New Jersey, on the other hand, requires immediate notification of all overdrafts to state authorities.[44] In Massachusetts, the BBO did approve an overdraft notification proposal and recommended its adoption by the Supreme Judicial Court.[45]

The duty to notify the client promptly that the attorney is in receipt of funds in which the client has an interest is clearly stated in Model Rule 1.15 (b) and in Model Code DR 9-102 (B) (1). This duty belongs to the attorney. A few states have gone on to require that insurance companies that make payment to an attorney on behalf of the attorney's client also notify the client that the check is in the mail.[46] In Massachusetts, the BBO did not approve an insurer notification proposal. The BBO chair observed that such a scheme would not only send an unwelcome message that attorneys cannot be trusted, but also would not ultimately deter those attorneys bent on theft.[47]

In addition to the noted preventative measures, one other element of client protection ought to be mentioned. Several states have established client security boards (CSBs).[48] These boards make disbursements to clients who have been victimized by lawyer theft. Money paid out by such boards is usually made available through annual lawyer registration fees. For instance, in Massachusetts, the CSB is estimated to receive approximately $1.25 million annually from the approximately $5 million collected in registration fees. Most of the remainder goes to funding the activities of the Board of Bar Overseers.[49]

Whether and to what extent any of these measures geared toward protecting an attorney's clients' funds can or should be made to apply to investment managers or others in the financial markets is an issue best left to those expert in those fields. Suffice it to say that the requirements of the fiduciary's responsibility to those whose money is held in trust demand an enforcement mechanism that minimizes conflicts of interest, promotes accountability, and punishes wrongdoing. This result, which may be imposed by law, is firmly supported by ethical theory.

PROFESSIONAL CONDUCT IMPOSED BY THE BAR AND ITS ROOTS IN ETHICAL THEORY AND MORAL DEVELOPMENT

The American Bar Association's Model Rule of Professional Conduct and Model Code Rule 1.15 is a clear and simple expression of absolute integrity regarding property that is held on behalf of another: "[it] shall be kept in a separate account."[50] This rubric avoids even the perception of wrongdoing by prohibiting the commingling of the client's funds with that of the fiduciary. Since the Bar Association and its Board of Bar Overseers promulgated this rule, one could query its philosophical underpinnings.

NATURAL LAW ETHICS

Thomas Aquinas, the founder of natural law, in his "Treatise on Law" stated, "[l]aw is nothing else than an ordinance of reason for the common good, promulgated by him who has care of the community."[51] Since our community relies upon the legal system and its practitioners to be beyond reproach, one could argue the rule of "a separate account" is an "ordinance of reason for the common good." Natural law lawyers contended there are "natural connections" between law and moral norms.[52] Within this natural law construct it would appear the Model Code Rule has its foundation in ethics and a moral orientation toward society.

KANTIAN ETHICS

A Kantian analysis, found in his Categorical Imperative, would question the morality of a fiduciary who commingles funds on the basis of universalizing that practice. Kant stated, "I ought never to act except in such a way that I can also will my maxim should become a universal law."[53] The commingling attorney or other fiduciary would have to defend his conduct within Kant's Categorical Imperative by arguing *all* who hold funds on behalf of others should be able to mix them with their personal and/or business accounts. This is simply an untenable position. Kantian ethics would further condemn commingling funds on the basis that the client's merged property is at risk, and this practice does not respect the client as an end in itself. Kant argued, "act in such a way that you always treat humanity, whether in your own person or in the person of any other, never simply as a means, but always at the same time as an end."[54] As members of the community, clients have the right to expect that fiduciaries will care for their property and account for its use. Consider the Garabedian case[55] where the attorney paid his personal income tax with a $6,000 retainer. Since the action of entrustment of funds to a fiduciary has intrinsic value beyond its consequences in the trust we give to another, the fiduciary's conduct of commingling funds is never justified by his motives. This deontological theory would obviate excuses of misappropriation on the basis of "good faith."

RAWLSIAN ETHICS

The "separate account" and "complete records of such account funds [to] be kept by the lawyer" has its ethical and philosophical roots in distributive justice. The Bar Association and the various state licensing authorities, usually the state's highest court, act on behalf of the state to establish rules of professional conduct for its legal practitioners as they distribute the benefits and resources of the legal system to society. John Rawls, in his book *A Theory of Justice*, has advanced Kantian ethics and the ethical theory of deontology.[56] Rawls argues that we should evaluate social transactions by imagining a "veil of ignorance" regarding our status in society that would prevent us from exploiting social and natural circumstances to our own advantage. Those in Rawls's "original position" exploring the justification of commingling funds would not know their "place in society . . . class position or social status, nor . . . [their] fortune in the distribution of natural assets."[57] This principle of functioning in the original position behind a veil of ignorance requires one to engage in "role reversal." The fiduciary should ask "if these were my funds would I want them to lose their identity and be commingled?" and "would I expect an accounting of this property entrusted to my care?" Rawls forces us to acknowledge that distributive justice demands we cannot economically benefit at the expense of others.

Rawls's neo-Kantian theory is especially relevant in our contemporary society which constantly seeks to review and rewrite traditional terms of the social contract.[58] Rawls's idea of the original position posits a group of men and women who come together to form a social contract. He contends that a group that is temporarily ignorant of its own social status will always act out of self-interest and will be intuitively guided by the social principles of equal liberty and equal opportunity. Query: do the "separate account" and "recordkeeping" rules adhere to these social principles? Rawls has been criticized on the basis that his social principles are conservative and some, aware of their own talents, may prefer another choice.[59] Although Garabedian could argue his professional integrity would assure repayment of the $6,000 retainer—used to pay his personal income tax—to his client, at best, he would be then acting as a self-enlightened egoist and not at a high level of ethical conduct.

Rawls's greatest contribution is that his theory of justice extends the contractarian metaphors of Locke's, Rousseau's, and Kant's moral vision. They all argue that a just society is best governed by a social contract determined by the consent of all.[60] Rawls's social contract goes beyond that democratic principle and includes liberty and economic opportunity that are linked to autonomy. According to Rawls, the capacity of persons to develop their lives forms the basis of self-respect and is a primary good.[61] Mr. O'Leary's escapade illustrates the dangerous consequences of ignoring Rawls's principles.

KOHLBERG'S STAGES OF MORAL DEVELOPMENT

Lawrence Kohlberg's stage theory of moral development[62] would characterize the Model Code Rule as a stage six postconventional level of morality. This stage draws on Kant's Categorical Imperative where morality is based on adherence to universal moral principles that govern social cooperation.[63] Kohlberg would find Rawls's theory of justice appropriate for his sixth stage of moral development. The basis of the American Bar Association's Model Rules of Professional Conduct's "separate account and full accounting rule" would be at Kohlberg's highest level of moral reasoning.

One could find other ethical justifications for the American Bar Association's Model Rule of Professional Conduct and Model Code 1.15.[64] Lawyers and other fiduciaries should recognize that their part of the social contract may be demanding but social justice dictates strict compliance for the welfare of their own profession and the common good.

CONCLUSION

Fiduciary trust is a distinctive requirement of our business life. It is a pervasive expectation because it presupposes the fiduciary to whom we have entrusted our financial well-being will somehow function at the highest ethical standard. In the last few decades the public has become more aware of the illegal and unethical behavior of financial and legal representatives. They are generally not placated by the argument that "most fiduciaries are honest and moral practitioners." The legal, accounting, and financial professionals must become extraordinarily sensitive to the moral and ethical principles patent in the fiduciary relationship.

Continuing the education of the profession and articulation of the ethical principles and theories that support fiduciary responsibilities are essential. Some practitioners will disagree with the high ethical standards adopted by their professional associations. But the debate will make them more sensitive to the ethical principles that shape our professional culture. The perception of wrongdoing maintained by the general public must be corrected. It is not enough to cite professional codes of ethical responsibility if the general practitioners are unconvinced of their relevancy. Our professional organizations should work openly with their clients and customers to assure them of realistic participation in the ethical rule-making process.

The problem lies not with fiduciary responsibility that is being eroded by a few unethical professional representatives, but with a general public perception that the elite who deal with other people's money cannot be trusted. We can rebuild the professional culture of the fiduciary only by understanding legal precedent, codes of professional conduct, and their underlying ethical principles. We must make sense of what has seemed to be unrelated legal duties and ethical responsibility. The challenge to the professions is to make fiduciary responsibility consonant with their own roots in ethical theory and moral behavior and hence, with our tradition of committed caring professionals.

NOTES

1. 2 Frederick Pollock and Frederick W. Maitland, *The History of English Law* 221 (2d ed. 1898) (Cambridge: Cambridge University Press, 1952).

2. Ibid. See also J. H. Baker, *An Introduction to English Legal History* 301 (2d ed.) (Butterworth Legal Publishers 1979). Baker explains that a manorial bailiff was an estate manager and that a guardian in socage was one appointed, often a near relative, to look after the estate of an under-age heir. In either case, the trustee could be made to account for his stewardship of his client's money and other property.

3. The writ of account filed on behalf of the client would direct the trustee to "justly and without delay render to the plaintiff" an account for the time during which the trustee was the plaintiff's bailiff and receiver of the plaintiff's money. 2 Pollock and Maitland, *supra* note 1.

4. An action in account resulted in just that, an accounting. To actually recover money and other property from the agent, the action of account had to be followed up by a second action, often the action in debt. Because of the shortcomings of this two-action process, lawyers began to treat a failure to account as a theft in itself. Thus, a single action in conversation was brought. As time progressed, courts entertained other single actions to protect the right of a client, including actions in trover and assumpsit. In assumpsit, by 1689, it was held that the receiver of money as an agent was understood to promise an account to the one whose money was held. Thus, the action of assumpsit alone was sufficient to recover the client's property. Baker, *supra* note 2, at 301–305.

5. For a brief summary of the attorney's duty, see "Safeguarding Client Funds," *LLR Quarterly*, October 1993, at 3–5.

6. "The Rise and Fall of Timothy O'Leary," *Massachusetts Lawyers Weekly*, July 13, 1992, at 41.

7. On February 4, 1992, O'Leary pleaded guilty to eighteen counts of perjury, embezzlement, forgery, and filing false income tax returns; on April 16, 1992, he went to jail. On June 26, 1992, the Massachusetts Supreme Judicial Court disbarred O'Leary.

8. Amy Dockser Marcus, "Thievery By Lawyers Is On The Increase, With Dupped Clients Losing Bigger Sums," *Wall Street Journal*, November 26, 1990, at B1.

9. Barbara Rabinovitz, "Chiefly Speaking," *Massachusetts Lawyers Weekly*, December 6, 1993, at 29, 35. Massachusetts Board of Bar Overseers counsel Michael Fredrickson reported in 1992 that the amount of money paid out by the Clients' Security Board, a body whose responsibility it is to compensate clients for attorney theft, is "up dramatically," but that the number of offending lawyers is fairly stable; see "The Consequences of Commingling Funds," *Massachusetts Lawyers Weekly*, July 13, 1992, May 57.

10. For the complete text of Model Rule 1.15, see *ABA/BNA Lawyers Manual on Professional Conduct*, sec. 45:101–102 (No. 131, 1993) [hereinafter *ABA Manual*].

11. For the complete text of Model Code DR 9–102, see *ABA Manual, supra* note 10, sec. 45:102.

12. For a discussion to the variations to Rule 1.15, see *ABA Manual, supra* note 10, sec. 45:102–105. For the complete rule as adopted by the Massachusetts Supreme Judicial Court, see *Massachusetts Supreme Judicial Court Rule 3:07, DR 9–102 (1994)*.

13. *ABA Manual, supra* note 10, sec. 45:101.

14. Ibid., sec. 45:502.

15. *Black v State Bar of California*, 18 Cal. Rptr. 518, 368 p. 2d 118, 122 (1962).

16. Ibid.

17. *ABA Manual, supra* note 10, sec. 45:101.

18. *Matter of Garabedian*, 415 Mass. 77, 612 N.E. 2d 1133 (1993).

19. Ibid., at 1135. In Massachusetts, according to Board of Bar Overseers counsel Michael Fredrickson, conversion of unearned legal retainers results in the second largest category of awards made by Clients' Security Board; he asserts, however, that many lawyers who convert retainers do so out of ignorance of the fact that retainers become the lawyer's property only after being earned, and not simply upon being paid over by the client; see "Lawyer Thefts Cost $625,000," *Massachusetts Lawyers Weekly*, December 2, 1991, at 1.

20. *See generally ABA Manual, supra* note 10, sec. 45:109–110 (a legal retainer becomes the property of the attorney when it is earned); *In re McDonald Brothers Construction, Inc.*, 114 B.R. 989, 997–1002 (Bankr. N.D. Ill. 1990) (provides a useful discussion of the various types of legal retainers and when each is deemed to be "earned" by the attorney).

21. Massachusetts is one such state; see *Massachusetts Supreme Judicial Court Rule 3:07, DR 9–102 (A) (1) (1994)*.

22. *Committee on Professional Ethics and Conduct v Gross,* 326 N.W. 2d 272 (Iowa 1982).

23. *Black v State Bar of California, supra* note 15, at 122; Attorney Grievance Commission of *Maryland v Sliffman,* 330 Md. 515, 625 A. 2d 314, 319 (1993); *In re Maran,* 402 A. 2d 924 (N.J. 1979).

24. *Matter of Garabedian, supra* note 18, at 1135. Likewise for the proposition that attorney discipline will result from commingling cases absent any harm to the client, see also *Matter of Fleischer,* 102 N.J. 440, 508 A. 2d 1115 (1986), and *Matter of Brown,* 427 S.E. 2d 645 (S.C. 1993).

25. *Matter of Fucetola,* 101 N.J. 5, 449A. 2d 222 (1985).

26. Ibid., at 224.

27. *Disciplinary Proceedings against Hetzel,* 118 Wisc. 2d 257, 346 N.W. 2d 782 (1984).

28. *Matter of Fleischer, supra* note 24.

29. Ibid., at 1120.

30. *North Carolina State Bar v Sheffield,* 326 S.E. 2d 320, 326 (N.C. Ct. App. 1985).

31. For the complete text of the ABA's Model Recordkeeping Rule, see *ABA manual, supra* note 10, sec. 45:1004–1005.

32. *ABA Manual, supra* note 10, sec. 45:1006.

33. *Matter of Fucetola, supra* note 25. The Bergen County Ethics Committee had recommended a private reprimand in Fucetola's case, but the Disciplinary Review Board countered that recommendation with one of public reprimand, which the New Jersey Supreme Court followed.

34. *Black v State Bar of California, supra* note 15; *Matter of Hennessey,* 93 N.J. 358, 461 A. 2d 156 (1983).

35. *Matter of Loventhal,* No. 93-037BD (Mass. Sup. Jud. Ct. Jan. 15, 1993); *Matter of Shyavitz,* No. 92-021BD (Mass. Sup. Jud. Ct. Jan. 15, 1993).

36. *Committee on Professional Ethics and Conduct v Gross, supra* note 22 (at least 60-day suspension); *Attorney Grievance Commission of Maryland v Sliffman, supra* note 23 (one-year suspension); *Matter of Garabedian, supra* note 18 (90-day suspension); *North Carolina State Bar v Sheffield, supra* note 30 (three-year suspension); *Disciplinary Proceedings against Hetzel, supra* note 27 (one-year suspension).

37. *Matter of Williams,* 711 S.W. 2d 518 (Mo. 1986); *Matter of Fleischer, supra* note 24.

38. *ABA Manual, supra* note 10, sec. 45:1001.

39. Ibid., sec. 45:1002.

40. Ibid., sec. 45:1002–1003. These states include Arizona, Delaware, Florida, Idaho, Maine, Maryland, Minnesota, Nebraska, New Hampshire, New Jersey, New Mexico, North Carolina, Virginia, Washington, and Wisconsin. Random audits occur in New York's First and Second Departments.

41. Barbara Rabinovitz, "Bar Targets Lawyer Theft; Fee Hike Of 40%, Rule On Overdrafts Asked By BBO," *Massachusetts Lawyers Weekly,* July 13, 1992, at 1.

42. *ABA Manual, supra* note 10, sec. 45:1003–1004. These states include California, Connecticut, Florida, Idaho, Maryland, Minnesota, Montana, New Jersey, New York, North Carolina, Rhode Island, Vermont, and Virginia.

43. Ibid., at 1004.

44. Ibid.

45. Barbara Rabinovitz, *supra* note 41. As of this writing, the Massachusetts Supreme Judicial Court has not yet acted on the overdraft notification requirement; see "Dishonored Check Rule Goes to Supreme Judicial Court," *Massachusetts Bar Association Lawyers Journal*, July/August 1994, at 3.

46. Susan Roberts Boyle, "Lawyer Theft Committee Issues Recommendation," *Massachusetts Lawyers Weekly*, May 25, 1992, at 3. New York and Pennsylvania are two states which require insurers to notify claimants that settlement proceeds have been mailed to claimants' attorneys. The New York rule requires simultaneous written notice whenever payments are for $5,000 or more.

47. Barbara Rabinovitz, *supra* note 41.

48. Amy Dockser Marcus, *supra* note 8.

49. Barbara Rabinovitz, *supra* note 41.

50. Model Rule 1.15 is referenced in *ABA Manual, supra* note 10.

51. T. Aquinas, *Summa Theologica* (1266–73), I–II. p. 90, art. 4, in 2 *Basic Writings of Saint Thomas Aquinas* (Pegis ed.) (New York: Random House, 1945).

52. D. Lyons, *Ethics and the Rule of Law* 74 (1984).

53. I. Kant, *Groundwork of the Metaphysics of Morals* 70 (Paton ed.) (New York: Barnes & Noble, 1969).

54. Ibid., at 16.

55. *See supra* note 18 and accompanying text.

56. J. Rawls, *A Theory of Justice* 11 (Cambridge, MA: Harvard University Press, 1970) (stating that the purpose of his philosophy is "to present a conception of justice which generalizes and carries to a higher level of abstraction the familiar theory of social contract as found . . . [in] Kant.").

57. Ibid., at 136.

58. Ibid., at 137.

59. Dworkin, *The Original Position*, 40 U. CHI. L. REV. 500 (1973).

60. Ibid., at 504.

61. Richards, *The Right to Die*, 22 WM. & MARY L. REV. 327 (Spring 1981).

62. *See generally* L. Kohlberg, *The Psychology of Moral Development* (San Francisco: Harper & Row, 1984).

63. *See generally* J. Rest, *Moral Development: Advances in Research and Theory* (Westport, CT: Praeger Publishers, 1986).

64. *See generally* L. Fuller, *The Morality of Law* (1964); and H. L. A. Hart, *The Concept of Law* (New Haven, CT: Yale University Press; Oxford: Clarendon Press, 1961).

5

Some Ethical Issues in Financial Markets

Patricia H. Werhane

Most people, most institutions, and even most politicians and governmental officials are decent, well-meaning people. Ethical issues sometimes occur not because people are evil or even greedy, but because the way in which they view a situation belies its ethical import. The model of financial markets one adopts and the way one thinks markets operate or should operate affect one's perception of those markets and whether and how one focuses on the ethical issues. Part of this model or perception is derived from the political, ideological, and economic context (in the cases I shall discuss, the United States), and part from individual mores, corporate culture, or more global perspectives. Often, ethical dilemmas arise because of a narrow perception of what is at issue, or because one has failed to see clearly how one's model or point of view concerning financial markets may be incomplete, narrow, or even erroneous. Sometimes that perspective does not include a moral point of view. That is, managers, traders, CEOs, financial analysts, and bankers do not think clearly about the normative implications of their decisions and actions—how they will affect (positively or negatively) the well-being of other people and other institutions, nor how their actions may or may not treat people fairly and respect them and their rights as human beings. This "moral muteness" in turn can have dilatory economic as well as moral effects.

In what follows, I shall use two illustrations to exemplify some of the kinds of issues in financial markets that arise, issues that face individuals, corporations, and some that are caused by the political system itself. Ordinarily, discussions of financial markets center around insider trading, mergers, the savings and loan crisis, and so on. Much has been written about these topics. So the issues I shall deal with are institutional investing and municipal bond trading to illustrate how a particular approach one adopts or presupposes in framing an issue impacts on its ethical substance and implications. In each instance I shall show how another, more inclusive framework, might better serve to alleviate the ethical dilemmas that arise in each case. Hopefully, the moral frameworks dealing with these cases will have general applicability in other contexts as well.

INSTITUTIONAL INVESTING

Lens, Inc. is a small activist-oriented institutional investment firm led by Robert Monks, its founder. In late 1990 Lens began pressuring Sears, Roebuck and Company, a corporation whose stock was part of Lens's investment portfolio, to focus on its core business rather than attempt to combine a financial supermarket with a department store. After almost two years of pressure, Sears announced that it would concentrate on its retail business and sell Coldwell Banker, its real estate operations, as well as 20% of Dean Witter and Allstate, its principal financial holdings. Lens claimed that its efforts generated more than $1 billion in shareholder value because the price of Sears stock rose sharply over the two years. But the rise in the stock price generally followed the rise in the S&P 500 during the same period. Only two points [of that stock price rise] are clearly from Lens's efforts: the company's stock substantially lagged the S&P 500 before the campaign began, and the stock rose almost $4 on the day Sears announced it was selling its financial businesses.[1]

Institutional investors have become increasingly important in the United States. The majority of voting shares of publicly traded stock is now owned by institutional investors: private, municipal, and state pension funds, employee stock option plans, mutual funds, and other large institutions that invest vast sums of money for their institution, their clients, or employees. A single institutional investor can own and vote large blocks of stock of any company, and thus influence its direction and decision making. Institutional investment is usually carried out by an internal or external investment manager. An active investment manager can give its investor–shareholders a substantive voice in corporate policy, and this new phenomenon has changed the traditional twentieth-century "hands-off" shareholder–manager relationship. As an owner or shareholder, having a voice in what happens to the company in which one owns shares would appear to restore the classic tradition of owner control that characterized early management arrangements of the eighteenth and nineteenth centuries. Indeed, from that perspective, shareholders, as owners of a corporation, have responsibility for its direction, and institutional investor activism is a justifiable method for the exercise of that responsibility.

However, this model of investor activism relies on the nineteenth-century model of entrepreneurial ownership wherein the owner or owners of a company were also its top management. Thus, it is an oversimplification of what is at issue. The twentieth-century division of corporate ownership and management changes the structure of corporate decision making, placing the onus of responsibility on managers as agents for the shareholders. Indeed, it would be messy, at best, if all shareholder–owners ran the companies they owned. This does not imply that investor activism is unjustified, but that phenomenon may require rethinking the division of ownership and management that has pervaded during the last 60 years. Institutional investors and their investment managers play the role of outside directors, and like outside directors they are viewed both as external consultants and as pariahs by internal directors and managers. Institutional investors are not always experts in corporate management, finance, marketing, or other areas in which they offer advice. Because of this lack of expertise, many CEOs and boards of directors question the value of investor activism and view this kind of activity as unnecessary meddling.

The relationship between institutions and their investment managers is a complexification both of the shareholder–management relationship and of the trader–shareholder relationship. Professionally, investment managers represent their institutional clients, and their primary aim is to maximize the return on clients' investments. If an institutional investor veers from that goal that can only occur with the permission of her clients, since such activism is paid for out of clients' investment money. Because institutional investor activism is costly to clients, if it does not increase the stock price or return on investment, *or* if it is engaged in without client permission, then it is at best a questionable procedure given the professional role of the investment manager. In the Lens case it is not clear that Lens maximized the return for its clients nor involved them in the decision process. Did Robert Monks at Lens attack Sears in an attempt to raise its stock price for his clients, or was his interest in Sears motivated by other of his own financial interests?[2] When investment managers use clients' money to engage in corporate activism, they act on the basis of their considered judgment of the value of this intervention, and they must do so with due diligence of the possible conflict of interest between their interests and those of their clients. There is less financial conflict when the investment manager is an employee of the institution she represents. Nevertheless, zeal to intervene, particularly when one is managing a large fund with controlling shares, sometimes overrides good judgment.

Investment managers are agents for their institutional clients, that is obvious. But, an investment manager might protest, how can one accurately assess the interests of clients, say, pensioners, who are as dispersed as stockholders? One cannot call up 300,000 clients of TIAA-CREF, for example, to get their opinion on investor activism, nor do mail ballots always solicit adequate responses. However, a helpful way to analyze one's practices is from a moral point of view, approaching questions involving institutional activism such as these from what is called an impartial perspective, imagining how one would react to a client's inquiry and defending one's actions. Impartiality is crucial, because unless one can disengage oneself from the context of a specific decision, one's decisions are parochially embedded such as to result in the very kinds of business decisions that invite moral and even sometimes fiscal failure. It is obviously impossible to completely disengage oneself from every perspective, but one can usually step back from a particular situation and ask some acute questions. For example, would a reasonable person think this activism makes sense given the particular corporate situation? Will this activity hold up against basic standards for acceptable behavior, for example, are you being fair to corporate management, to the board, to other shareholders, to employees and customers, and to the best interests of your clients? Is this the kind of action you can defend in public to the constituents you represent? Does your decision or action best represent your clients' interests even at the expense of your own?[3] Will this decision pass the "television" test, that is, would you mind seeing it on television? Is this an action that is necessary for the success of the company in which you are investing? for the survival of the industry? Is this the only option? How might you and your institutional clients make changes? These sorts of questions along with communication with institutional clients help to assure diligent restraint and responsible action.

MUNICIPAL BOND TRADING

Let us consider a more difficult set of cases that involve entrapment in a system of political pressures, a set of scenarios that *Business Week* has recently called "Institutional Back-Scratching on the Street." When a state or local government needs to raise money, particularly for projects such as schools, highways, or hospitals, it often issues municipal bonds or "munis." The actual bond issues are handled by underwriters, typically investment banking firms who issue and sell the bonds to their clients and other interested investors. Municipal bonds are desirable investments because they are tax exempt in most states, their yield is high, most of these bonds are rated as to their value and likelihood of maturing (e.g., by letters such as "B," "A," "AA," etc.), many are insured, and there is an extremely low default rate, even on low-rated, uninsured bonds.[4] The problem is as follows. According to *Business Week*,

For decades, Wall Street investment bankers and state and local politicians have enjoyed a mutually beneficial relationship. Politicians dispense more than $1 billion in taxpayer dollars a year to the Street in fees to underwrite municipal-bond issues. The Street, in turn, sends politicians millions in campaign contributions.[5]

Two examples:

The US Attorney's office and the SEC are looking into whether Merrill Lynch & Co. bestowed financial favors on a tiny Clementon (N.J.) brokerage firm to win $2.0 billion worth of New Jersey municipal bond business. At issue is whether the firm, Armacon Securities, helped Merrill get business through Armacon's part owners, Joseph C. Salema, who happened to be the NJ Governor James Florio's chief of staff. All parties deny any wrongdoing or that they are targets of the investigations. Salema had said his Armacon stake is in a blind trust.[6]

Last September just as a $210 million [Chicago] Cook County bond issue was about to hit the market, underwriters and attorneys on the deal got a message from County Board President Richard J. Phelan's chief fund raiser. . . . On stationery emblazoned with "Citizens for Phelan" a Democratic fund-raising committee asked bond advisers for $1500 contributions to three Phelan political allies. . . . "Citizens for Phelan" . . . has already collected over $400,000 from bond professionals who work on Cook County deals including $91,500 from Goldman Sachs and its employees. That is almost 25% of Phelan's entire $1.75 million campaign war chest.[7] (Holland and Light, 1993: 46–47)

What is wrong with this quid pro quo arrangement? It is not illegal, and in fact municipal bond underwriting is unregulated. Nevertheless, there is an obvious possible conflict of interest on the part of politicians. Contributions to these politicians leads to the strong likelihood that there will be favoritism to donors rather than competitive bidding based on the merit of the underwriting contracts. The quid pro quo arrangement, then, reinforces questionable political behavior. Moreover, some underwriters also act as financial advisors to municipalities where they underwrite the issue—another possible conflict of interest.

Third, this system is costly to taxpayers, because municipalities do not always get the best price for the underwriting fees. For municipal bond investors, insufficient disclosure is coupled with the fact that there is no public market for trading; so one does not always pay the best price for the bonds. From the underwriter's perspective, one is involved in giving political contributions that are not always voluntary nor to a party of one's choice. These firms are "held hostage to the system," doing what almost no underwriter would think was the "right thing." Thus, almost every stakeholder, except the politicians, suffers as a result of this practice.

Municipal bond underwriting is an interesting phenomenon, because most underwriters were involved in some payoff scheme. In fact, however, most underwriters do not approve of these procedures, but they feel trapped. If an underwriter does not contribute, the company is unlikely to get the underwriting. It is tempting to criticize underwriters for being moral cowards, and that is correct. Yet, as part of a system that itself is corrupt, it appears that a single person or a single company can do little to stop the phenomenon. So companies are trapped because of the political system of contributions and payoffs, and for many years there seemed to be no vision of another model with which to deal with this dilemma.

The municipal bond cases illustrate a central moral dilemma. How does one, as a manager or board member, take moral responsibility in representing the best interests of one's depositors, one's loan customers, one's clients and investors, the institution, and shareholders? That is, how does one shake loose from this scenario in the face of difficult issues without becoming a sacrificial lamb of regulation, political greed, or changing financial markets? The short answer is, with extreme difficulty. However, I shall suggest a longer answer, which is by no means foolproof but is at least an attempt at tackling this difficult issue.

As I suggested in connection with institutional investing, a condition for taking moral responsibility is to get at a distance from one's own point of view or the point of view of one's colleagues, one's constituents, and/or the institutional or regulatory framework in which one is operating. If one can take a critical approach to issues and decisions, without displacing them from their proper historical and social context and keeping in mind the variety of stakeholders in each situation, one can often develop new models for dealing with old problems. Any decision requires not merely working one's way through a particular situation, but also appealing to, or setting precedents for, other decisions. Such reasoning helps the manager to step back, evaluate a particular situation, and work her way out of dilemmas, some of which are created out of conflicts arising from the very ingredients of business in which that manager or director flourishes. Whether a decision maker means to or not, business decisions are made in a public arena. Thus, even apparently unimportant decisions set precedents, precedents that other managers and other institutions follow. To give some obvious examples, contributing to political campaigns by one underwriter sets a precedent for further contributions. These activities create models for other similar actions, precedents are set, and it is difficult to change that.

Keeping these qualifications in mind, in outline form a framework for moral decision making might include the following.

1. Moral decisions have to do with relationships between individuals or between individuals and institutions. Therefore, stakeholder analysis is crucial. One cannot approach decision making in financial markets without considering those persons and institutions affected by and affecting lending, investing, trading, underwriting, and other financial market activities.

2. From an impartial perspective, a moral decision is "legislatible," that is, it sets a precedent for what one thinks should be rules applying to everyone in a particular set of contexts.

3. A decision should meet a "reasonable person standard." It should be the kind of decision one could publicly defend, both for its practicality and because it is the kind of decision you would expect others to make in a similar context. This does not mean that the decisions one makes will always be accepted by all

parties, but that the aim is a decision and a plan of action that is most likely accept*able*, all things considered.

4. Moral decisions are also contextual. So a moral decision must take into account the peculiar circumstances of the situation at hand, the personality and social history of the participants, the context of the decision, its institutional and regulatory framework, and the historical and cultural precedents that preceded that situation and decision.

5. Any acceptable decision must meet what I would call "moral minimums," that is, those negative "bottom lines" beyond which one would ordinarily agree that no action should be undertaken. They include, at the least, the following. First, a decision and subsequent action should not improve one's situation, for example, that of a politician, or an investor, if it worsens the situation of others, such as one's clients, depositors, a municipality, a corporation, unless each party to the interaction is fully informed, and in an equally competitive situation. Second, a decision should not be unfair to or violate the rights of individuals, groups of individuals, or those who would be affected by similar decisions. For example, abrupt regulatory changes are sometimes unfair to institutions that have operated by another set of rules. Third, if doing business requires dealing with and contributing to the well-being of people or institutions who are breaking the law or violating the public trust or the trust of their clients, one needs to be sure that this is a last-resort activity for which there is no other alternative.

In practice, to take into account all of these factors is admittedly tedious and difficult. But, sometimes, when you can step out of your role as a manager, investor, or trader you expand your horizon and can get another perspective on a particular crisis, which provides a window to another model for dealing with this issue and thus a new solution. The resolution of the municipal underwriting affair is one such concrete example.

In October 1993, seventeen of the largest Wall Street underwriting firms instituted a voluntary ban on campaign contributions and announced guidelines for putting this into effect. Under the sponsorship of the SEC chairperson Arthur Levitt, they agreed to put an end to contributions to state and local campaigns by their firms, by their political action committees, employees, and senior management. Any exceptions require disclosure of contributions and no contribution can be made to a political candidate or official with whom one is doing business. To date, 42 of the largest underwriting firms have subscribed to the voluntary ban, and the Municipal Securities Rulemaking Board, a self-regulatory organization, is developing a rule that prohibits municipal bond companies from doing underwriting for two years if they violate the ban.[8] This move took creativity and imagination; it required fresh thinking on this problem. It was risky, because one was not sure of the extent of the buy-in by all underwriting firms, and, like most decisions, it is not a perfect solution. Small firms, particularly those who live in small communities where part of being a good citizen is making political contributions, are questioning the decision. But it is a way to stop the political entrapment and corruption, perhaps the only way, except through excessive regulation.

MORAL LEADERSHIP

Engaging in a moral dialogue, being morally imaginative, and taking into account moral minimums is risky; one may fail—fail morally and/or fail financially. Such thinking requires being able to rethink and radically reformulate or "reengineer" one's point of view. I want now to conclude by describing a positive example of such risk-taking and reengineering, the development of the South Shore Bank of Chicago.

The South Shore Bank is located in the South Shore area of Chicago covering a neighborhood population of about 80,000. Before the 1960s the neighborhood was made up of lower-middle-class and middle-class apartments and houses and one four-block-square section of mansions. The neighborhood was primarily Jewish, and there was a tradition of staying in the neighborhood, moving up to more affluent areas as one's economic status improved. In the 1960s, there was a mass migration of blacks into the northern cities and a subsequent "white flight" from certain neighborhoods, including South Shore. By 1970 the population of South Shore was primarily black and poor and it was predicted that within five years the neighborhood would become one of the worst slums in Chicago. The South Shore Bank, whose deposits had been steadily falling to $42 million, was for sale, and in 1973 a group of entrepreneurs led by Ronald Grzywinski borrowed enough money to buy the institution for under $4 million. Today, still located in South Shore, this bank has assets of almost $180 million; it is profitable, although not wildly so, and its net loan losses in 1991 were .12 percent, the lowest for any bank of its size. Yet until recently, most of its loans were to the South Shore neighborhood. (Two years ago it moved into a second low-income neighborhood in Chicago, the Austin neighborhood, and it has also opened a bank and a program in rural Arkansas.) How is this possible?

What the bank did was to focus its attention on housing and to lend money to people willing to rehabilitate buildings in South Shore. It also set up a series of subsidiaries, one of which concentrates on real estate development, another on minority business enterprises, a nonprofit institution that works with state and federal programs to rehabilitate and develop housing for low-income residences, and a subsidiary that serves as a consulting firm for these other projects. It has raised money through what it calls "development deposits," encouraging wealthy people from other neighborhoods to open accounts at South Shore. Today South Shore, still primarily black except in the mansion area which is 40:60, is a viable place to live. Drugs and gangs are virtually absent, and more than three-quarters of the residences and apartments are restored and inhabited.

It took imagination, moral imagination, to engage in a project that no other Chicago bank at that time would engage in, in a neighborhood that leading sociologists had written off, particularly when the project is neither a government project nor a charity but is a for-profit and a profitable enterprise, and to see the low-risk element in this kind of venture. The South Shore Bank team had to rethink the traditional banking model which, for the most part, was fiscally conservative. For its part, South Shore Bank officers do not claim to be Mother Theresas. Rather, they argue, they lent money to people and enterprises that were less risky than many Third World recipients of big-bank loans.[9] From a moral point of view, South Shore Bank developed its stakeholders: its customers and the community; it respected their interests and in the process became very successful.

Finally, why should one try to become a moral leader? Why take the "high road" when making money in financial markets is so easy? This is highly speculative; I would suggest that sometimes, *just sometimes*, if one sets a standard and one is a leader, positive changes will occur that benefit more stakeholders and benefit them more in the long term. Sometimes, then, if one takes the risk of leadership, one sets a positive precedent, and changes occur, changes that alter our way of thinking about business; creative reengineering changes that are morally appropriate and financially successful as well.

NOTES

1. Robert C. Pozen, "Institutional Investors: The Reluctant Activists," *Harvard Business Review* (January-February 1994): 253–63.

2. Ibid.

3. See Bernard Gert, *Morality* (New York: Oxford University Press, 1988), especially chapters 1 and 4. Gert would not formulate the framework in the way I do, but his work had influenced my analysis as has the work of Ronald Green, particularly his essay, "The First Formulation of the Categorical Imperative as Literally a 'Legislative' Metaphor," *History of Philosophy Quarterly* (1991): 163–179.

4. See Susan E. Kuhn, "Munis: the Last of the Tax Havens," *Fortune: 1991 Investor's Guide*, pp. 189–192.

5. Leah Nathans Spiro, Larry Light, Chuck Hawkins, and Geoffrey Smith, "Back-Scratching on the Street," *Business Week*, May 24, 1993, p. 233.

6. Ibid., p. 122.

7. Ibid.

8. See Jonathan Furebringer, "Bond Firms Disclose Guides for Banning Political Gifts," *New York Times*, December 9, 1993, pp. D1, D18; Mercedes M. Cardona, "Political Gifts Ban Considered," *Pensions and Investments*, November 1, 1993, pp. 2, 58.

9. See Richard Taub, *Community Capitalism* (Boston: Harvard Business School Press, 1988) for a detailed analysis of the South Shore Bank and its development.

II

Ethics and Financial Disclosure

6

Ethical Issues in Financial Reporting for Nonprofit Healthcare Organizations

Nancy M. Kane

DIFFERENCES IN THE INFLUENCE OF PRODUCERS AND USERS OVER ACCOUNTING DISCLOSURES IN FOR-PROFIT VERSUS NONPROFIT FIRMS

The primary users of publicly reported accounting information in the for-profit sector are investors, who assess the likely future return of an investment in an organization and appraise the performance of management (Anthony, 1983). If the audited financial statements of an investor-owned organization fail to "present fairly the financial position" of the organization, the public accountants run the very real risk of being sued, especially if individual investors are harmed financially. The threat of investor lawsuits provides counterpressure to the influence of management over the public presentation of financial results. While management can always switch accounting firms when there is significant disagreement over presentation issues, sophisticated investors expect an explanation for the switch. In addition, the Securities and Exchange Commission (SEC) plays a consumer-protection role over the public disclosures of publicly held, for-profit firms. Thus, in the for-profit environment, the professional ethic of the public accountant is supported by the relative balance in influence between producer and user interests. This support has clearly not eliminated misrepresentation of accounting information; reforms of the for-profit accounting environment have been called for in the wake of a number of unanticipated financial calamities, the most recent being the savings and loan industry scandals. However, the nonprofit world lacks even this minimal degree of disincentive regarding inadequate and misleading financial reporting.

In the nonprofit healthcare environment, the $300 billion nonprofit hospital industry represents nearly 5 percent of the gross domestic product (Prospective Payment Assessment Commission, 1993). Tax dollars support these organizations, both in terms of tax subsidies and direct payment for services provided. There are no individual investors; taxpayers, as a class, are the investors; donors, as specific individuals, also are investors. However, taxpayer–investors have relatively little influence over the presentation of accounting information. There is no SEC, no individuals claiming financial harm, and no source of demand for public disclosure if the accounting firm is changed. Management, on the other hand, can exert enormous influence over the public accountant, by virtue of being able to hire and fire, subject only to the knowledge of the board of trustees. Thus, the professional ethics of the public accountant must operate in a very different climate; one that, in my opinion, is detrimental to the interests of users of public accounting information, and to the constituencies they serve.

EXAMPLES OF THE FAILURE TO MEET USER'S ACCOUNTING INFORMATION NEEDS OF NONPROFIT HEALTHCARE ORGANIZATIONS

The Needs of Users of Nonprofit Healthcare Organizations

The "investors" of nonprofit healthcare organizations are the diffuse community of taxpayers and donors contributing to such institutions. This community, as it relates to a specific nonprofit institution, is not well-defined or formally organized to represent its informational needs. To a certain extent, the media make an effort to both define and address the informational needs of the public. The government (federal, state, and local) has significant informational needs, both as formally organized representations of the community and as a significant payer for the services of these organizations. Finally, the board of trustees is another formally organized representation of the community with critical informational needs. However, hospital trustees historically have shown a tendency to identify with the institution more than with the community (Stevens, 1989).

Investors, as users of publicly available accounting information, ask the following types of questions:

- Are revenues adequate to provide a given level of services without excess profit or a loss?
- Are tax subsidies and donations being used to meet the charitable purposes for which they were given?
- What resources are available to these nonprofit institutions, and how are they being used to address the needs of the community?

While publicly available accounting information should shed some light upon the answers to these questions, in too many instances the financial statements fail to provide important information that users have a right to expect. Some examples of inadequate and misleading accounting information discovered by this author in the course of reviewing hospital financial statements are described below.

Specific Examples

The Adequacy of Revenues

Over the period from 1984 to 1988, nonprofit acute general hospitals in Massachusetts reported operating profit margins well below national averages (Kane, 1991). However, undisclosed in the income statements of those hospitals was the amount of revenue set aside in "reserve" for the possibility of unfavorable third party (i.e., Medicare, Medicaid, Blue Cross) cost report settlements, which take from one to ten years to resolve. While it is consistent with the principle of conservatism to underestimate revenues under uncertainty, it is not consistent with the notion of material disclosure that a half a billion dollars in revenues were set aside as reserves over the five-year period without footnote or comment on the potential impact on profits. Over the same period, a cumulative $28 million operating loss was reported. The cumulative operating loss became the focus of public debate over the adequacy of the regulated hospital payment system (Knox, 1991). Even sophisticated creditors and bond rating agencies were misled into thinking that Massachusetts hospitals were suffering under an inadequate payment system (Moody's, 1991); and media reports of that era focused on the "heavy losses" and subsequent budget cuts as further evidence that the hospitals were not able to meet essential financial needs. By 1988, the fiscal "crisis" of the hospitals compelled legislators to pass new hospital payment legislation that was favorable to the hospitals—so favorable that the industry backed the legislation, which, among other things, required private payers to pay higher hospital charges to offset reductions in government payments. Clearly, state policy makers were concerned, and responded to the state hospital association's steady assertions that the industry was in crisis. The assertions by the industry of impending financial crisis continued through 1990 (Massachusetts Hospital Association, 1990).

Yet between 1986 and 1990, these same hospitals added 6,800 net new jobs (Knox, 1991). Between 1984 and 1989, they were able to invest $2.8 billion in new capital assets, lowering their age of plant by 30 percent (Kane, 1991). And, as it turned out, in subsequent years, most of the third party "reserves" were settled in the hospitals' favor. However, unlike the creating of the reserves, the recognition of the reserves as revenues was separated out as a distinct element on income statements, and highlighted in footnotes, so that users would not be "misled" into thinking the hospitals were making too much money in the current year.

The tendency to understate current performance serves management's interests, from the perspective of political persuasion and the maintenance of a nonprofit image for purposes of donations and third party payers on the lookout for excess profits. However, it is clearly misleading to the users of accounting information. In this case, the reporting bias eventually was disclosed by the media; public disillusion with the credibility of hospital financial statements was the result.

The Charitable Return on Tax Subsidies

Increasingly of concern to cities, counties, and states is the question of whether tax subsidies granted decades ago to nonprofit hospitals are merited in terms of the charitable services now provided by the hospitals. Charitable services are traditionally defined as services provided to medically indigent patients without expectation of payment, or with expectation of payment below cost (Catholic Health Association of the United States, 1989).

Thus, an important accounting element for government agencies concerned with monitoring tax-exempt status is the amount of charity care provided by a hospital. With the hospital accounting guidelines (AICPA, 1990), hospitals are expected to disclose the amount of charity provided in a footnote, separate from bad debt, which is to be reported as an expense. Before 1990, hospitals were expected to report charity, still separate from bad debt, as a revenue deduction on the income statement. Very few hospitals did this; in fact, very few hospitals separated charity from bad debt in their books, unless forced to by a third party payment system that made the distinction a condition of additional payments.

Quite a few nonprofit hospitals provide very little "charity" care as defined above (GAO, 1990). However, this fact is often not disclosed in the audited financial statements. One common treatment is to combine charity with other elements, such as third party, contractually agreed-upon discounts (generally a very large number), state-mandated payments to a "free-care pool" to subsidize hospitals that really do provide charity services, or bad debts (a number often two to three times as large as the charity figure). In too many audited financials, only the combined number is disclosed.

The frustration of users of hospital financial statements trying to assess and compare traditional charity levels of hospitals is captured well in the judge's opinion in a tax-exempt challenge against a Pennsylvania hospital: "(The Hospital) contends that it provides uncompensated charity care to the community. . . . (the Hospital) could not, however, state the number of patients written off voluntarily as charity patients after only one billing. (The Hospital's) "uncompensated care" includes patients who simply do not, or cannot, pay their bills. These "uncompensated care" patients . . . are aggressively pursued by (the Hospital) through every avenue of the collection process. (The Hospital) has sued the very patients that it would now have this court deem objects of charity." (*School District of City of Erie v. Hamot*, 1989).

It is not clear what rationale public accountants use when they agree to allow charity services to be booked and reported in an obfuscated manner. While the amount of charity may well be immaterial in relation to total revenues or revenue discounts, that fact in itself is important to users of the information.

Identifying the Resources of the Organization

In this era of increasing concern over unmet health needs of poor urban areas, of uninsured workers and their families, and of constantly escalating costs of health insurance, hospitals are often asked to do more to address serious unmet health needs of the community. While many hospitals rise to the occasion, some of the wealthiest hospitals claim that they do not have the resources to address local community needs. Investigation into the availability of nonprofit hospital resources has revealed a number of accounting practices that hinder public understanding of the financial resources of their community-owned organizations.

One major problem has been the failure of some hospital financial statements to disclose the assets, liabilities, and income of very large, often cash-rich affiliated entities, despite accounting guidelines recommending such disclosure (AICPA, 1990). Thus, in 1992 a major teaching hospital that is very active in fund-raising activities issued hospital financial statements that acknowledged the existence of a parent holding company, but failed to disclose the assets or income of the consolidated entity. This oversight obscured the fact that the hospital had transferred most of its cash assets to the parent in earlier years; and that the parent had invested those cash assets to reap substantial capital gains and investment income each year. Thus, the parent entity had over $360 million in unrestricted cash assets as of 1992, as well as an annual net income of over $26 million generated by the parent entity and its nonhospital subsidiaries. The articles of incorporation of the parent state that it "shall operate exclusively for the benefit of . . . 'the Hospital' and its affiliated organizations . . . in the conduct of their charitable, educational, and scientific functions." (Children's Medical Center Corporation, 1990). Yet none of the parent entity's financial facts were revealed in the hospital audits, despite the guidelines of the AICPA (AICPA, 1990), which clearly state that

A separate organization is considered to be related to a health care entity if one of the following conditions is met: . . . (Condition b.2) The health care entity has transferred some of its resources to the organization, and substantially all of the organization's resources are held for the benefit of the health care entity.

According to the AICPA guidelines, when a separate organization is related to a healthcare entity, the healthcare entity is required to consolidate or combine financial statements; however, in this case, the healthcare entity didn't even offer a footnote disclosing summarized financial data of the related organization.

A related problem is the difficulty users have in discerning the general availability of assets, particularly cash assets, within the hospital or even the parent entity. Many hospitals have cash assets that are restricted by donors for endowment, specific purposes, or capital replacement and expansion purposes. Other cash assets are limited as to use by agreements with outside creditors. Finally, cash may be set aside by the board for board-designated uses (such designations can also be changed by the board). Board-designated assets plus uncommitted cash represent assets whose use is subject to the discretion of management and the board. These asset distinctions are clearly important to users concerned with the hospital's discretionary financial capacity, for a variety of interests (i.e., unions, public health agencies, community health centers).

However, some hospitals have chosen to report these assets under categories that fail to make the critical distinctions described above. Some have chosen to combine all forms of limitation (restricted, limited by contractual agreements with creditors, and board-designated) into one element, "current portion of assets whose use is limited," with no further distinctions made. Tens to hundreds of millions of dollars have been reported in this combined element by a number of hospitals. Others have created new and ambiguous names such as "unexpended endowment income funds," which have the effect, if not the intent, of keeping the outside user in the dark as to the nature of asset restrictions.

These reporting practices clearly do not serve the purpose of users of publicly reported accounting information. While they may well serve the needs of management, such practices undermine public confidence in the professional ethics of the public accountant.

SUMMARY AND CONCLUSIONS

Failure to fully disclose important elements of hospital financial position and performance carries very little penalty for the public accountant. In contrast to the potential sanctions of management, which include losing the account, users have only the most cumbersome and indirect means of influence, such as media pressure or government-regulated reporting requirements to supplement audited financials. The results are not healthy—a disillusioned public, management that is insulated from public accountability for its use of community resources, and boards that choose institutional over community priorities.

A central question is whether the ethical position of the public accountant dealing with the nonprofit organization can be bolstered by education alone, or whether a rebalancing of the producer–user influence over the public accountant's professional judgment is required. Should accounting guidelines promulgated for this sector direct more disclosure in areas previously left to the public accountant's discretion? Should states expand the traditional role of charitable oversight (often exercised by state attorney general offices) to a more active one of accounting and performance review of the largest nonprofit organizations? Do we need an SEC equivalent for the nonprofit sector?

It seems unlikely that the accounting profession can "heal thyself" under the circumstances. Most accountants are undoubtedly aware of proper disclosure procedures; the problem is getting their paying customers to agree to them. In terms of accounting guidelines, there is some room for greater directness, such as specific instructions on how to report the practice of third party reserves. However, most of the misleading information reported here ignored existing guidelines indicating more appropriate disclosure.

It thus appears to be necessary to invoke some governmental intervention into the producer–user balance. As a starting point, the nonprofit hospital reporting environment would be greatly enhanced by a federal law requiring timely public availability of audited financial statements of all nonprofit hospitals, preferably in some central location in each state or a federal agency. Currently, hospital financial statements are treated as confidential information in a number of states (Siegrist, 1992).

However, simply improving availability may not improve practice without the formation of visible, accounting-literate constituencies representing the public interest. Such constituencies could be created within departments of state attorney general offices, many of which are already charged with assuring the charitable nature of nonprofit organizations. The function of these departments would be to issue annual reports on the financial positions and performances of the largest nonprofit organizations (hospitals and possibly others), much as Wall Street analysts describe publicly held firms. Alternatively, cities and towns could elect to require their local hospitals to present their financial statements once a year in "public hearings" which are attended by accounting-literate community representatives.

A national solution such as the SEC may be less likely to generate the level of interest that a local, community-based group would have. While it would be helpful to have nationwide reporting standards and some sanctions for when they are not upheld, the real "investors" in nonprofit healthcare organizations are the local communities they serve. The ideal combination would be a watchdog community agency with a natural interest in the local nonprofit hospital, with a reasonable level of accounting expertise, and a standard (national) means of exerting influence when the accounting statements are not reasonably presented.[1]

None of these suggestions are perfect or cost-free. The ideal may simply not be feasible. The more local the public forum, the less likely the requisite accounting literacy will be present. However, it is time to start down the road of altering the producer–user balance, so that the professional ethics of the public accountant has some room to operate.

NOTE

1. My colleague, Professor Marc Roberts of Harvard School of Public Health, suggested that hospitals or related entities should be required to issue a public prospectus upon initiation of any major fund-raising campaign. At the same time, individual donors should be given the right to litigate should the accounting information in the prospectuses be materially misleading. The SEC would oversee the production of these prospectuses just as it does those issued for the tax-exempt debt.

REFERENCES

American Institute of Certified Public Accountants (AICPA). (1990). Audit and Accounting Guide "Audits of Providers of Health Care Services." Chicago: Commerce Clearing House, Inc.

Anthony, Robert N. (1983). *Tell It Like It Was: A Conceptual Framework for Financial Accounting.* Homewood, IL: Richard D. Irwin, Inc.

Catholic Health Association of the United States and Lewin/ICF. (1989). Social Accountability Budget for Not-for-Profit Healthcare Organizations. St. Louis, MO and Washington, DC.

Children's Medical Center Corporation. (1990). Form 990 Return of Organization Exempt from Income Tax.

General Accounting Office (GAO). (1990). "Nonprofit Hospitals: Better Standards Needed for Tax Exemption." *GAO/HRD-90-84.* May 30.

Kane, Nancy M. (1991). "Hospital Profits, a Misleading Measure of Financial Health." *Journal of American Health Policy 1* (1): 27–35.

Knox, Richard A. (1991). "Are Hospitals Crying Wolf?" *Boston Sunday Globe,* February 3, p. 73.

Massachusetts Hospital Association. (1990). *A Financial Analysis of Massachusetts Hospitals 1981–1986.*

Moody's Public Finance Department. (1991). Review of Hospital Bonds. State of Massachusetts (February).

School District of the City of Erie and the City of Erie and the County of Erie v. the Hamot Medical Center of the City of Erie, Pennsylvania and Hamot Health Systems, Inc. and Erie County Board of Assessment Appeals. (1989). Opinion of Judge Levin.

Siegrist, Richard. (1992). Source Book on Information Availability. Deliverable submitted under HCFA Cooperative Agreement #99-C-98489/9-08.

Stevens, Rosemary. (1989). *In Sickness and in Wealth: American Hospitals in the Twentieth Century.* New York: Basic Books.

7

The Ethical Implications of Financial Derivatives

David Mosso

INTRODUCTION

I assume that derivative financial instruments are themselves ethically neutral. However, I recognize that derivatives do pose ethical issues for their purveyors and users, and also for the purveyors' and users' accountants. My focus is on accountants and their role in financial reporting. My remarks are in three parts:

• The ethical implications of derivatives
• The ethical context of financial reporting
• The FASB's approach to derivatives

THE ETHICAL IMPLICATIONS OF DERIVATIVES

Accountants' dither about derivatives starts from the fact that derivatives can be acquired for little or no cash investment, yet they carry a huge gain or loss potential. Because there is no investment to record (or very little), derivatives are often called off-balance-sheet instruments. For traditional financial instruments, and nonfinancial assets and liabilities as well, a balance sheet is the capstone of a reporting system and is a prime source of information about risk. At a minimum, it tells you the amount of an investment that can be lost. A balance sheet is one of the most important tools for communicating financial information. It doesn't say much about derivatives, and that is a problem for accountants.

The plot thickens when you consider that accounting sometimes varies according to the purpose for which a financial instrument is held. For example, for some purposes, an instrument might be carried on the balance sheet at its original cost, in which case any change in its market value is ignored until the instrument is disposed of. For other purposes it might be carried at its current market price (called marking to market), in which case changes in its market value go to income each reporting period.

Now, the ethical worm begins to squirm. The purposes for which a financial instrument may be held are ethically biased. Contemplate the following spectrum of purposes, which range in descending order from good to bad, ethically speaking:

- *Held for investment.* Good. Solid citizens save and invest.
- *Held for hedging.* Pretty good. The entity is a risk reducer. On the other hand, it did take on a big risk to begin with.
- *Held for risk management.* Chic, but problematical because risk can be managed to go up as well as to go down.
- *Held for dealer inventory.* Neutral until you know whether the dealer is Goldman Sachs or a penny stock boiler room.
- *Held for trading.* Okay for Salomon Brothers, but bad for mom and pop S&Ls.
- *Held for speculation.* Frowned upon, except for the folks in the open outcry pits.
- *Held for gambling.* Bad. No entity has ever done it, if absence from notes to the financial statements is a good indicator.

A derivative could be classified in any one of those seven purpose categories. The point of walking you through that spectrum is to show that different purposes have different ethical connotations. What it's called affects how investors react to it. I saw a cartoon recently that illustrates that point. When asked how he had invested pension fund money, a portfolio manager replied "short-term governments." Then he observed, in an aside, that short-term governments sounds better than lottery tickets.

Not only does the purpose classification affect investor perceptions, it can affect the accounting. Purposes on the good end of my spectrum tend to get to defer losses (gains too, but that isn't a result much sought after). Purposes on the bad end tend to get mark-to-market accounting, which spews out losses and gains as they occur. Now managers usually don't like mark-to-market accounting because it causes volatility of earnings. Earnings volatility connotes greater risk and higher cost of capital. It may also prompt embarrassing questions from investors who do not necessarily share management's long-term perspective (in which large losses are always followed, sooner or later, by larger gains). To complicate matters further, none of the purpose categories can be rigorously defined. We have to look for fragmentary clues. For example, we can sometimes identify a speculator— someone who bets against a central banker, and wins. But we usually can't tell whether a purpose classification is descriptive of the underlying activity until it is too late. Moreover, classification is based on management's stated intent, which is not auditable.

All of these factors create an ethical tension among managers trying to put the best face on their financial statements, investors trying to get behind the facade in order to assess future prospects, auditors trying to add credibility to the financial statements and avoid malpractice litigation, and accounting standard setters trying to provide guidelines for useful financial reporting. Let me turn now to the ethical context of financial reporting.

THE ETHICAL CONTEXT OF FINANCIAL REPORTING

Like all professions, certified public accountants (CPAs) have a formal code of ethics. Unlike most professions that I know of, however, the CPA is not primarily responsible to the client. Primary responsibility is to the public. The precept, as stated in the CPA's code of ethics, is as follows: "When members [of the profession] fulfill their responsibility to the public, clients' and employers' interests are best served." You can readily see a source of ethical tension there—it is not easy to bite the hand that feeds you. But biting is required of an auditor if the client tries to feed tainted information to the public by way of the financial statements.

The ethical essence of the accounting profession is captured in the auditor's opinion on financial statements, which addresses the question of whether the statements "present fairly . . . in conformity with generally accepted accounting principles."

"Fairness" is the auditor's ethical objective, but fairness is defined in terms of generally accepted accounting principles. And that is where the Financial Accounting Standards Board (FASB) enters the picture. FASB standards are the top tier of generally accepted accounting principles.

The FASB mission is to improve financial reporting by establishing standards that lead to information that is useful for economic decision making. Like the accounting profession, the FASB's responsibility is to the general public. The FASB is committed to putting the interests of those who rely on audited financial statements above any special interest. In our society, essentially everybody relies on audited financial statements, directly or indirectly, because those statements are the foundation of the body of information needed by the capital markets for allocating resources efficiently.

In pursuing its mission to improve financial reporting, the ethical objective of the FASB is best captured in the single word "neutrality." The FASB strives to set standards for information that is free from bias toward any predetermined result. Thus, for example, we would not set standards for accounting for derivatives designed either to encourage or discourage the use of derivatives, or to make the accounting for similar derivatives transactions more onerous for one kind of entity than another.

This precept of neutrality creates tensions at times between the FASB and its constituents, and between different groups of constituents. For example, tension might arise between investors who want more information about derivatives in order to assess the relative merits of investment opportunities and managers who want to be left alone to conduct their business without revealing their strategies to competitors. And both groups might be miffed at the FASB—one because the FASB required too much, the other because it required too little. Tensions like those are not ethical in nature at their core, but when a maelstrom of controversy surrounds a financial reporting issue, the ethical principles of fairness and neutrality are sorely tested. I know of no better example than the current controversy over a derivative financial instrument called "executive stock options."

That in brief is the ethical context for financial reporting of activity in derivative financial instruments. In summary, the ethical imperative for financial reporting of derivatives is *fair presentation* of *neutral information* for *economic decision making*. I will turn now to what the FASB has done and is doing in response to that imperative.

THE FASB's APPROACH TO DERIVATIVES

I can think of only two practicable ways to address both the need for information about derivatives and the shortcomings of the balance sheet in dealing with derivatives. The first is to require more footnote disclosures of information that will help assess the risks of derivatives. The second is to require derivatives to be marked to market, which effectively moves them onto the balance sheet and provides current income information. Neither of these is a sure-fire way to forewarn of financial explosions, but they should help. Risk measurement technology is developing rapidly and that may lead to new tools to enhance the usefulness of financial statements. In the meantime, we muddle along with the tools we have.

Some time ago the FASB issued a new standard, Statement 119, requiring additional disclosures about derivatives. It is effective for year-end 1994 financial statements of large companies and year-end 1995 for smaller companies. The Statement builds on standards issued in 1990 and 1991. These standards all deal with footnote disclosures, with no effect on the balance sheet or income statement. As they apply to derivatives, the principal requirements are as follows.

- By category of derivative, that is, by class of instruments, by business activity, by type of risk, or by some other category that is consistent with the way derivatives are managed, disclose:

  —The face or contract amount or notional principal

  —The nature and terms of the instruments, including a discussion of credit and market risks, cash requirements, and accounting policy

- Those disclosures would be done separately for derivatives held or issued for:
  —Trading purposes
  —Nontrading purposes
- For trading instruments, these additional disclosures are required:
  —The average fair value of positions during the period along with ending fair value
  —The amount of net gains or losses from trading
- For nontrading instruments, these additional disclosures are required:
  —A description of the objectives for holding the instruments, and the strategies for achieving the objectives
  —A description of how the instruments are reported in the financial statements
  —For derivatives that hedge anticipated transactions, a description of the hedged transactions and hedging instruments, the amount of gain or loss deferred, and under what conditions that gain or loss would be taken to earnings
- For derivatives and all other financial instruments a single note must disclose their fair value along with their carrying amount. That information must be broken down by trading and nontrading. Netting of instruments is not permitted except in tightly circumscribed instances.

As extensive as those disclosures may seem, the main criticism has been that they do not go far enough. In particular, the Securities and Exchange Commission and others would like more quantification of risks. The FASB considered some quantification requirements but decided that it could not do the necessary research and deliberation in time to get a standard in effect for year-end 1994 financial statements. The rash of derivatives disasters this past year gave a sense of urgency to getting some disclosure requirements in place quickly, even though they might be less than optimal. We will continue to look at quantification possibilities for the future.

Beyond footnote disclosures, the FASB is looking at recognition and measurement of derivatives in the balance sheet and income statement. It is doing that as part of its project on hedging—or risk management, to use fashionable lingo. That project still has many unresolved issues, but a tentative decision has been made to mark all derivatives to market. Gains and losses would be taken to earnings unless they met specified qualifications for risk management purposes, in which case they would be deferred in some manner.

Everything that the FASB has done so far concerns only free-standing derivatives. The use of structured notes and other forms of embedded derivatives is the current rage and we haven't scratched the surface of the problems they present. You may have noticed that the FASB has some affinity to the generals who fight yesterday's war. By the time we get a problem solved, it has often become yesterday's problem and some new problem has come up front and center. I can only assure you that we will continue the pursuit of a good way to account for the risks and opportunities of derivatives even though our chances of catching up with the financial engineers are slim.

NOTE

Expressions of individual views by members of the Financial Accounting Standards Board (FASB) and its staff are encouraged. The views expressed in this chapter are those of Mr. Mosso. Official positions of the FASB on accounting matters are determined only after extensive due process and deliberation.

8

Confidentiality in a Professional Context with Especial Reference to the Accounting Profession in Australia

P. B. Jubb

INTRODUCTION

Respect for the privacy of knowledge obtained in a professional capacity is asserted by professions in their codes of ethics and conduct. Known as confidentiality, the assertion is usually hedged with provisos, vaguely expressed and suggesting rarity, thereby allowing for it to be overridden. An Australian sample of such statements is provided in the appendix.

Leaders of professional bodies are likely, through their offices, to be fully exposed to the frailties of confidentiality, but many rank and file members may only acquire that awareness by involvement in a real conflict situation. It is likely to be dismaying to learn in such a context that one is obliged, on pain of severe penalty, to violate undertakings to a client and avowed ethical standards by revealing confidential information.

The professional codes lack precision, probably by intent. The literature on the subject, apart from that concerning caring professions, appears sparse. Could it be that in noncaring professions a perception prevails that this ethical issue is not a serious one, or that the substantive matters it raises are legal and not ethical, or that members have the capacity to resolve the conundrums when they arise? It seems worthwhile, therefore, to try to explore the meaning, implications, and limitations associated with confidentiality.

PRIVACY, CONFIDENTIALITY, AND TRUST

Privacy is one of a number of rights said to derive from the principle of respect for the dignity of human beings. Rights are meaningless without corresponding obligations, so one's privacy restricts the freedoms of others. The right of privacy is the right not to be invaded. It extends to our space and to information concerning or held by us. Assault on our bodies is another form of privacy invasion, as is mind penetration. Privacy is not an unfettered right. It can be waived by informed consent and it needs to be weighed against other rights when conflicts arise.[1]

Confidentiality is distinct from privacy but is a derivative of it. Rights and duties attaching to confidentiality would be meaningless unless there was a right to privacy in the background. Confidentiality is linked to information privacy, especially information about a person's attributes and actions; and arises when the person imparts such private matters to another. The information transfer must be volunteered; communication under duress would fall within privacy invasion and is not a special case of confidentiality. Like any right, confidentiality is circumscribed by other rights with which it may clash or be incompatible.

A fourfold justification of confidentiality presented by Bok (1988: 232–233) consists of autonomy over personal information, the acceptability of sharing secrets, a pledge or promise of silence, and social utility. The first two are aspects of respect and appear to be instances of what is entailed in the right of privacy. The pledge is a new dimension, while social utility is proposed as an arbiter between rights, which serves to prioritize confidentiality and determine its limits. The justification, all aspects of which are admitted to be problematic, is thus a blend of ethical reasonings, derived from rights/duties and consequences, which Bok then employs to address three major problems; confidences imparted by persons who may lack full autonomy, confidences about threatening intentions, and misuse of confidentiality to protect the professional adviser.

Trust is not part of the language in Bok's paper, yet trust is highly pertinent to two of the justifications. Secrets would not be shared willingly, except in desperation, in the absence of trust; while the pledge to silence articulates its acceptance. Trust is also a factor to be weighed in the social utility cost/benefit analysis because it is indispensable to routine social interaction (Pellegrino, 1991: 69). We expect people to honor promises, obey the law, and so forth, and most of our experience confirms that this is the case; thus it is rational to assume that other road users will drive on the correct side, even though experience shows that, occasionally, some do not. What is just described may be designated general trust, an all-pervading, indispensable degree of faith in human nature which even the most cynical must acknowledge.

However, it is more conventional to associate trust with those special relations between individuals in which one party voluntarily makes himself vulnerable to the other. One such category is the marital relationship, another is that between client and professional; and an instance, one especially though not solely identified with both the above bonds, is confidentiality.

Trust in selected individuals is not crucial to our social functioning, though without it our lives would be seriously diminished. It is usually relied on in nonroutine circumstances and after careful reflection.

This chapter attempts to examine confidentiality in terms of trust, and to isolate the differences, if any, that arise when confidence is placed in a professional as distinct from a fellow human. The relationship examined is that between adviser and the person seeking help and the problem principally addressed is onus of disclosure. Other confidential relationships, say between advisers, and other problems, like abusing the confidence for personal gain, are not explored. Greater specification will increase understanding of confidentiality and sensitivity to it, and help professionals with their judgments about the constraints limiting it. It is hoped that this chapter makes a small contribution to that enhanced awareness.

A CONFIDENTIALITY MODEL

A model of interpersonal confidentiality is depicted in Figure 8.1. It purports to describe situations in which secrets are entrusted to ordinary people. They may be chosen for some special skill or knowledge but more likely they are singled out for their qualities of kindness, maturity, practicality, sympathy, nearness, and so on.

The basic structure of the model is the participants and a two-way information flow between them. Its core is the mutual trust between the participants, which reminds us that confidentiality belongs to the class of trust relationships. The model is essentially a closed one because, while participant behavior may be affected by external stimuli, informer and confidant can only communicate with each other. However, the ability to contact external resources may be a negotiated option. The model elements are now enlarged upon.

The informer is a person who senses a need to impart information to a chosen other person in order to relieve a particular pressure. Motives driving the informer will vary, but include: to unburden an item of knowledge, to protect knowledge by placing it in safekeeping, to remove or reduce a personal uncertainty, and to get advice on how to resolve a problem. The communication is made voluntarily and the initiative for it comes from the informer.

The confidant is the person chosen to receive the communication; chosen because of the trust that the informer places in the confidant's capacities.

Informer and confidant usually are, but need not be, single persons. Exceptions include couples, families, or other collective informers; a congregation hearing a public confession, such as occurs at AA meetings, qualifies as a group confidant.

The communication itself is described by the expression "*confide information.*" The primary distinguishing attribute of the communication is that

Figure 8.1
A Model of Person-to-Person Confidentiality

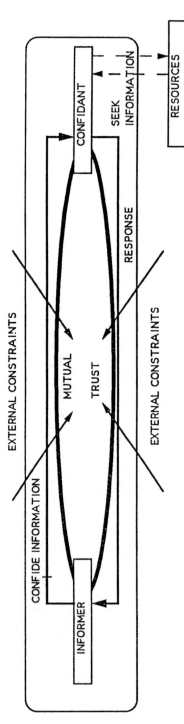

the information imparted is perceived by the informer to be very sensitive. The second major feature, the promise, explicit or otherwise, that the confidant will not disclose the information flows naturally from the first. Since the aim is to elicit a suitable response from the confidant, it is important that the informer's communication conveys his or her motives and sensibilities concerning it.

The response from the confidant may be a passive one, that is, it may be sufficient simply to hear, share, and be empathetic to the communication. More commonly, the confidant will take an active role by providing additional knowledge, guidance on problem solving, or facilitation of the informer's own problem-solving capacity.

Mutual trust is the communication context and is a necessary condition if the communication is to have a satisfactory outcome. It embraces the content of general trust but has added dimensions. The informer, in choosing the confidant, trusts that person to have the capacities attributed to her and to use them in formulating an appropriate response; and to respect the confidential nature of the communication, an expression which includes the following negative duties:

- not to use the confided information to personal advantage;
- not to assign the case to another without the informer's consent;
- not to reveal the confidential communication without the informer's consent.

As was mentioned earlier, only this last quality is subjected to examination.

Mutuality is used to indicate that the confidant must also place trust in the informer. This encompasses the general trust inherent in social intercourse but goes further. I suggest that a confidant trusts that informers:

- believe in the sensitivity of the communication;
- convey it truthfully and completely to the best of their ability;
- allow probing by the confidant in order to clarify the communication;
- do not exploit the trust relationship for ulterior motives.

Reciprocity is a valuable property of trust. It redresses somewhat the power that secret knowledge gives to the confidant, who also faces exposure to exploitation. That is, acceptance of the confidence carries risks. The more equal the parties are in their dealings, the better the prospect for a healthy trust relationship between them.

A final note on mutual trust is that it is a relationship that is negotiated. The informer chooses the confidant and does so by direct discussion with that person, or by relying on a recommendation or the confidant's general repute. The confidant agrees to act as such and has opportunity to decline, at the outset or later, if the relationship fails to achieve its objective. Only rarely might such negotiation be formal or precede receipt of the information; confidences are often blurted out to a friend, neighbor, or family member. Rather, the suggestion is that, over time, exchanges take place that forge the basis for the mutual trust which may be called upon and given without notice. This potential immediacy adds weight to the claim that the confidant must also trust the informer, since there may be no opportunity to refuse a particular confidence before it is given.

In providing a response, the confidant may wish to seek assistance from other sources, described in the model as *resources* and depicted as outside the boundary of the confidentiality relationship. However, a human resource consulted by the confidant, in a nonhypothetical manner and with consent of the informer, would be equally bound to confidentiality and would, thereby, become part of that relationship.

External constraints are forces which demand disclosure. In the context of trust between ordinary people, such constraints are most likely to be other ethical obligations which appear to the confidant to be incompatible with confidentiality. Ethical conflicts represent dilemmas which can only be resolved by ranking the competing obligations or their perceived outcomes. In such ranking, confidentiality tends to fare poorly, disclosure often being coupled with the claim that it is for the informer's own good. If the subject matter of the confidence is serious enough, pressure from administrators or legal duties may also emerge as external constraints. In such cases, confidentiality has little chance of prevailing, particularly if the competing obligation can threaten the confidant with penalties.

THE MODEL IN A PROFESSIONAL CONTEXT

The attempt, so far, has been to use the model to describe confidentiality as a purely ethical problem. However, once we extend the discussion to include confidences between an informer and a professional confidant, new aspects, not necessarily of an ethical character, enter the relationship. Each element of the model is reconsidered in the new context which leads to some revision of the model, as shown in Figure 8.2.

The attributes of informer and confidant are not altered by the latter being a professional, provided we are still talking strictly of a person-to-person dialogue as, say, between a client and therapist. However, it is frequently the case that the informer is (spokesperson for) some kind of corporate entity; for instance, a company seeking investment advice or a welfare agency seeking legal help on behalf of a class of victims. A professional dealing with an agent enters relationships with client and agent, both of which may raise expectations of confidentiality, but which must surely collide when agents have exceeded or abused their authority. It is equally probable that the confidant is a member, as employee or principal, of a professional firm, practice, or agency.

Figure 8.2
A Model of Client/Professional Confidentiality

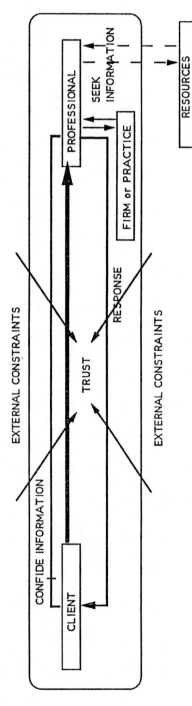

Corporatization adds greatly to the complexity of the confidentiality relationship. One reason is that many persons are, or are potentially, caught up in it. On the confidant side, it is to be expected that any principal, not just the one consulted, may be privy to the confidential communication through peer support mechanisms. Clerical staff responsible for preparing or handling records also have access to the information in a condensed form, yet support staff are not bound by their employers' professional code. The extent to which confidants (feel obliged to) share private communications may surprise many informers and suggests an onus on the professional to alert the client at the outset.

A second complexity is that the informer is not necessarily the client. The case of the agent informer was identified above. Other such situations can arise, like the client who, considering the acquisition of another entity, engages its accounting advisor to audit the other entity.

Characteristics of confiding and response communications can differ when the framework is that of professional and client. The confidence may not be imparted freely, such as when a person is ordered to undergo counseling or psychiatric treatment. Second, confidential and other nonsensitive communications may be transmitted together. The professional needs to be alerted, by experience or by the informer, to those that are of a private nature. Finally, a professional is nearly always asked for an active response, such as advice or a specific service.

The essential elements of mutual trust between informer and confidant, previously enumerated, continue in place when the latter is a professional; nevertheless there are important differences, partly because there is an extended array of external constraints on the trust relationship to be considered later, but also due to changes in the relationship itself. Three such changes are now considered.

First is the fact that most client/professional relationships are formalized in a contract. The contract introduces a legalism into the relationship which shifts emphasis from the ethical domain or may even supplant it entirely. Thus, with respect to professionals, confidentiality has been absorbed into the common law, via the influence of the old equity courts, as an implied contractual term (Finn, 1977). Also the simple fact of fee-for-service places the relationship on a commercial footing. Professional practices are businesses after all, but some commentators (Trade Practices Commission, 1992, 1994; Lederman, 1994) believe commercialism has become their guiding principle. Moreover, it is commonplace that a professional provides service to one party but receives the fee from elsewhere. The doctor who is paid by an insurer and the legal aid lawyer are examples; or, given that some professional practices are global, diversified firms, fees may come from the client but primarily for other, nonconfidential or less sensitive services rendered. Such situations imperil mutual trust, since the professional faces ambiguity about client identity, or divided loyalty. Contract and enterprise, then, are new dimensions in the trust relationship; they downplay the ethical domain and may even remove it from consciousness; they are potential threats to the mutual trust on which confidentiality is claimed to depend.

The choice process is a second change. While many clients do select professionals from personal knowledge or recommendation, many others select on price, Yellow Pages advertising, or other criteria that have no seeming connection with trust in the person. Rather, in such cases the client is trusting the regulatory machinery that governs the professional's training and accreditation. One more variation is when the selection is made not by the client but by the payer of the bill.

The third difference is professional skepticism. The simple confidentiality model revolves around mutual trust but a professional may not, sometimes must not, assume client frankness. Thus, auditors risk negligence suits if they accept auditee statements at face value; doctors should examine patients rather than accepting the patient's own diagnosis; journalists should check stories before going to print. There is an onus to seek out information beyond that imparted by the client. Skepticism is necessary, partly to enable the professional to provide good service to the client, but especially because most professionals have and profess obligations to parties other than the client. The suggestion, then, is that the trust underlying confidentiality in a professional context is not mutual but one-directional. If true, the scales of power are tilted even more in favor of the professional.

A major resource for professionals is their peer group. The professional firm or practice is depicted as a separate resource and inside the confidentiality relationship on the assumption that clients know and expect that those they consult will, as needed, seek assistance from immediate colleagues.

There are many more external constraints on the confidentiality relationship in the professional context, to a large extent because professionals are known to receive confidential information and because, for professional and contractual purposes, they need to keep records of client communications. These constraints arise because the professional, by virtue of that status, has responsibilities to colleagues, the professional association, and the community beyond and, perhaps, overriding those owed to clients. The obligations are additional to those owed by anyone in a society in accordance with its general ethical standards; they are part of the baggage that comes with professional membership, along with its specialized culture and codes.

Other obligations are imposed on professionals by law simply because they do or should have knowledge that is sought. A legal duty to disclose is usually couched in terms of public interest and it is hard to defy, since professions aver a concern for the public interest and use the concept to justify their status in society. The public's right to know (journalistic leaks), the administration of justice (notifying a court of client perjury), registering cases of notifiable diseases, reporting reasons for critical audit opinions are a few of the public interest circumstances alleged to justify disclosing confidences, all but the first being disclosures required by laws.

Summarizing thus far, the professional confidentiality model differs from the original in that it represents a more complex network in which parties, including corporations, may engage through agents; and where client and informant may be different persons. The model also proposes one-directional trust because the relationship is multidimensional. There is an implication that the quality of trust is inferior for this reason and also because it often lacks the personal touch; instead, the client may place its trust in corporate agencies that accredit personnel and practices within the firms that provide professional services.

A TENTATIVE APPLICATION OF THE MODEL

These models are helpful only if they offer insights into the range of circumstances in which confidentiality is asserted. Consider journalism, for instance. The ethical code of the Australian Journalists' Association (AJA, n.d.) prohibits revelation of confidential sources, in defiance of the law, if necessary (see Appendix). The position, an extreme and absolute one which is presently under review (AJA 1993) and under attack by the intelligence services (Brough, 1994) has resulted in the jailing and fining of five journalists since 1990 (Flint, 1993). In all cases the information from the undisclosed source related to corruption within the police or major financial institutions. In the most recent case, claims were made, but not resolved, that the information provided to the journalist was false and known to be so by the source. Journalistic confidentiality is a poor fit to the professional model. There is no client as such and no contract or fee; the informer's identity is the secret while publication is the motive for the communication; the journalist confidant is usually chosen with care, though the media vehicle's image and policies may also influence the choice. The circumstances of the communication can be such as to place the journalist in considerable risk and this one feature suggests that the person-to-person model, in which mutuality is the prevailing form of trust, is more fitting for journalism. That being so, there should be little doubt that disclosure would be the right and ethical course if the claimed facts were true. An informer had no right to lie to the journalist nor to dupe the latter into disseminating falsehoods. The informer's action would be an abuse of the mutual trust, an exploitation and nullification of the confidentiality bond.

In the concluding section, the models are related to the accounting profession, with which the author is most familiar. Accountants perform many roles. Here, compulsory audit is singled out because this function is the source of most conflicts and the public scrutiny of the profession. Businesses may opt for audit by an external agency, but the high profile audit is one that is imposed on a business by regulation. In Australia the typical such audit is of a public company and it is prescribed by the Corporations Law. The auditor's prime task is to express an opinion on the acceptability of the company's published financial statements. The opinion is to be based on evidence that is sufficient and competent to sustain it, and on the auditor's independence of spirit and action. Auditor/auditee dealings are said to occur within a professional and client relationship. Consider now how the model components apply to the case of obligatory audit.

The client is a corporation. However, a corporation has many competing players or stakeholders, so which of these is the client? The profession's response to this question is schizophrenic. Economic self-interest is a strong incentive for auditors to identify the client with company management, which appoints the auditors, sets fees, and pays them[2] (Dhaliwal et al., 1993; Farmer et al., 1987); and the attitude of the profession to management consultancy indicates its aversion to policies which limit the members' earning power (ICAA, 1988). The empirical academic literature provides reinforcement; it typically portrays the client or its officers and employees as the auditee. But tradition and legal duty point to shareholders as the ultimate client; the nineteenth-century watchdog metaphor is still valid (Lopes, 1896). Subsequently imposed duties to disclose violations, of covenants to trustees for creditors, and of regulations to the Australian Securities Commission and Australian Accounting Standards Board (Corporations Law ss 332 [9-10], 332A, 334), indicate a limited recognition of secured creditors and the agency as auditor clients. The spread of the accountability net may in time point to all stakeholders being captured by the term audit client.

Information is supplied by its staff, by others it so authorizes, and through the auditor's own enquiries and searches of public and company records. In general, the information is not volunteered, but if required by the auditor the client cannot deny the auditor's right of access and must provide it or else terminate the auditor's appointment. Thus, the informer confides in the auditor involuntarily, in response to pressures and rules set by the governing regulation.

Typically, the auditor is also a corporate body with principals and employed professional and support staff. The client company's choice of auditor can depend on many factors but, with acceptance by the profession of competition and advertising, public image and price have obviously gained importance; while globalization of the big accounting firms has led to many auditor choices being made by the client's (offshore) parent company. Personal trust may be forged on the job but it seems to have little to do with the initial choice of auditor. It may even appear as an undesirable threat to independence, which I suspect lies at the heart of proposals for obligatory and frequent auditor rotation.

From the foregoing it will be apparent that the communication to the auditor is not one of an informer confiding sensitive data in the hope of receiving help. Rather, the scenario is an informer handing over the data only on demand, probably with reluctance, and either supplying the barest minimum needed to satisfy strict obligations or burying it in a morass of spurious material. As the communication is not voluntary do not expect it to be accompanied with explanatory motivations or helpful extras. The scene painted here is one where the client has something to hide; extremely valuable data, say trade secrets, or misconduct. If there is nothing to hide a client tends to cooperate fully, if only to get the auditors out of the way quickly.

While a client may remind the auditor that certain data provided are to be kept confidential, for example, employee pay rates or salaries, in general the auditor has the task of identifying that which is sensitive and that which is not. The usual reaction is that auditors treat all information gathered as confidential, even though much of it is routine. Note too that sensitive information may have been withheld by the client but discovered by the auditor's independent enquiries or analysis of the evidence or by a tip-off. Do the same confidentiality conditions apply to concealed as to provided information?

The auditors main response is the opinion on the accounts. The opinion, though addressed to shareholders, is a public statement included in the company's financial reports, which are available to anyone through their publication and also filing with the ASC. An unfavorable opinion must be supported by frank explanation, which is potentially damaging to the client and necessitates disclosures that the client would not wish. It is important to realize that opinion rendering lays a duty on the auditor to breach confidentiality, to appreciate that this violation is inherent in, indeed is the raison d'être of auditing and that it is, or should be, commonplace.

The characteristics of the parties and their interactions raise serious doubt about the supposed trust between them with respect to secrecy. Look at this from the point of view of client, of auditor, and the human quality of the relationship. By virtue of her function the auditor should be on the side of shareholders and other users of the published statements. The client submits to audit and supplies information to the auditor under compulsion. Therefore, a rational client, anxious about its secrets, would be expected to attempt concealment rather than confide in the auditor.

The auditor's duties require exercise of skepticism to a high degree. Client-supplied information is to be checked and corroborated; audit procedures, tests, and sampling techniques are aimed at finding errors and their causes. Auditors who presume that they are fully and frankly informed by their clients, or presume that clients do not have agendas of their own for the audit, do so at their peril.

The process of auditor appointment is to a considerable extent impersonal and divorced from perceived human qualities of the persons who do the work. Moreover, once appointed the auditor is supposed to establish and maintain independence. To trust in the client's good faith becomes a questionable attitude, suggestive of cosiness and complacency; audit independence is more redolent of vigilance and the distancing of oneself from the client.

Put together, these factors make a strong case for denying any trust between client and auditor with respect to maintaining secrecy, and these factors are caused by the external constraints which in the client/auditor case are so forceful as to overwhelm the trust that might otherwise exist. The most important constraint is the auditor's legal duty of disclosure. Its dominant form of course is the primary duty to report an opinion to external parties. Two other, less public, disclosures have also been mentioned. In addition, auditors who seek consent to their resignation must supply reasons to the regulators; and they have the right to defend themselves at a shareholders' meeting if client management seeks to have them dismissed. Finally, auditors do not benefit from legal privilege, therefore they must furnish documents or appear as witnesses in response to lawful subpoenas. In giving their evidence auditors should not behave as client advocates. All such disclosures are compulsory violations of client confidences.

Obligations to fellow professionals also impinge on confidentiality. Two instances are given; there is a professional duty to inform a replacement auditor of known or suspected circumstances which would make it improper for the incoming auditor to accept appointment; and auditors of subsidiaries must provide information to the parent's auditors, who are responsible for the audit of the consolidated statements.

CONCLUSION

Auditors do owe confidentiality to clients but in a very restricted sense. It warns the auditor not to use the client information for personal gain nor to be careless about maintaining security over it. In this sense the duty is legal (*Parry-Jones v. Law Society* [1969] 1, Ch. 1) not just ethical. But keeping secrets, the main quality of confidentiality, is undermined by the auditor's goal of insuring full and adequate disclosure. In a competent and honest business environment the occasions may be rare in which an auditor has to make disclosures detrimental to the client. In our recent past the indicators are that such disclosures ought to have been numerous. But whether they are frequent or not is not the issue. A good watchdog barks at all comers whether they be innocuous visitors or the rare would-be intruder. So should auditors be wary of all clients because renegades are not easily identifiable.

The climate described is inimical to trust and without trust secrets are not offered but extracted. This, I believe, lies at the heart of one of the most difficult ambiguities facing auditors, their roles toward clients and others. The auditor benefits from a close and trusting relationship with clients, but how to achieve this without prejudice to independence and other constituents? It is incumbent on the accounting profession to give consistently clear signals to its members that independence is paramount. Its bland statement on confidentiality in the Appendix is one that blurs the signal and contributes in no small way to a perception that duties to the client take precedence. Maybe the profession's fundamental ethical principle of confidentiality should be replaced or tempered by a principle of disclosure.

APPENDIX: A SAMPLE OF STATED ETHICAL POSITIONS ON CONFIDENTIALITY

Australian Journalists Association (n.d.)

In all circumstances they [i.e., members] *shall respect all confidences received in the course of their calling.*

Australian Psychological Society (1986)

This code nominates responsibility, competence, and propriety as three general principles of professional conduct. Propriety includes the following:
Psychologists must respect the confidentiality of information obtained from persons in the course of their work as psychologists. They may reveal such information to others only with the consent of the person or the person's legal representative, except in those unusual circumstances in which not to do so would result in clear danger to the person or to others. Where appropriate, psychologists must inform their clients of the legal or other contractual limits of confidentiality.

Business Council of Australia (Bosch, 1993)

Directors frequently acquire information not generally known to the public or other businesses such as trade secrets, processes, methods, advertising or promotional programs, sales and statistics affecting financial results. This information is the property of the Company and it is improper to disclose it or to allow it to be disclosed to any other person unless the disclosure has first been authorized by the Company.

Institute of Chartered Accountants in Australia (1990)

The profession proclaims that members and affiliates should be governed in the conduct of their professional relationships with others by the Rules of Ethical Conduct which are based upon the following fundamental principles: integrity, objectivity, independence, technical standards, confidentiality, personal competence, and ethical behavior. The confidentiality principle is worded thus:
They should respect the confidentiality of information acquired in the course of

their work and should not disclose any such information to a third party without specific authority or unless there is a legal or professional duty to disclose it.

Law Society of ACT (n.d)

5.1 A practitioner should strive to establish and maintain the trust and confidence of his or her client.

5.2 Without the consent of the client, a Practitioner should not in any way detrimental to the interests of the client directly or indirectly reveal or use any information which the practitioner receives as a result of the retainer nor lend or reveal the contents of the papers in any instructions to any person, except to the extent:

(a) required by law, rules of court or court order, provided that where there are reasonable grounds for questioning the validity of the law, rule or order the Practitioner should first take all reasonable steps to test the validity of the same; or

(b) necessary for replying to or defending any charge or complaint as to conduct or professional behavior brought against the Practitioner or his or her partners, associates or employees or to respond to a requirement under subsection 22.2 [which concerns reporting to the Law Society in respect to complaints raised against the Practitioner].

NOTES

1. This paragraph on privacy is indebted to Pinkard (1982).

2. For present purposes, no distinction is made between management and directors. The formal procedure is that management nominates auditors and shareholders appoint in meeting. Typically, the members appoint the nominated person or firm; challenge is extremely rare.

REFERENCES

Australian Journalists Association (AJA). (n.d.). "Ethics: How to Complain." Media Entertainment and Arts Alliance.

Australian Journalists Association Ethics Review Committee. (1993). "Issues Paper." Sydney: Media Entertainment and Arts Alliance, December.

Australian Psychological Society. (1986). "Code of Professional Conduct." Parkville Victoria.

Bok, S. (1988). "The Limits of Confidentiality," in J. C. Callahan, ed., *Ethical Issues in Professional Life.* New York: Oxford University Press, pp. 230–239.

Bosch, H. (1993). *Corporate Practices and Conduct,* 2nd ed. Sydney: Business Council of Australia.

Brough, J. (1994). "Journalists' Code under Threat." *Canberra Times,* August 30.

Callahan, J. C., ed. (1988). *Ethical Issues in Professional Life.* New York: Oxford University Press.

Corporations Law, 1990 as amended to 1994, AGPS.

Dhaliwal, D. S., J. W. Schatzberg, and M. A. Trombley. (1993). "An Analysis of the Economic Factors Related to Auditor-Client Disagreements Preceding

Auditor Changes." *Auditing: A Journal of Practice and Theory* 12 (2): 22–38.

Farmer, T. A., L. E. Rittenberg, and M. Trompeter. (1987). "An Investigation of the Impact of Economic and Organizational Factors on Auditor Independence." *Auditing: A Journal of Practice and Theory* 7 (1): 1–14.

Finn, P. D. (1977). *Fiduciary Obligations.* Sydney: Law Book Company.

Flint, D. (1993). "Putting the Pen to the Sword." *Sydney Morning Herald*, September 9, p. 13.

Institute of Chartered Accountants in Australia (ICAA). (1988). "Professional Independence." *Rules of Ethical Conduct.* Members' Handbook, vol. 4, ICAA, March.

———. (1990). "Definitions, Principles, and Discipline." *Rules of Ethical Conduct.* Members' Handbook, vol. 4, ICAA, December.

Law Society of the Australian Capital Territory (ACT). (n.d.). "Guide to Professional Conduct and Etiquette," as amended to 1992.

Lederman, G. (1994). "Lighting the Fuse." *Charter 65* (June): 70–72.

Lopes, L. J. (1896). *In Re The Kingston Cotton Mill Company Ltd.* [1896] 1, Chapter 6.

Pellegrino, E. D. (1991). "Trust and Distrust in Professional Ethics." In E. D. Pellegrino et al. (eds.), *Ethics, Trust, and the Professions.* Washington, DC: Georgetown University Press.

Pinkard, T. (1982). "Invasions of Privacy in Social Science Research." Reproduced in J. C. Callahan (ed.), *Ethical Issues in Professional Life.* New York: Oxford University Press, 1988, pp. 225–230.

Trade Practices Commission. (1992). *Study of the Professions—Accountancy.* Canberra: AGPS, July.

———. (1994). *Study of the Professions—Legal.* Canberra: AGPS, March.

III

Trust, Responsibility, and Control: Cases and Analyses

9

Accounting for Fraud: Auditors' Ethical Dilemmas in the BCCI Affair

Nikos Passas

INTRODUCTION

Markets depend on corporations' financial statements to assess and monitor their standing. In this sense, annual reports are an essential self-regulatory mechanism. Yet, how reliable are companies' annual reports? Many recent events highlight how official accounts and audit reports often present a distorted picture of reality. Misconduct at Polly Peck International, Robert Maxwell's empire, Kidder Peabody, a number of savings and loan institutions in the United States, the notorious rinky-dink department deals at Citicorp (Dale, 1984; Hutchison, 1986; Miller, 1993) are cases in point. The financial statements of many public companies have included serious inaccuracies (Henriques, 1992). Other companies have legally manipulated their accounts in order to achieve Chapter Eleven protection against creditors, competitors, or labor unions, although their operations were highly profitable in the years in question (Delaney, 1992). The problem is not limited to business organizations. Bettino Craxi, former prime minister of Italy, while testifying as a witness in a corruption trial before television cameras, admitted knowledge of illegal financing of political parties: "The whole system was corrupt . . . *Everyone knew the parties' balance sheets presented to parliament each year were a sham*" (*Financial Times*) [hereafter *FT*], February 2, 1994: 2; emphasis added).

Such cases demonstrate how easy it may be for management to deceive, but they also raise the question of accountants' responsibility. While the phrase "true and fair view" is the foundation of the accounting profession, a precise definition of those terms has been elusive. In many instances, auditing firms find themselves shouldering a great deal of blame for their

clients' sorry state of affairs. For example, as the Zurich affiliate of Rothschild Bank fired KPMG Peat Marwick, the Swiss Federal Banking Commission was reported "likely to ask how it [KPMG] could have failed to
notice and draw attention to some of the problems at the bank" (FT, November 20, 1992: 18).

Legal actions brought by the U.S. government against auditing firms for
professional negligence in giving clean accounts to insolvent thrifts has led
to settlements amounting to hundreds of millions of dollars. For example,
in 1994, Deloitte & Touche agreed to pay $312 million in settling fifteen
lawsuits; in 1992, Ernst & Young paid $400 million (FT, March 16, 1994:
4). In the ever-evolving saga of corruption in Italy, Montedison has sued
Price Waterhouse for $611 million for serious negligence (FT, April 19,
1994: 18). The South Australian government was reported prepared to sue
Price Waterhouse for A$1.1 billion over its audit of the collapsed Beneficial
Finance (Economist, August 20, 1994: 5).

A result of these developments is that the Big Six refuse to serve smaller
institutions trying to go public. Lawrence A. Weinback, Arthur Andersen's
CEO, stated that "Liability risk has gone so far, it's not worth the risk to
audit some small companies, IPOs, and small banks. The risk-reward trade-
off is out of whack" (Newsweek, March 1, 1993: 76).[1] So, some companies
sued auditors who dropped them as clients.

This paper examines some legal and ethical issues regarding the audit
and liquidation of international corporations by using the collapsed Bank
of Credit and Commerce International (BCCI) as a case study. After BCCI
was shut down in July 1991, the losses were estimated by the liquidators
at $12 billion, which made most observers wonder how it was possible for
a Ponzi scheme of this proportion to go on undetected for more than a
decade. With victims spread throughout the world, but primarily in the
Third World and the United Kingdom, regulators and accountants came
under pressure to explain why it took so long for drastic action to be taken
(Bingham Report, 1992; HMSO, 1992; Kerry Report, 1992). As the most
investigated bank in the world (Passas, 1993, 1995; Passas and Groskin,
1993), BCCI is a gold mine of reliable information rarely accessible to
researchers wishing to explore the role of accountants in contemporary
global markets. Although many firms performed different roles while BCCI
was operating in 72 countries, three of the Big Six feature prominently in
the affair. Groups of firms from Price Waterhouse (PW) and Ernst & Whinney (E&W; now part of Ernst & Young [E&Y]) were the chief accountants
for the BCCI group of banks and foundations around the world. Touche
Ross has been appointed to liquidate the assets and distribute them equi-
tably to BCCI's creditors. The aim of this paper is to outline questions
raised for accountants in various functions they performed in the whole
affair and point to directions in which answers can be sought.

THE EXTERNAL AUDITORS: TRUE AND FAIR VIEW
IN A WORLD OF VIRTUAL REALITY

The main parts of BCCI's complex organizational structure were a Luxembourg holding company, which controlled a bank incorporated in Luxembourg (BCCI S.A.), a bank in Grand Cayman (BCCI Overseas), and a number of locally incorporated banks around the world (e.g., Canada, Egypt, Japan). An important part of the BCCI network was the ICIC (International Credit and Investment Company) Group, which consisted of holding companies and a bank incorporated in Grand Cayman, subsidiaries, charitable foundations, and a staff benefit fund. Management control of ICIC was exercised by a small team of top BCCI executives.

In the late 1970s and especially early 1980s, BCCI faced serious problems. In the course of its frantic growth, it took imprudent risks by offering substantial loans to select clients without conventional guarantees. These loans were not serviced and caused concern that the borrowers' bankruptcy might destroy BCCI itself. A second major source of concern was significant losses incurred at BCCI's treasury department, which was investing unwisely and at a level violating BCCI's internal rules. The loss caused a deeper crisis that was kept secret until 1986, when PW reported it to the Institut Monétaire Luxembourgeois. Bank of England officials also found out about it the same year.

As it turned out, mismanagement was compounded by systematic fraud, a Ponzi scheme operated by a few top BCCI executives in collusion with clients and shareholders. Unrecorded deposits, deceptive accounts, circuitous transactions, and inside loans were occurring mainly at BCCI Overseas over many years.

Should the auditors have uncovered the misconduct earlier? Should they have resigned, carried out further tests, insisted on better internal controls or qualified BCCI's accounts? How extensively should they have worked with the regulators without breaching client confidentiality?

Until 1987, the audit responsibility for the BCCI group of companies was split primarily between PW and E&W firms. PW audited ICIC Overseas, BCCI Overseas, and BCCI Emirates, while E&W audited the BCCI SA side and the group's consolidated accounts (Bingham, 1992). Frustrated by its incomplete audit responsibility (i.e., lack of access to other parts of the group) and concerned about serious lapses of internal controls, E&W (a partner of Whinney Murray Ernst & Ernst) wrote a letter in April 1979 to the president of BCCI indicating it would refuse to continue. The letter also noted that E&W could accept reappointment if concerns were addressed and "on the assumption that the fee on which we agree represents a fair reward for our services" (cited in Jack, 1994: 7). Although E&Y argues that its concerns were met at the time, E&W did not receive the requested audit responsibility. Yet, it continued to audit until 1986, when it reiterated the threat to resign because risk concentration and the other problems still remained. Another letter written by E&W in April 1987 indicated to BCCI that "they were entirely willing to continue to act as BCCI group auditors provided that they were appointed as sole auditors to the group." Their letter stated that "their continued involvement was no longer conditional on changes in management and reporting" (PW, 1992: 10).

Termination of the split auditing situation had been urged by bank regulators as well. So, in June 1987, PW accepted the appointment as the auditor for the entire group. Since then, it has written fifteen reports on BCCI, some of them pointing to false and deceitful accounts, grounds for concern about top managers' integrity. The clearest reference to fraud was made in a June 1991 draft report. Yet, no qualification of these problems appeared in the audit reports for years 1987–1989 (the 1989 report contained only a qualification relative to possible liabilities following BCCI's indictment for money laundering in Florida).

In the aftermath of BCCI's closure, criticism of the auditing firms came from all sides, including the accounting profession (Aldous and Hamedani, 1991). Numerous signs of trouble, the argument goes, should not have gone unheeded: persistent rumors on tax fraud, money laundering, bribery, currency transaction violations, and so forth; complex structure with a dominant chief executive; suspect accounting; an aging computer system; undocumented loans and many transactions with related parties; liquidity problems.

BCCI's shutdown has been justified on the basis of a PW draft report (under Section 41 of the Banking Act 1987) finding that BCCI's accounting records failed to meet the required standard and there was no proper or adequate system of controls for BCCI's business management. Why was this problem not unveiled by the ordinary audit process? Why was this not found out in the course of earlier PW inquiries commissioned by regulators before 1991? Should frauds have been detected earlier? Was the 1990 audit report adequate in view of the facts PW knew in that year? Was PW's role as auditor of the bank compatible with its assistance for management restructuring and advising the Abu Dhabi government? These were questions to be examined by the Joint Disciplinary Scheme, a disciplinary committee operated by the three leading accountancy bodies in Britain, that would look into the "conduct and competence of members and member firms" relative to BCCI. On December 21, 1993, however, PW won a deferment on the grounds that the inquiry would prejudice the outcome of civil litigation against it. Thus, despite the obvious public interest served by an early study of these issues, the inquiry is unlikely to proceed before the next century.

A very vexing question is how PW expressed private concerns to BCCI managers over the 1989 accounts, but went on to give a relatively clean bill of health, with a footnote noting that Abu Dhabi authorities, the main shareholders, had "advised the directors of their intention to maintain the group's capital base while the reorganization and restructuring necessary for its continuing development is undertaken" (PW, 1992: 25). PW felt comfortable with this arrangement, especially because British and Luxembourg regulators knew of the uncertainties involved in the venture, and because those responsible for discovering false and deceitful transactions were about to be removed.

PW argued that the footnote in the 1989 accounts was adequate. That is, unless something was seriously wrong at BCCI, the government of Abu Dhabi would not have given such assurance. However, the rest of the note deals with mundane accounting matters and the significance of the note could be easily missed. It is noteworthy that the meaning and significance of the note differs due to discrepancies between U.S. and U.K. accounting standards—in the United States it would not have been sufficient.

Both PW and E&Y firms have been sued by Milberg Weiss, a U.S. law firm, on behalf of all BCCI depositors (*Hamid et al. v. Price Waterhouse & Co., et al.,* 1991). Among the allegations in this RICO suit against 77 defendants were that E&Y and PW firms in Luxembourg, the United Kingdom, and the Caymans knew of or recklessly disregarded facts and financial misstatements that violated accounting principles; they should have qualified BCCI's accounts; they accepted BCCI's prohibition to communicate between the two firms and no Urdu speaking examiners could be hired, although important documents were written in this language; they did not press BCCI to disclose material facts and allowed it to misrepresent its financial condition to regulators and the public for years. In addition, the suit alleges that a former PW partner accepted inappropriate payments for assistance in falsifying BCCI accounts and that PW accepted loans from BCCI and grew dependent on BCCI fees.

E&W is also criticized for not disclosing the reasons for withdrawing as BCCI auditors, but most arrows are clearly directed at PW, who audited the parts of the BCCI group where the most serious misconduct took place.

PW did indeed receive loans or credit facilities in two African countries, as well as in Panama and Barbados from its audit client, and two of its partners in the Cayman Islands had deposits with the bank. Former BCCI executives have accused PW of being negligent in its duties and/or incompetent to detect the frauds (Kerry, 1992). PW argues that "these transactions had been on normal commercial terms and that they had in no way affected its audit judgments on BCCI" (*FT*, March 23, 1994: 8). At a BCCI-related trial in London, one PW witness "admitted that his firm had failed always to use best-practice methods when auditing the BCCI books" (*FT*, February 26/27, 1994: 6). It is noted, nevertheless, that it was ultimately a PW report in October 1990 (as well as the draft S.41 report) that paved the ground for BCCI's closure, civil suits, indictments, and prosecutions in the United Kingdom and the United States.

PW's general stance is that is was duped. Concentration of executive power in the hands of BCCI's president and its CEO, the credibility of BCCI's board of experienced directors, the very rapid growth of BCCI internationally, and the lack of resources for regulators in Luxembourg and the Cayman Islands were important factors preventing PW from discovering frauds. A senior PW partner has argued that unraveling the fraud was like piecing together a huge jigsaw puzzle without having the picture: "Over time you get an idea of what the picture looks like, but it gets ever more difficult. You are dealing with deception and manipulation of information both inside and outside the company. Wherever you turn, whatever you are looking at, all is unreal. You are living in a world of unreality." He also made it clear that his firm is not surprised at the criticisms: "Of course we won't come out of this smelling like roses. . . . Everyone involved will be criticized and we will get our fair share of unfair criticism" (cited in Waller, 1991: 6).

Some argue that PW should have done what Arthur Andersen did with respect to Capcom, a BCCI affiliate trading in securities: They resigned as Capcom's auditors after issuing a damning report for 1988 referring to lost papers, dubious loans, illegal transactions, and fraud. Strong critics of PW note that the firm would not wish to lose such a lucrative client by qualifying its accounts—PW's worldwide audit fee for 1988 was $4,700,000 and was estimated to increase by 6 percent for 1989 (PW, July 31, 1989 letter to Dr. A. Hartmann, member of BCCI's board of directors: 5).

At any rate, PW's difficult position regarding the 1989 accounts can be better appreciated by looking at several of its reports and its understandings leading up to the nonqualification. Auditors serve shareholders, other stakeholders, the directors, and the executive management. In addition, they often serve regulators' interests. The BCCI case makes abundantly clear that these roles can be incompatible with each other and that they may conflict with the interests of depositors.

Concerns about concentration of loans, some of which were hardly ever serviced, wanting management and computerized information systems, had been repeated by PW over the years and were known to BCCI's directors and managers. Further, the Bank of England, the Institut Monétaire Luxembourgeois and the main shareholders (that is, the Abu Dhabi ruler and related parties) were also aware of the problems. Several reports, notes, and letters from and to PW were placed in the public record by Senator Kerry (see U.S. Senate Committee on Foreign Relations 1992, Part 1: 261–488; 1992, Part 4: 95–232). It is instructive to review them because they reveal the extent of knowledge of misconduct and mismanagement at BCCI long before the Section 41 draft report of June 1990. PW agreed to sign off the accounts only when Abu Dhabi agreed to support the restructuring of BCCI. Giving a clean opinion in this case, however, amounted to arguing that "if a rich shareholder says he will prop up a company, it doesn't matter what the financial statements say" (Truell and Gurwin, 1992: 292).

British case law suggested that auditors have no duty of care to lending banks and their duty is confined to shareholders (*Al Saudi Banque v. Clarke Pixley* [1989] and *Caparo Industries v. Dickman* [1990], respectively). The problem is, thus, that there is nobody to prepare statements with depositors' interests in mind (Dale, 1992). Even if shareholders are perceived as the main clients of the accounting firm, does their knowledge of problems eliminate the need for detailed public reports? In turn, if managers are seen as the main clients, what sense would it make to alert them to their own misconduct and abuses, leaving the public unaware?

Moreover, many argue that auditing a bank is not the same as with other companies. A PW senior partner stated rather bluntly that "you can not qualify a bank." There is some merit in this point, because a run on the bank can be thus precipitated with catastrophic consequences. Yet, PW's April and October 1990 reports to directors and regulators clearly show a near-complete lack of internal controls and raised serious questions about BCCI's senior management. It is neither sound public policy nor a service to prospective depositors to let things stand. If in this case the accounts should not be qualified, whose accounts ever will? The problem is that, if bank accounts are known to almost never be qualified, the credibility and usefulness of external audits are substantially undermined. If audit reports cease to be a reliable source of information, how can markets assess the creditworthiness and health of financial institutions? Hence, ensuing uncertainty can destabilize markets.

Another PW-related problem was a potential conflict faced by Robert Bench, the vice chairman of PW(U.S.)'s world regulatory advisory group for banks. Bench, a former official of the Office of the Comptroller of the Currency (OCC), had read at least two documents containing important information on BCCI. The first was a report on the Bank of America's investment in BCCI in the late 1970s. The report had detailed BCCI management problems and questionable loans from that time (U.S. Senate Committee on Foreign Relations, 1992, Part 4: 15–23). The other was a CIA memo indicating that BCCI secretly controlled the First American Bank, which was based in Washington, DC and had branches in several states (Kerry Report, 1992: 283–284).

In 1987, Bench joined PW and in 1988 he was one of the partners responsive to BCCI for its compliance needs in the United States following the bank's indictment for money laundering. This indictment raised many red flags for bank regulators who wanted to know whether other internal control failures existed at BCCI. Given the frequent research into foreign holdings of U.S. banks conducted at the time of the Third World debt crisis and the myriad of intelligence documents he reviewed while at OCC, Bench did not recall the specific BCCI-related documents (Kerry Report, 1992).

However, had he remembered what he knew about the nominee arrangements at BCCI, had he connected in his mind that Clark Clifford and Robert Altman, the heads of BCCI's legal defense team, were also running First American Bank, he would have suspected that BCCI had violated U.S. law. This was because BCCI had assured Federal Reserve officials that it would have no role in the financing or control of the takeover of Financial General (later renamed First American Bankshares) by Middle Eastern investors. In fact, PW (U.K.) knew also that BCCI had lent hundreds of millions of dollars to those who ostensibly owned First American. The only guarantee for these loans were the shares in First American. As the loans were not serviced, BCCI had control of the shares.

So, the firms that had been appointed as single auditors of the BCCI group had people working for them who, collectively, had knowledge of BCCI law violations, while they were advising BCCI on its compliance efforts relative to money-laundering prevention. Had all these connections been made, a serious conflict would have arisen between knowledge of misconduct and U.S. confidentiality duties to BCCI's legal defense team (see engagement agreement in PW letter to Altman, Wechsler, Banoun and Barcella dated March 8, 1989 in U.S. Senate Committee on Foreign Relations, 1992, Part 4: 53–58).

A wider issue pointed up by this case, thus, is the independence of external auditors who provide management advisory services to their clients. In such situations, the auditors could effectively audit their own work or the work of their partners, an additional conflict of interest (Armstrong, 1993: 107–109; Briloff, 1994; Weiss, 1992: 12).

THE INVESTIGATORS

Accountants have a crucial role to play in uncovering financial offenses and management fraud, particularly because the technical wording and cryptic messages contained in annual reports make it hard for outside observers to fully understand what is going on. In some cases, sham transactions become obvious very quickly. Other cases require analysis of accounts, balance sheets, and information contained in forms institutions must file according to the law. The degree of difficulty in following the money trail depends on the sophistication of the perpetrators. Auditors shy away, however, from the task of looking for fraud, possibly because they do not wish to alienate clients (Weiss, 1992: 10). There is a fundamental conflict in reporting the wrongdoing of people who pay you to examine their operations.

Accountants working for the government, on the other hand, may be tempted to breach the trust of their employers. Mark Braley, for example, was one of eleven accountants seconded from Coopers & Lybrand Deloitte to the Serious Fraud Office (SFO) for its BCCI investigation. Four weeks later, in October 1991, he and Bernard Lynch, an independent accountant also on the SFO team, were arrested and charged with conspiracy to pervert the course of justice by removing, substituting, defacing, or copying documentary evidence relative to that investigation. The court was also told that the two men tried to sell documents to a lawyer representing a suspect. In October 1992, they were found guilty and sentenced to three years each in prison.

SERVING TWO MASTERS: FROM WATCHDOG TO FRAUD CHASER

In the United States, regulators have their own bank examiners. Supervisors of several countries in continental Europe rely on external bank auditors. The United Kingdom is somewhere in between (Dale, 1992). Under the terms of the Banking Act, the Bank of England charged PW with investigative work relative to BCCI, while PW was its auditor and restructuring advisor as well. It certainly makes sense and sounds cost-effective to assign the task of investigation to a firm already familiar with the company in question. Most familiar is the firm that audits the books of that company. Yet, how compatible are these tasks?

There is some inherent conflict in that special reports under different sections of the Banking Act are needed when things appear to be wrong. This suspicion as well as the rare cases of qualified reports indicate a failure of auditors to influence management: "A qualified report is not only an expression of the auditors' opinion that the directors have failed to comply with the law. It is also an admission by the auditors that they have failed effectively to influence the directors" (Fowle, 1993: 26). In this light, Section 41 or other reports may not be best commissioned from the institution's own external auditors (comp. HMSO, 1992: 34).

PW, however, "believe that had we not been able to combine the various roles it may not have been possible for us to make so much progress in discovering the full extent of the fraud" (PW, 1992: 21). Others argue that this auditor-regulator relationship can also bear better results than the U.S. arrangements. In the United States, passing information on to regulators would involve breach of confidentiality duties to the client. The client might even bring legal action if the accounting firm is too cooperative with regulators. Under U.S. professional rules of the AICPA and the SEC, when auditors detect misconduct that management does not correct, the most they can do is resign from the audit and insure that regulators are informed by the client about the reasons behind the resignation.[2]

The rather different standards by which auditors operate in different countries have generated multiple hurdles to regulators, law enforcement, and congressional investigators in the BCCI investigations in the United States. It is not hard to see why many of those committed to bringing out all the facts surrounding BCCI were at times incensed by refusals of accountants or other bodies overseas to share documents and other evidence. The Kerry Report (1992) illustrates well such frustrations. Nevertheless, it must be stressed that international cases frequently create situations where accountants or other professionals will violate the law of the country of residence if they cooperate fully with those from a requesting country with different laws, cultures, and traditions. PW (U.K.) has found itself in such a spot as well.

THE LIQUIDATORS

The question of high fees (in 1994 down to £31.2m) has been repeatedly raised with Touche Ross, the court-appointed liquidators. The victims had been warned about the huge sums paid to lawyers and spent on provisional liquidation (*FT*, October 26–27, 1991). As a member of the British Parliament (Mr. Darling) remarked, "I understand that, as ever, rapacious accountants and lawyers are having a field day with what funds remain in the bank. This matter must be investigated" (House of Commons [HC], Hansart, 1992, Nov. 6: col. 543). As another Member of Parliament (Mr. Vaz) put it, the first scandal was the fraud at BCCI because of the Bank of England's failure in its duty to protect them; "The second scandal will be the liquidators becoming rich on the victims' money while the Government stand by and watch" (HC Hansart, 1992, Nov. 6.: col. 560).

The liquidation costs in the period July 6, 1991 to January 6, 1992 were £77.4m. Concorde flights were seen by Touche as a matter of "survival," as it was necessary for a negotiator to be "in more than one place at the same time"; holidays were paid to personnel to keep their performance of high quality; Touche Ross charged £127 per hour, which was "market, commercial rates" for recruiting "the best quality people and not just anyone who was available" (*FT*, February 22–23, 1992: 7).

A report produced at the high court suggested that the provisional liquidators had incurred overhead and expenses costs of $200 million before the end of 1991 (*FT*, December 3, 1991). Touche disclosed that its bill in the first eighteen months was £108 million, of which £82.1 million was fees; its weekly fees fell from £1.45 million a week to £600,000 a week with about 450 staff working on the case down from about 650 at its peak (Tehan, 1993a, 1993b). According to a report to the Department of Trade and Industry, only the English side of the liquidation up to January 1994, including legal and other fees, amounted to $360 million; of this, $169.2 million was remuneration for the English liquidators (English Liquidators, 1994). The conflict that arises in this situation is that the longer this affair lasts, the better off the firm will be. Catastrophic as it has been for hundreds of thousands of depositors from the Third World, the collapse of BCCI represents a bonanza for Western accountants and lawyers.

A second issue relative to liquidation processes is that of legal action against other accounting firms. Touche Ross has also sued PW and E&Y—originally for $8 billion, but in March 1994 bringing the claims up to $11 billion—for material misstatements regarding 1985, 1986, and 1987. Had they not breached their duties to shareholders, had they not failed to detect and report irregularities dating back to 1977 and 1979, respectively, the suit alleges remedial action would have prevented the gigantic losses.

This lawsuit may not have been an easy course of action for Touche to take. After all, few accounting firms dominate the international market. If they show undue aggressiveness against colleagues, they may well find themselves in the shoes of defendants in future cases when a client of Touche's is being liquidated. It is not wise to throw stones at others while living in a glass house (Peters, 1993).

Also, given the domination of the Big Six, it is conceivable that one auditing firm may sue another whose insurance liability company is audited by the former. In such a case, success in getting the most for depositors would possibly entail the serious financial trouble of the insurer. The amounts in the BCCI liquidation are unusually high. However, let us take a hypothetical example: If PW's insurer were a syndicate of the Lloyd's of London and the same syndicate were audited by Touche, Touche would have a terrible dilemma. In the current turmoil, some of Lloyd's syndicates may be unable to cope with another huge liability loss. If such a crisis leads to bankruptcy, Touche could lose a valuable client and could theoretically find itself in PW's situation (Peters, 1993).

Liability payments are made first from accounting firms' own resources, then liability insurers who become less and less affordable. Further, Andrew Jack reports, "the 'Big 6' firms are all members of two secretive mutual insurance companies based in Bermuda. One is called Pail (Professional Assets Indemnity Limited), and the other Padua (named after the Italian city credited with creating double-entry bookkeeping). These two mutuals plug certain 'gaps' in the cover offered by external insurers. That covers the firms up to about $150m" (Jack, 1992: 14).

The size of liability suits is another burning issue. Is it fair to have the auditors bear the full financial responsibility of misconduct carried out by management? Should they, in other words, bare the losses or bear the losses? A senior partner at PW argued that "It is quite clear that, following some spectacular corporate collapses and the ensuing epidemic of legislation, the major firms are now facing claims of such size that one or more of them could be bankrupted" (Brindle, 1994: 14). His argument is that auditors should not shoulder more blame than is theirs and not be sued for 100 percent of a company's losses. If this change is not made, the whole industry may suffer the consequences of major auditing firms going under by not having their accounts substantiated and therefore being unable to attract investment.

Coresponsibility with management may confuse the relative independence accountants ideally bring. The auditors' role is to comment on accounts presented to them by management. "If you move to a position where reporting is in the first place the duty of auditors not directors, this denies the auditors' essential role as objective commentators and effectively makes them another tier of management" (Fowle, 1993).

On the other hand, the innocent victims' perspective must not be neglected in this debate. When guilty managers are personally bankrupted or in prison, depositors who relied in good faith on published reports can only turn against those who can make restitution.

In addition, the argument made by PW (U.S.) that it cannot be held liable for business conducted by its U.K. or other partners has also been criticized. There is no doubt that major accounting firms operate under different rules and regulations overseas. However, totally separating their responsibility when it comes to legal action "is tantamount to saying 'let the buyer beware' when they do business with my firm elsewhere—even though people should rely on my name for uniform quality," according to Douglas Carmichael, an accountancy professor at the City University of New York's Baruch College (*Wall Street Journal*, June 20, 1991: A3).

CONCLUSIONS

In short, the BCCI affair highlights a series of problems relative to the auditing of multinational corporations and dilemmas faced by accountants in their roles as external auditors, investigators, and liquidators. The foregoing case study illustrates the risks of split auditing; international discrepancies of auditing standards; lack of clear responsibility to creditors; ambivalence toward auditors' responsibility and duties to regulators; potential problems emanating from the revolving door between regulators and accounting firms; deals with clients; potential conflicts of interest between auditors and liquidators; and temptations to exploit positions of power for personal gain.

The policy implication is that unless such fundamental problems are resolved, or their effects minimized, the danger of the BCCI type of disaster will remain high. At the very least, accountants and investigators need a more complete understanding of each others' duties, responsibilities, and constraints, and clear guidelines on how to resolve ethical dilemmas when they arise.

Given the increasing internationalization of trade and commerce, there is a pressing need for more standardization of auditing guidelines, responsibilities, and duties across national borders. The differences between the U.S. and U.K. standards have made it difficult for regulators and criminal investigators to achieve full cooperation from auditors who had to respect confidentiality and secrecy rules in their respective jurisdictions.

A lesson for the Bank of England is to decrease its dependence on an institution's auditors and expand its own investigative role. Steps have been taken in that direction following the Bingham Report recommendations. The Bank may also consider the appointment of auditors other than the client's for special reports.

BCCI, just like the S&L debacle in the United States, is a painful reminder of accountants' obligation to serve the wider society and not to focus exclusively on their clients (Briloff, 1986, 1990). External auditors should look for fraud with the help of internal auditors, and should not be prevented by confidentiality requirements from reporting fraud to the authorities. This responsibility has remained outside the scope of the auditors chiefly because of the profession's wishes. Public pressure and demand by the clients of accounting firms could make it an explicit objective of the audit function (Sorensen et al., 1980: 224–225). A widespread recognition of this duty will assist the auditors, too. If other accounting firms have the same duties, auditors' fears of losing their clients will be reduced. This will make it easier for them to confront uncooperative management and counter its resistance.

A measure of responsibility toward depositors must be introduced as well, although increased auditing and liability costs must be considered (Dale, 1992). The issue of limits of liability to the point of auditing firms' responsibility needs also to be settled in an equitable fashion.

Instead of spending so much energy in debates about liability losses, accounting firms should perform more adequate risk assessment before they undertake a client's audit. More accountability will help improve risk assessment procedures and increase vigilance with obvious societal benefits. Accountability can be further fostered by introducing a rotating audit system, according to which new firms will examine a company's files every few years. The costs of such a measure can be contained through better bookkeeping, making the transition smoother and affordable (Weiss, 1992: 12).

Finally, steps must be taken to address the problems caused by the revolving door connecting auditors, regulators, and clients. We need to insure that conflicts of interests are minimized by providing a set of norms as a yardstick against which moral dilemmas may be handled or resolved.

NOTES

1. This "liability crisis" should not be exaggerated. Out of the record-setting $400 million penalty paid by Ernst & Young, for example, $300 million were covered by insurance. The rest was to be paid over four years. A $25 million a year penalty for a company with $2.2 billion annual income from fees in the U.S. is more manageable than it appears at first sight (Tait and Jack, 1992).

2. Change of professional rules in the British direction met with strong resis-

tance which reflected fears that government agencies could gain easy access to internal accounts; the notion that the IRS might do that deflected attempts at reform.

REFERENCES

Aldous, H., and H. Hamedani. (1991). "BCCI Collapse: Auditing at the Crossroads." *Financial Times*, August 16, p. 23.

Armstrong, M. B. (1993). *Ethics and Professionalism for CPAs*. Cincinnati: South-Western Publishing Co.

Bingham Report. (1992). *Inquiry into the Supervision of the Bank of Credit and Commerce International*. London: HMSO.

Briloff, A. J. (1986). "Accountancy and the Public Interest." *Advances in Public Interest Accounting* 1: 1–14.

———. (1990). "Accountancy and Society: A Covenant Desecrated." *Critical Perspectives on Accounting* 1: 5–30.

———. (1994). "Our Profession's 'Jurassic Park.' " *The CPA Journal* (August): 26–31.

Brindle, I. (1994). "Auditor Liability Must Have Limit." *Financial Times*, May 3, p. 14.

Dale, R. (1984). *The Regulation of International Banking*. Cambridge: Woodhead-Faulkner.

———. (1992). "Reflections on the BCCI Affair: A United Kingdom Perspective." *International Lawyer* 26 (4): 949–961.

Delaney, K. (1992). *Strategic Bankruptcy: How Corporations and Creditors Use Chapter 11 to Their Advantage*. Berkeley: University of California Press.

English Liquidators. (1994). *Bank of Credit & Commerce International SA ("BCCI SA") (In Liquidation)*. (Report to the Secretary of State for Trade and Industry Pursuant to Regulation 12 of the Insolvency Regulations 1986 for the Period 16 January 1993 to 15 January 1994).

Financial Times. Various issues.

Fowle, M. (1993). "Time for Auditors to Come Out of Their Shells." *Financial Times*, February 19, p. 26.

Henriques, D. B. (1992). "Falsifying Corporate Data Becomes Fraud of the 90's." *New York Times*, September 21, pp. A-1, D-2.

HMSO. (1992). *Banking Supervision and BCCI: National and International Regulation* (HC (1991–92) 177). Treasury and Civil Service Committee, Fourth Report. London: HMSO.

Hutchison, R. A. (1986). *Off the Books: Citibank and the World's Biggest Money Game*. New York: William Morrow.

Jack, A. (1992). "Auditors Count the Cost of BCCI." *Financial Times*, October 1, p. 14.

———. (1994). "BCCI Audit Doubts Go Back to 1979." *Financial Times*, February 16, p. 7.

Kerry Report. (1992). *The BCCI Affair*. Washington, DC: U.S. Government Printing Office.

Miller, R. B. (1993). *Citicorp: A Bank in Crisis*. New York: McGraw-Hill.

Passas, N. (1993). "Structural Sources of International Crime: Policy Lessons from the BCCI Affair." *Crime, Law and Social Change* 20 (4): 293–305.

————. (1995). "The Mirror of Global Evils: A Review Essay on the BCCI Affair." *Justice Quarterly* 12 (2).

Passas, N., and Groskin, R. B. (1993). "BCCI and the Federal Authorities: Regulatory Anesthesia and the Limits of Criminal Law." *Society for the Study of Social Problems Annual Meeting*. Miami Beach.

Peters, E. (1993). "BCCI: Making a Case for RICO Class Action Cases." *Symposium on Cross-Border Banking Offenses and Regulation: Policy Lessons from the BCCI Affair*. Philadelphia: Temple University.

PW. (1992). *Memorandum Submitted by Price Waterhouse in Response to Questions From the [House of Commons Treasury and Civil Service] Committee*, February 5, 1992.

Sorensen, J. E., H. D. Grove, and T. L. Sorensen. (1980). "Detecting Management Fraud: The Role of the Independent Auditor." In G. Geis and E. Stotland (eds.), *White-Collar Crime: Theory and Research*. Beverly Hills, CA: Sage, pp. 221–251.

Tait, N., and A. Jack. (1992). "Past Turkeys Come Home to Roost." *Financial Times*, November 27, p. 21.

Tehan, P. (1993a). "£108m: The Bill, So Far, for BCCI Liquidators." *The Times*, March 3.

————. (1993b). "Touche Ross Defends BCCI Fees." *The Times*, March 3, p. 21.

Truell, P., and L. Gurwin. (1992). *False Profits*. Boston and New York: Houghton Mifflin.

U.S. Senate Committee on Foreign Relations. (1992). *The BCCI Affair*. Hearings before the Subcommittee on Terrorism, Narcotics, and International Operations. Washington, DC: U.S. Government Printing Office.

Waller, D. (1991). "Auditor Faces Scrutiny Over Actions." *Financial Times*, July 8, p. 6.

Weiss, M. I. (1992). "Why Auditors Have Failed to Fulfill Their Necessary Professional Responsibilities—And What to Do About It." *The Abraham J. Briloff Lecture Series on Accounting and Society* (School of Management, SUNY at Binghamton): 1–14.

10

Was Maintaining the Executive Payroll at PTL an Example of Auditor Independence?

Gary L. Tidwell

The release of Jim Bakker from federal prison not only drew national attention,[1] but it also spurred a renewed interest in the facts that led to the downfall of Bakker and his PTL organization. The PTL case provides an opportunity to examine the narrow yet complex issue of auditor independence as that issue relates to an outside auditing firm maintaining its client's executive payroll.[2] The author will specifically examine the requirement that auditors "should avoid situations that may lead outsiders to doubt their independence."

PTL's independent auditor from 1977 to 1984 was Deloitte Haskins and Sells (DH&S), and from 1984 to 1986 the firm of Laventhol and Horwath (L&H) served as PTL's "independent" auditor. DH&S gave PTL a clean audited opinion for the fiscal year ending May 31, 1984, while L&H qualified its report concerning an ongoing IRS examination for the years 1985 and 1986. Both firms maintained PTL's executive payroll.

AUDITOR INDEPENDENCE: THE BASICS

Independence represents the most basic benchmark of the auditing profession. Were it not for independence and the fact that independence undergirds all audit functions, the auditor's attest function would be meaningless. Instead, an auditor's opinion has meaning because the public places confidence in auditors' ability to make decisions objectively and independent of management.

The concept of auditor independence does not only affect the way CPAs are treated in their various professional roles; the public expects auditors and accountants to exhibit integrity and the highest of ethical standards. In the alternative, when auditors compromise their independence, they undermine investor confidence in the reliability of financial statements and threaten the integrity of securities markets. Independence is, therefore, perhaps the most important auditing standard in existence today.

It is not surprising that the critical issues of auditor independence have not only been extensively documented in the professional literature, but even the U.S. Supreme Court has addressed the independence issue:

By certifying the public reports that collectively depict a corporation's financial status, the independent auditor assumes a public responsibility transcending any employment relationship with the client. The independent public accountant performing this special function owes ultimate allegiance to the corporation's creditors and stockholders, as well as to the investing public. This "public watchdog" function demands that the accountant maintain total independence from the client at all times and requires complete fidelity to the public trust. (*United States v. Arthur Young*, 465 U.S. 805, 817-18 [1984])

Generally Accepted Auditing Standards (GAAS) require, among other things, that an auditor be independent (American Institute of Certified Public Accountants [AICPA], Professional Standards, Vol. 1, AU 150.02, 220.03). Consequently, if the auditor is not independent, the auditor is precluded from issuing an opinion and must disclaim an opinion (AU 504.08–.10).

GAAS (AICPA, Professional Standards, Vol. 1, AU 220.03) states that:

It is of utmost importance to the profession that the general public maintain confidence in the independence of independent auditors. Public confidence would be impaired by evidence that independence was actually lacking and it might also be impaired by the existence of circumstances which reasonable people might believe likely to influence independence. To be independent, the auditor must be intellectually honest; to be *recognized* as independent, he must be free from any obligation to or interest in the client, its management or its owners. . . . Independent auditors should not only be independent in fact; they should avoid situations that may lead outsiders to doubt their independence.

GAAS states that the precepts concerning independence that have been codified in the AICPA Code of Professional Conduct "have the force of professional law for the independent auditor" (AICPA, Professional Standards, Vol. 1, AU 220.04). Article IV of the Code requires the auditor to be independent not only in fact, but also in appearance when providing auditing and attestation services.

Independence in fact entails "intellectual honesty" and the absence of any obligation to any potential users of financial statements. On the other hand, independence in appearance is "the perception of the auditor's independence by parties interested in the audit reports" (Berryman, "Auditor

Independence: It's Historical Development and Some Proposals for Research," *Ethics in the Accounting Profession* S. Loeb, ed., 1978 141, 155.

The distinction between these two different types of independence is that independence in fact questions the auditor's state of mind, while independence in appearance considers the state of mind of persons other than the auditor. The appearance that an auditor attempts to convey may not be that which is perceived by an observer. However, an auditor must not only be independent in fact, but also independent in appearance to others.

Finally, Article IV of the AICPA Code also provides that "[i]n providing all other services, a member should maintain objectivity and avoid conflicts of interest."

INTERPRETATION OF STANDARDS

There has been a plethora of scholarly articles on the issue of independence in fact as well as independence in appearance as this concept relates to auditors. Most of these articles consist of extensive and well-documented studies that relate to independence issues and perceptions of independence, given various hypothetical factual situations. As one author correctly predicted, "(a)rticles on independence may continue to be published because few of the previous works agree on the major conclusion reached" (St. Pierre, "Independence and Auditors Sanctions," *Journal of Accounting, Auditing and Finance* (1984, 257).

However, there has been substantially less written concerning actual cases where questions are raised concerning situations that may lead outsiders to doubt an auditor's independence. Unfortunately, most of these cases are litigated cases, involving numerous causes of action. Typically, these cases are not analyzed by those who are in academia or by those who are not parties to the case.

FACTUAL BACKGROUND OF PTL

With a $52 deposit, Trinity Broadcasting System opened its first bank account in Charlotte, North Carolina, on December 7, 1972. Trinity Broadcasting eventually incorporated in South Carolina as Heritage Village Church and Missionary Fellowship, or "PTL." From this meager $52 beginning, PTL (Praise The Lord, or People That Love), under the leadership of Jim and Tammy Bakker, emerged as a major religious organization. PTL received donations of approximately $400 million from 1982 through 1987. By 1986, PTL claimed it was the third largest theme park in the United States, right behind Disneyland and Disneyworld, and had in excess of six million visitors.

However, despite the outward appearance of financial prosperity, the government would later contend and prove that Jim Bakker was actually perpetrating a massive wire and mail fraud. The government contended that an overt act of this fraud was the excessive salary and bonuses received by Bakker and select others at PTL. Bakker was ultimately found guilty and sentenced to eight years' imprisonment. Specifically, Bakker was charged with fraud in the sale of 152,903 fully paid lodging partnerships, providing at least $158 million in revenue for PTL. Beginning in 1984 and continuing until his resignation in March 1987, Bakker and others at PTL continued to solicit its television viewers and mail partners to become a "Lifetime Partner." Generally, one could become a PTL lifetime partner for a one-time "gift" of $1,000 to PTL. Each lifetime partner and his immediate family would be able to stay in a luxurious hotel at PTL for four days and three nights, for the balance of the life of the lifetime partner. In addition to making numerous mailed solicitations and almost daily television solicitations concerning the benefits of becoming a lifetime partner, PTL told its followers that there were limits on the number of people who could become lifetime partners.

For example, Bakker and others said there could only be 25,000 lifetime partners in the Heritage Grand Hotel. However, in reality, at least 66,683 memberships were sold, producing at least $66,900,000.[3] In another PTL hotel (The Towers), Bakker said only 30,000 lifetime partnerships were available, but instead he sold at least 68,755 memberships producing approximately $74,221,751.[4] Furthermore, over $95,100,000 of the total funds received were used for nonconstruction expenses.[5] The oversale began as early as July 7, 1984, and continued until March 1987.

Rather than building the facilities (the Grand Hotel was built and was operational, but The Towers was never completed) and setting aside funds to provide for the obligation to the lifetime partners, the PTL drew down the funds almost instantaneously to meet the daily operation expenses. These operational expenses included the executive payroll.

EXECUTIVE COMPENSATION AT PTL

PTL's subsequent bankruptcy,[6] and Jim Bakker's criminal conviction for what the government contended was the largest consumer fraud prosecuted as a wire and mail fraud in U.S. history[7] has received extensive publicity. Others at PTL, to include Richard Dortch, senior vice president and co-defendant with Bakker, were also found guilty of wire and mail fraud. David Taggart, vice president and administrative assistant to Bakker, was convicted of income tax evasion.

In all of the judicial proceedings, the compensation of the top key executives was one of the focal points of the various trials. Excessive compensation or private inurement was a critical factor in causing the federal bankruptcy judge to hold the Bakkers and David Taggart personally liable to PTL for breaching their fiduciary duty to the corporation.

Table 10.1
Actual Compensation versus Reasonable Compensation
(Federal Bankruptcy Court)

In Re Heritage Vil. Ch. & Missionary Fellowship
92 B.R. 1000 (Bankruptcy D.S.C. 1988).
DOLLAR AMOUNTS HAVE BEEN ROUNDED

I   Jim Bakker

Year	Actual Compensation	Reasonable Compensation	Personal Inurement
1984	$1,197,352	$133,100	$1,064,252
1985	$1,065,123	$146,410	$1,458,713
1986	$1,886,895	$161,051	$1,725,844
1987	$2,667,108	$177,156	$2,489,952
Total	$7,356,478	$617,717	$6,738,761

II   Tammy Faye Bakker

Year	Actual Compensation	Reasonable Compensation	Personal Inurement
1984	$220,963	$119,790	$101,173
1985	$262,586	$131,769	$130,817
1986	$290,358	$144,946	$145,412
1987	$459,433	$159,440	$299,993
Total	$1,233,340	$555,946	$677,394

III   David Taggart

Year	Actual Compensation	Reasonable Compensation	Personal Inurement
1984	$260,759	$69,878	$190,881
1985	$678,150	$131,769	$546,381
1986	$942,986	$144,946	$798,040
1987	$1,011,491	$159,440	$852,051
Total	$2,893,386	$506,033	$2,387,353

Table 10.1 shows the total amount of actual compensation, reasonable compensation, and resulting personal or private inurement that Jim Bakker, Tammy Faye Bakker, and David Taggart received as determined by the federal bankruptcy court.

The federal bankruptcy court, after considering PTL's management and certain executive compensation, and expenditures, found and concluded "that the acts and conduct of the defendants jointly and severally constitute, at a minimum, gross negligence. In actuality, the conduct of the defendants surpassed any standard of negligence and in truth, was intentional, wanton, capricious and reckless. The parties have failed to perform their duties honestly, in good faith, or with any reasonable amount of diligence or care."[8]

Consequently, the bankruptcy court found Jim Bakker liable for $4,926,242, Taggart liable for $1,048,175, and Tammy Bakker liable for $677,397. Joint and several liability was assessed against Jim Bakker and David Taggart in the amount of $1,036,000.

Ultimately, PTL's tax exempt status was revoked because of private inurement. That is, the IRS found excessive compensation and benefits were inuring to the benefit of certain PTL employees and this is in violation of the IRS Code, Section 501(c)(3).

In Jim Bakker's criminal trial, the government contended that the salary, bonuses, and lifestyle of Bakker, largely financed with PTL funds, provided him with the incentive to perpetrate this fraud.

Certainly, a major component of the Bakkers' compensation package were the salaries, bonuses, and minister's benefit association (MBA) contributions made by PTL for its executives. Those components were introduced as evidence at Jim Bakker's criminal resentencing in tabular form (see Table 10.2).

It is interesting to compare these levels of compensation with compensation the Bakkers' received in earlier years. For example, in 1977, Bakker received a base salary of $24,000, a housing allowance of $2,868, and an annuity contribution of $6,864. Tammy Bakker received an annual salary of $8,000, and in 1977 the Bakkers' net worth was $24,000.

EXECUTIVE PAYROLL

How was executive compensation determined and how were executive payments made at PTL?

According to the minutes of the PTL Board of Directors, the president of PTL (Jim Bakker) is assigned the "duty and responsibility of determining salary and amenities for each of the non-Board Members" of PTL. This means Jim Bakker had ultimate responsibility for setting the compensation of everyone at PTL with the exception of the board members, and he and Dortch were board members. In his depositions, Bakker stated he did not set salaries but relied on the personnel department and Richard Dortch to set salaries and determine bonuses. Bakker also testified he did not know who set Dortch's salary. The PTL Board of Directors set Bakker's salary and authorized certain executive bonuses.

As early as September 1981, Jim Bakker's salary was raised by the PTL Board of Directors to $102,000, and Tammy Bakker's salary was $52,000 per year. Jim Bakker was given a $25,000 bonus and a company car which the board recommended should be a "Cadillac or Lincoln."

Table 10.2
Salaries, Bonuses, and MBA Contributions Paid by PTL to or on Behalf of the
Bakkers

Jim Bakker

Year	Salary[1]	Bonus	MBA	Total
1984	$270,822	$640,000	$121,690	$1,032,512
1985	$314,673	$550,000	$145,348	$1,010,021
1986	$313,567	$790,000	$132,500	$1,236,067
1987	(not available)	$450,000[2]	$55,208	$505,208
	$899,062	**$2,430,000**	**$454,746**	**$3,783,808**

Tammy Bakker

Year	Salary[1]	Bonus	MBA	Total
1984	$94,355	$100,000	_	$194,355
1985	$99,034	$148,512	_	$247,546
1986	$99,951	$265,000	_	$364,951
1987	(not available)	$170,000	_	$170,000
	$293,340	**$683,712**	_	**$976,852**

Combined

Year	Salary[1]	Bonus	MBA	Total
1984	$365,177	$740,000	$121,690	$1,226,867
1985	$413,707	$698,512	$145,348	$1,257,567
1986	$413,518	$1,055,000	$132,500	$1,601,018
1987	(not available)	$620,000	$55,208	$675,208
	$1,192,402	**$3,113,512**	**$454,746**	**$4,760,660**

1. Includes salary, housing and/or automobile allowances, excess group term life insurance
   premiums, etc.
2. Includes $150,000 payment obtained through David Taggart, 1/87.

The arrival of Richard Dortch as a PTL board member and his subsequent employment as PTL executive vice president in 1983 began an era
of secrecy and confidentiality in executive compensation. Three confidential
checking accounts were controlled by executives of PTL. The Executive
Account, the Executive Payroll Account, and the Parsonage Account were,
according to the federal bankruptcy judge, "not subject to usual PTL audit
procedures and, in many instances, funds were withdrawn from these accounts without explanation or receipts."[9] David Taggart contended his

business receipts were in a "shoe box at home" as he continued to draw business expense advances of $10,000 in cash.

The minutes of the PTL Board of Directors reflect that bonuses were approved by the board. The amounts of bonuses approved by the board were not recorded in the body of the minutes, but they were, in accordance with Richard Dortch's instructions, recorded on a one-page addendum attached to the minutes. The board of directors never saw the addendums and were told the minutes could not be removed from the board room.

At Jim Bakker's criminal trial, the testimony of seven of PTL's board members was that they never approved bonuses to Jim Bakker of the magnitude that were reflected in the minutes. Bakker testified he was out of the room at the time bonuses were discussed and voted on.

AUDITORS AND THE EXECUTIVE PAYROLL

PTL's executives were paid from the Executive Payroll Account that was administered by PTL's outside accounting firm. As previously noted, for the fiscal year ending May 31, 1984, PTL's auditor was Deloitte Haskins and Sells, and for the years 1985 and 1986, Laventhol and Horwath served as outside auditors.

DH&S, and subsequently, L&H maintained the check register and prepared checks for the account from which approximately twenty to thirty PTL executives were paid from approximately 1982 through 1987. At the time each accounting firm was hired by PTL, it prepared payroll checks, certain bonus checks, and other checks representing compensation payments to PTL executives after being directed by PTL management. PTL sometimes prepared compensations and bonus checks on its own. Neither accounting firm exercised any discretion with respect to the disbursement of funds from the Executive Payroll Accounts and neither firm signed any of the checks written on the account.

In documents filed with a U.S. Federal District Court, DH&S stated the following concerning its involvement with the PTL Executive Payroll Account:

The sum total of Deloitte's activities were that Deloitte would fill in the date, payee and amount of the check and record information for PTL's tax records. The checks would then be forwarded either to PTL's attorneys or to PTL for signature. This limited role in connection with the account resulted from Deloitte's careful investigation of its professional responsibilities. When Dortch requested that Deloitte administer the account, Deloitte went to the books and investigated the impact on its audit services of performing that task. It determined that it could do so as long as it did not sign any of the checks or set compensation for any of the employees to be paid through the account. As a result, Deloitte never signed any of the checks or possessed a PTL signature stamp.

In documents filed with the same federal court, L&H stated the following concerning its involvement with the PTL Executive Payroll Account:

No Laventhol partner or employee decided who was to be paid from the Executive Payroll Account. No Laventhol partner or employee determined the amount of compensation which was to be paid to any PTL employee. Such managerial, discretionary decisions were made by PTL's officers and directors, who then communicated them to Laventhol personnel for mechanical and clerical execution. No Laventhol employee or partner had any check-signing authority on the Executive Payroll Account at any time, and no Laventhol employee or partner ever had possession of any PTL facsimile signature stamp.

The audit manager of L&H testified that while he was aware of the bonuses from reviewing the minutes, he became aware of Bakker's salary from reading about it in the newspaper.[10] However, he never talked and, to his knowledge, no one at L&H talked to the board of directors (other than Bakker and Dortch) to confirm salaries or bonuses in the minutes. Likewise, the compensation and bonus checks prepared by DH&S were never discussed with the full PTL Board of Directors. Instead, the checks prepared by the firms were sent by courier to PTL's lawyers or to PTL for signature.

As already discussed, the board of directors (except Bakker and Dortch) contended they never approved the compensation that was ultimately paid to Bakker. Typical of the board's testimony, one board member testified that he was "astonished" to find out just recently about the big salaries, bonuses, and expenditures.[11] Board members also testified that they would not have approved the bonuses received by Bakker if they had known of PTL's true financial situation.[12]

Besides raising issues of private inurement and the awarding of bonuses from funds fraudulently raised, PTL could not afford the bonuses and opulent lifestyle the Bakkers were enjoying at the expense of this nonprofit corporation.

PTL's Chief Financial Officer continually warned of PTL's financial demise in memos to Bakker, Dortch, and others. For example, on March 12, 1984, the CFO wrote a memo to Bakker stating, "Our payroll is too high and can not be sustained by General Funds any longer. American Express has to be paid very soon, as we are cut off until we pay $85,000 . . . pushing Security Bank to increase our line of credit." The very next day Jim Bakker was awarded a bonus of $390,000. By September 13, 1984, the CFO was writing to Bakker indicating that he had met with the DH&S audit partner in charge of the PTL account. Specifically, PTL's CFO wrote, "[t]he main concern expressed in the report is whether PTL will be able to continue as 'a going concern' based on current assets of only $8.6 million against $28.5

million in current liabilities. There is a concern whether PTL will be able to meet its debt obligations during the coming year."

On October 17, 1984, the CFO warned Jim Bakker that they were "in a false euphoria. We must cut back on spending or continue to use tower funds to maintain operations."

PTL was able to continue its existence from the oversale of lifetime partnerships, and then using those funds for current operations, to include executive salaries and bonuses.

Finally, it is interesting to note the response of PTL's attorney when he received the PTL executive payroll checks from DH&S. As previously noted, the accounting firm would, based on instructions from PTL, prepare the executive payroll checks but would not sign the checks. Instead, the checks would be sent to PTL's outside counsel for the purpose of stamping the PTL authorizing signature on each check.

However, outside counsel refused to sign the checks, even on behalf of PTL, and reasoned that his signing the checks might be taken as an act of affirming or approving the compensation being received by PTL executives.[13]

CONCLUSION

Readers of this book may contend that the actions by DH&S and L&H were proper, given the minutes and related addendums reflecting apparent board approval of compensations. Furthermore, there is no evidence from any source that the accounting firms were put on notice that compensation to Bakker and other executives had not been approved by the PTL Board of Directors.

However, given the magnitude of certain key executives' compensations in this tax exempt organization, and the requirement to insure auditor independence in appearance, both firms should have at least verified compensation amounts with the *entire* PTL Board of Directors. This verification, while not specifically required by the accounting literature, but rather as an act of independence and professional skepticism, might have prevented one of the overt acts in furtherance of this fraud, and/or resulted in the firms' withdrawing from the engagement. Unfortunately, this was not done.

In the future, independent auditors should verify, with the full board of directors, all acts that might cause third parties to question auditor independence. If the board of directors approves acts that raise issues concerning the lack of appearance of auditor independence, then the firm should withdraw from the engagement.

It is only by remaining extremely sensitive to acts that may compromise the appearance of independence of auditors that auditors can maintain their critical role of being a public watchdog, and increase the public's confidence in the accounting profession.

NOTES

1. "Jim Bakker a Free Man Today," *USA Today*, December 1, 1994, p. 3A; "Bakker Ends Prison Term In Fraud Case," *New York Times*, December 2, 1994, p. A8.

2. Other issues arising from the audits of PTL have been examined in: Tidwell, *Anatomy of a Fraud: Inside the Finances of the PTL Ministries* (New York: John Wiley & Sons, 1993); Tidwell, "The Auditor's Responsibility in Detecting Fraud: A Case Study of Laventhol and Horwath's Last Client: PTL," *Massachusetts CPA Review* (Spring 1995): 24–27; Tidwell, "Accounting for the PTL Scandal," *Today's CPA* (July-August 1993): 28–32; Tidwell, "The Anatomy of a Fraud," *Fund Raising Management* (May 1993): 58–62.

3. *U.S. v. Bakker* (Tr. 353, 6 Tr. 498)

4. *U.S. v. Bakker* (6 Tr. 380–1)

5. *U.S. v. Bakker* (6 Tr. 379–81)

6. PTL subsequently declared bankruptcy on June 12, 1987.

7. Affidavit of John C. Brugger, Fraud and Prohibitive Mailings Branch Criminal Investigations, United States Postal Services. This affidavit was submitted by the government at the time of Jim Bakker's resentencing hearing.

8. *In Re Heritage Vil. Ch. & Missionary Fellowship*, 92 B.R. 1000, 1016 (Bkrtcy. D.S.C. 1988)

9. Ibid., 1006.

10. *Teague v. Bakker*, No CC-87-514-M (D.N.C.), Tr. 3005.

11. *In Re Heritage Vil. Ch. & Missionary Fellowship*, 92 B.R 1000, 1008 (Bkrtcy. D.S.C. 1988).

12. Bakker testified that he was not present when the board voted on bonuses. Excluding Richard Dortch, the Board of Directors testified they never approved bonuses of the magnitude reflected in the addenda to the minutes. See *U.S. v. Bakker* and the testimony of PTL board members: Charles Cookman, Tr. 292–293; Amiee Cortese, Tr. 15, 19; Ernie Franzone, Tr. 850–854, 866; A. T. Lawing, Tr. 323–324; Evelyn Carter Spencer, Tr. 184–187; Don George, Tr. 1915–1921; and Efrim Zimbalist, Jr., Tr. 335, 336.

13. *Teague v. Bakker*, Tr. 3279–3280.

11

From Monitor to Master? Ethical Comments on the Regulation of Fraud Notification by Accountants

H. J. L. van Luijk

INTRODUCTION

On June 20 and 21, 1994, the Dutch Association of Certified Accountants and the Dutch Association of Accountants/Administrative Consultants arranged a special meeting for all their members. On the agenda on both days was just one point: a self-imposed rule obliging Dutch accountants to report to investigative authorities every case of serious and unrepaired fraud that had come to their knowledge while they were fulfilling their professional duties. There are restrictions to the rule. The fraud—be it fiscal, social, or other—has to be substantial, compared to the annual balance of the organization under scrutiny. The controlling activities of the accountant, through which he/she gets knowledge of the fraud, should be legally prescribed—not every firm in Holland has the legal duty to submit itself to an annual accountant's control. The accountant should first insist that damage be repaired within the firm and that repetition be excluded. When his endeavors prove unfruitful, he has to resign as the firm's accountant and report his resignation to the Central Investigation Service (C.I.S.), indicating the nature and amount of the fraud. The C.I.S., a governmental agency, in turn will notify fiscal authorities and/or other appropriate bodies. Next to the restrictions to the rule, there is an additional license. For also, when an annual control is not legally prescribed—as is often the case in small and medium-sized companies—or when the fraud is serious, but not substantial compared to the annual turnover of the firm, the accountant is entitled to proceed in the same way. To make such an initiative possible, the Dutch Association of Accountants has discharged, on this specific point, its mem-

bers of the duty of confidentiality contained in its professional rules of
conduct.

The self-imposed rule is the outcome of a long process. For years, the
Dutch government, the Ministry of Justice notably, tried to commit specific
professions to forms of cooperation in the war against crime. So, for example, since 1994, Dutch *banks* are obliged to report all "unusual transactions," cash transactions, that is, exceeding *f*25.000, which is the
equivalent of some $14,000. A year and a half ago, the Ministry sent a
Concept of Law to the Parliament, obliging *accountants* to report all kinds
of fraud. The profession was shocked, its resistance was fierce and successful. After a full year of negotiations, the Concept of Law was replaced by
the self-imposed rule mentioned above, a rule that came into force on July
1, 1994, given the fact that the majority of Dutch accountants were willing
to accept it.

The discussion of the possibility of legally obliging accountants to notify
fraud has again turned full spotlight on the tension which can exist between
the accountant's relationship with his *client*, on the one hand, and the position of the accountant as a representative of the *public interest*, on the
other hand. From time immemorial, accountants have been "monitors of
social traffic." The impression arose, when the Ministry of Justice prepared
the Accountants Fraud Notification Bill, that accountants had unexpectedly
been transformed from monitors to masters, without being consulted. This
was perceived as a severe imbalance. Steps toward a balanced regulation
now seem to have been taken in mutual consultation, and the worst is over.
So, it is time to look at the argument from a slightly more distant point of
view. What exactly was at stake, what arguments were put forward, and
whose sensibilities were offended? It is worth looking at the recent debate
in the light of such questions for two reasons. It can give us more of an
understanding of the public function of accountants under *present circumstances*, now that the fight against crime and crime prevention have become
crucial social concerns, and it can shed some light on the *process* used to
achieve the regulation.

I make no claims here to reconstruct the entire debate. Someone will
probably be graduating in a subject of similar scope, or someone will obtain
a doctorate in it in a couple of years. My approach is more modest. I am
examining the discussion from the point of view of *ethics*. What was at
stake and what has been achieved from an ethical point of view? My attitude is that an explicitly ethically oriented analysis sheds a special type of
light on the subject of the debate, the result achieved, and the method used
to achieve the result. I will proceed as follows: First, I enumerate the major
arguments which have played a part in the tussle about the legal notification
obligation. Then I go off on a tangent: I highlight a few ethical views which
may well not have a direct bearing on a potential obligation by accountants
to notify fraud, but which can shed some light on it. Bearing in mind the

arguments advanced and taking the ethical views as a backup, I then look at the outcome actually achieved: What is its moral weight and its moral significance? I conclude with brief comments on the process which led to the actual result.

ARGUMENTS AND ALTERNATIVES

I commence with the arguments which were advanced *against* the possibility of a legal notification obligation, for now listed without comment. These are, in random order:

1. *Fraud detection* is a *job for the authorities*; an accountant is not an unremunerated investigator and must not become one. It is usual among accountants to draw a distinction between the commercial and fiscal sides of annual accounts. From a commercial point of view, the annual accounts provide information for the administration and third parties with a view to policy decisions and market transactions. The fiscal side of the annual accounts provides (often the same) information in so far as it offers an insight into the financial situation of the bookkeeping as far as taxes are concerned. Market participants are the main interested parties in one type of information, while the tax man is interested in the other type. The majority of accountants and those who use their services subscribe to the view that tax inspection is not the domain of accountancy. Those who object say that the authorities are attempting to privatize tax inspection without paying for it or, worse still, by making accountants and their clients pay the price;

2. Since 1990, an *effective Directive 3.03* has been in force which gives clear directions as to how an accountant should react if he or she detects "fraudulent or unlawful activity of tangible significance" in preparing his or her account: the management or, if the management is itself involved, the supervisory body is informed; if measures are insufficient to neutralize the fraudulent activity, the accountant returns his assignment. Research carried out in 1991 showed that the Directive is being correctly applied; only in exceptional cases are assignments returned or does such prove necessary (see C. A. Regoort RA: "Opnieuw: fraudemelding door accountants," *De Accountant* no. 8/April 1993, 505);

3. The government's policy is disrupting the *relationship based on trust* between the accountant and his client and a one-sided emphasis is being placed on the trust function of the accountant for the benefit of the general public;

4. The *proposal is defective* as an instrument in combatting crime; organized crime will always find its own alternatives; for example, through bookkeeping systems which are not subject to compulsory auditing. As far as tax and national insurance fraud is concerned, there are already several options open to the government, such as by using annual accounts, which are filed in the trade register;

5. The normal exercise of the accountant's function regularly seems to lead to the rectification of fraudulent acts, in an internal procedure which may include the

corresponding notification to the appropriate point; the proposed *remedy* is therefore too *strong*;

6. When accountants are subject to a notification obligation, it can mean that book-keeping systems which are not compulsorily audited begin to demonstrate *evasive behavior* and look out for other forms of accounting support. This can detract from what is currently being achieved in places where accountants *are* being recruited, even if this is not compulsory;

7. Practices *abroad* do not reveal the far-reaching notification obligation proposed here.

The arguments advanced fall broadly within one of the following three categories:

- *considerations of effectiveness*: a notification obligation like the one proposed by the government has no added value; current practice is satisfactory; the proposal is counterproductive and leads to evasive behavior; the costs of the remedy are out of proportion to its return;
- *considerations based on the accountant's function*: the remedy distorts the relationship based on trust between the accountant and the client, which is essential for practicing the profession;
- *considerations based on the government's function*: the remedy makes the monitor into an unremunerated master, which is not what the monitor is for.

There is another, fourth category, which is regularly suggested, although it is not prominent in all considerations:

- *considerations based on the accountant's interests*: the legal obligation can cost them customers, some of whom make a beeline for accounting support which is not subject to compulsory notification, while others punish what they see as over-zealous notification by terminating the contract. They may even submit a claim for damages if the notification proves to be less justified than it originally appeared.

What about the arguments advanced *in favor* of the notification obligation? Again, these are presented in random order, without comment or incidental asides:

- an obligation to notify has a *preventive effect*;
- the *legal obligation* gives accountants some *backing* if they come up against fraudulent or unlawful activity;
- the high degree of trust which society places in an auditor, as guarantor of a reliable and sound financial sector, means *welcome social appreciation* of the profession, with unmistakable economic implications: it is a good thing to be trusted by society;

- a legal obligation *fits in* with what is increasingly happening in *practice*: a positive stance is expected of certain professions, including accountants, with respect to monitoring standards and fighting crime—tasks which may well be the primary responsibility of the government but for which we are increasingly calling each other to account, particularly those among us who operate in places where they can exert an influence on social developments.

The arguments in favor were slightly different in nature from the arguments against, or there was at least a noticeable difference in accent. Considerations of effectiveness played a role inasmuch as the expectation was expressed that a notification obligation would have a preventive effect. The backup, both moral and commercial, which a legal obligation can generate was also pointed out; the accountant can appeal to it and because of the mystique of guardian of a sound financial sector clinging to it, he will not be the worse for it. However, the *main emphasis* was on the concept of a *shared social responsibility*, which accountants in particular should not evade.

Before attempting to define the specific moral gravity of the arguments advanced, I am first of all making a detour to present three ethical considerations which may well not be directly related to a potential notification obligation on the part of accountants, but which can shed some light on it.

ETHICAL TINT

"Whistle-blowing"

An initial source of inspiration can be found in the current ethical notions of "whistle-blowing," ringing the bell or raising the alarm. Someone within an organization learns of activities which must be considered morally reprehensible. Does such a person have a moral obligation to raise the alarm *externally*? If so, how far does this obligation extend and which conditions have to be fulfilled for a moral obligation to be involved? From the point of view of business ethics in particular, these questions have been thoroughly discussed. In such cases the employees involved are aware of crimes against the environment, of unsound products which are nevertheless marketed, or of financial corruption against other market actors, on the stock exchange or against the government.

Current interpretations boil down to the following:

- someone has the moral *right* to raise the alarm whenever one of the following occurs:
  —serious damage caused to third parties
  —sufficient certainty of the facts

—all internal paths to achieve a solution have been trodden and have led nowhere

—the expectation that raising the alarm will not cause more damage than it prevents or remedies is justified, for the alarm-raiser himself, the organization, or society as a whole;

• someone has a moral *obligation* to raise the alarm whenever the above conditions are fulfilled and if, in addition

—he or she is under specific instructions to prevent damage, given his/her professional responsibility or social function, or when, no one else can prevent the damage (see for example, Richard T. De George, *Business Ethics*. New York: MacMillan, 1990, 200–216; Thomas I, White, *Business Ethics. A Philosophical Reader*. New York: MacMillan, 1993, 515–571).

So what light does this ethical theory-in-a-nutshell shed on any notification obligation on the part of the accountant?

We are already familiar with some of the conditions mentioned here from modern accounting practice, particularly in the light of Directive 3.03: There must be sufficient certainty about the facts, the first steps have to be taken *within* the organization, approaching the management or eventually the supervisory body, and there must have been "serious damage," a tangible interest. In business ethics discussions of whistle-blowing, "serious damage" refers primarily to life and health. In accounting practice and in the eyes of the authorities, pecuniary consequences can also be grounds for action.

Two considerations remain: The remedy must be related to the result achieved and, if there is to be a moral *obligation*, a specific professional responsibility should be at issue. This presents us with two questions: Is the price which the accountant or society pays not too high for the return on any notification obligation and do the professional responsibilities of accountants cover active intervention, or facilitate active government intervention? If we subsequently look for answers to these questions, we will first have to ask ourselves who is actually authorized to answer them. Who actually determines what is covered by the professional responsibility of accountants? The accountants themselves? The government? Society as a whole, represented by appropriate institutions such as the Parliament? First of all, however, let us turn our spotlight on two other ethical considerations.

Confidentiality and a Relationship Based on Trust

In discussions of the role of the accountant in established cases of corruption, the terms "confidentiality" and "a relationship based on trust" are quite regularly used as arguments. Confidentiality especially, and a professional obligation to maintain confidentiality in particular, is a subject which ethicists have discussed at great length. It is a standard belief that the obligation to maintain confidentiality does not apply without restriction in cases where third parties are threatened with serious damage. If a doctor learns that a patient is suffering from a serious contagious illness and the patient refuses to inform third parties at risk, the doctor not only has a moral right to inform interested parties, but actually a moral *obligation*. Equally, if he detects the potential focus of an infectious disease, he is *legally* obliged to inform the Public Health Inspectorate. A lawyer who hears from his client that he has committed a murder of which someone else is accused, or a banker who is reasonably certain that capital deposited has been criminally obtained—such individuals cannot casually invoke the principles of confidentiality and trust and, on that basis, refuse to take any action. We do not have to decide here how far the obligation to reveal information reaches in the various cases. What is important is that under certain circumstances, the professional confidentiality obligation is overruled by third-party interests.

Within this framework, two further terms are important which seem to cause quite a few problems in discussion, that is, self-incrimination and the betrayal of a relationship based on trust. Self-incrimination is initially concerned with the legal right which people have to be protected from making an enforced confession. People are entitled not to be put on the rack in order to incriminate themselves; they therefore have legal protection from an excessively keen government. Gradually, this has been interpreted as a legal right which implies that you cannot be forced to incriminate yourself. However, two comments should be made in this respect: First, a situation can occur where you do not have the *moral* right to make use of your *legal* right, for example, if someone else is punished for a crime which *I* committed. Then there is the question of what is understood by "obliged to incriminate yourself." If I am not in a position to wipe out the traces of my misdeed, sooner or later I will, out of necessity, be indicted, but appealing to the right against self-incrimination is not appropriate in this case. The (crooked) reasoning which is sometimes used goes as follows: My corruption is recorded in the books; I am obliged to submit my books for auditing; the auditor is obliged to make the information accessible; I am therefore obliged to indict myself. However, the reasoning should be: I am legally obliged to record my financial transactions faithfully. As a result of this legal obligation, the information contained in the books is public property, not in detail but in terms of scope, even if public accessibility would be detrimental for me. This does not force me to indict myself—a society which forced me to do so, using rack-like methods or gagging laws, is guilty of an attack on human dignity. But I am obliged to register my transactions and that is an obligation which society can indeed place upon me (see David Luban, *Lawyers and Justice. An Ethical Study*. Princeton: Princeton University Press, 1988, Chap. 10: Corporate Counsel and Confidentiality, 206–234).

The same morally false construction is sometimes used when the relationship between the professional and his client, which is based on trust, is appealed to. There can be no doubt that from a *psychological* point of view a close relationship based on trust is a great asset between a doctor and his patient, a lawyer and his client, or an accountant and his customer.

But this relationship based on trust is falsely used from a *moral* point of view if it is advanced to protect information which cannot be considered purely private, which is certainly the case when the information relates to the legitimate interests of third parties who will be harmed by confidentiality. A relationship based on trust can exist in one of two ways: when someone confides *information* to me, and when someone entrusts me with *his interests*. In one case, someone is giving me access to stores of knowledge which he on no account wants made public, and in the other case he is involving me in representing his interests because he trusts me, either as a person or because of my expertise. The same thing applies to both cases: The extent to which someone can enter into a relationship based on trust depends on the extent to which the function which he or she fulfills has a public character. A person betrays the integrity of his public function by keeping secret information which has public relevance or by concerning himself with a private promotion of interests which is at odds with his public obligations.

Civil Virtues

Considerations which can currently be found in social ethics concerning what are known as "civil virtues" are of a slightly different nature, for example, concerning shared responsibility and participatory market relations. The considerations cover a wide field but their outlines can be described reasonably well.

Two points of view are of central importance. The first relates to the *social definition of standards*. This is concerned with the perception that, in our society, moral standards have for a generation and a half no longer been defined primarily by authorities, regardless of whether the authority is formed by the church, the government, tradition, or science. To an increasing extent, what is decent and what is not and what can reasonably be expected of every participant in social traffic, is being determined in a *collective process of expectation molding.* This process takes place in many locations simultaneously and has diverse participants. The public debate plays an important role in it at both local and national levels. But we also came up against not-for-profit organizations and specific interest groups. This collective concern with what we can reasonably expect of each other is a relatively recent phenomenon and far from all individuals and groups are sufficiently able to cope with their task. Nonetheless, this ongoing process of standard definition insures that, as a society, we are certainly not without a foothold. The complaint that as a society we are sliding down the road of decaying and declining standards is seriously exaggerated.

A second perception from social ethics fits in with this comment. It is no longer concerned with *standard definition* as a collective *process*, but with *the maintaining of standards* as a collective *product*. The key points here are individualization and interdependence.

Individualization refers to the increased and increasing autonomy which people acquire in our type of society—financial, administrative, cultural, and professional—with its positive and sometimes worrying social consequences. Interdependence refers to the simultaneously increasing mutual dependence at national and global levels. In order to give some meaning to our sharply increased decision-making capacity, we need comprehensive cooperation arrangements which are substantially based on voluntariness. This is in fact a new situation with which we still have little experience: In order to achieve what we as autonomous, decision-making adults really believe is worthwhile, we cannot do without the cooperation of others—but such cooperation is difficult or impossible to enforce. This unique situation applies to many policy fields. It applies to an environmental policy in which we are supposed to find each other, it applies to a social policy regarding native inhabitants and ethnic minorities, and it applies in the area of reciprocal financial/economic responsibility. Even the minimum can often no longer be effectively enforced but is partly dependent on cooperation arrangements in mutual understanding (see Henk van Luijk, *Om redelijk gewin. Oefeningen in de bedrijfsethiek*. Amsterdam: Boom, 1993, Chap. 11: Rechten en belangen in een participatieve marktmaatschappij, 190–218).

In the past fifty years, it is not only standards which have shifted, but also the way in which we define and maintain standards. To some extent, we still have to get used to the unavoidable, shared responsibility for social traffic, to the renewed appeal to something like "civil virtues"—the character attitudes of autonomous individuals who themselves decide that they will not withdraw from shared responsibility and who together determine what legitimate reciprocal expectations are and which new perspectives are apparent. Does this rambling over ethical peaks and troughs put us in a position to grasp the moral weight of the arguments put forward for and against making accountants obliged to notify fraud? It is always worth a try.

ARGUMENTS RECONSIDERED

We saw earlier that the arguments *against* a legal notification obligation fell chiefly into four groups: The obligation is not effective or at least not indispensable; the confidentiality position of the accountant is at issue; preventing crime is a job for the government, so the accountant is not a master;

and business interests are at issue because an obligation to notify fraud brings the risk of losing customers. The arguments *in favor* of a notification obligation referred to its expected positive effect on the level of crime prevention, and placed the most emphasis on shared social responsibility which an accountant especially, given his public function, should not rashly shirk.

Upon closer inspection, our ethical detour has brought some order and balance to these various points of view. Without questioning the fact that a relationship based on trust is indispensable between an accountant and his client, first and foremost, professional confidentiality and trust do not apply without restriction. A limit is reached where the modus operandi of the party being audited clearly conflicts with a legal obligation and causes harm to third parties. Harm not only refers to cases of murder and manslaughter, but can also be expressed as a monetary value. The estimated scope of tax fraud is such that it considerably curtails the political and social policy space of the government, harming precisely those who rely the most on government packages. That is social harm which states a moral limit and makes active intervention necessary.

An additional argument can be derived from the ethical theory of whistleblowing, which says that people and professions in a specific position of effectively being able to raise the alarm are more obliged to do so.

But surely, is not the fight against crime first and foremost a job for the government? Yes and no. Yes—to the extent that when a crime has been established, the traditional repressive measures are preferably meted out by the government. No—insofar as the process whereby we determine what criminality requires collective watchfulness. Criminality and unlawful behavior are too important to leave their definition and prevention purely to the government; society as such must take up such matters.

On a more positive note, the new possibilities of citizenship which are emerging can be very strikingly embodied in practices which clearly imply that fraud is not a matter of course, for example, in some notification practices. In the meantime, the *legal obligation to notify fraud* is off the agenda. Instead, Directive 3.03 has been given the weight of a rule of conduct and is supplemented by notification to an external notification point. So who has won?

In this matter, that is not an interesting question. What is morally significant is that within the profession a method of *regulated reaction to fraud* has been found. It does justice to the professional image of reliability and independence which has always been associated with the character of an accountant. As monitors of social traffic, accountants are preeminently active in a position which embodies our joint concern for a sound, reliable financial sector. It is true that the accountant's profession has become more commercial in recent years, in both appearance and organization, which is no disgrace. But the independence and impartiality of the monitor are still given prominence, and that is no luxury. The ruling which has now been devised explicitly places the monitor in the middle, without adding the legal function of unremunerated master. The moral argument behind it is as simple as it is convincing: In today's social traffic, where the monitoring of standards and prevention of crime are combined in a collective task, the recognized monitor can only practice his profession on the basis of considered vigilance. The agreed ruling expresses this adequately.

This leads to one last finding. Not only the *content* of the agreed ruling demonstrates moral quality, but the *process* by which the ruling came about bears witness to moral consciousness. That process unmistakably bore the traces of negotiation. Well then, the perception is growing in ethics today that you can also negotiate with each other on what is morally desirable. This requires mutual readiness to take account of each other's interests and the will to reach a solution which is satisfactory for all parties, and which also reflects the viewpoint of the general interest, if necessary. The agreed ruling shows this will and readiness to a satisfactory extent. From now on, all parties can hold each other to the arrangements that have been made. From a moral point of view, that is a stronger foundation than an enforced law.

12

Unique Ethics Challenges in Defense Industry Auditing

Harry W. Britt

INTRODUCTION

Over the last few years, the role of many internal auditors in the defense industry has changed significantly. Traditionally, internal auditors have focused on accounting and operational controls. However, within many defense companies, auditors now routinely deal with ethics and compliance issues.

During the 1980s, public concern about the defense industry grew as investigations of major defense contractors and reports of procurement irregularities increased. Stories appeared in the press that raised questions about the business ethics of company managers, employees, suppliers, and vendors. Those stories included reports of procurement kickbacks, product substitutions, and labor mischarging. A picture emerged of a defense industry flawed with ethical misconduct.

As a result of the ethical problems in the 1980s, a group of leading defense contractors formed the Defense Industry Initiative (DII) on Business Ethics and Conduct. The DII effort is one of the most ambitious ethics undertakings by any industry in the United States. The DII signatory companies have taken their obligations seriously and have developed and implemented comprehensive ethics programs.

Defense industry contractual relationships have undergone a significant change. In today's climate, optimum compliance with ethical precepts as well as government regulations is vital. The internal audit function has become a valuable tool in monitoring compliance practices and informing management of any needed corrective actions.

ETHICS PROBLEMS IN THE DEFENSE INDUSTRY

During the 1980s, public mistrust of the performance of private contractors in the country's defense programs increased. Reports of questionable procurement practices included the falsification of time cards and test results, poor quality controls, waste, fraud, and overall mismanagement of defense contracts. Those reports led to a widely shared belief by the public and many officials in government that defense contractors were more concerned about profits than legal and ethical responsibilities.

One study indicated that, at one point, there were 131 separate investigations pending against 45 of the 100 largest defense contractors. The major issues included defective pricing, cost and labor mischarging, product substitution, subcontractor kickbacks, and false claims. As a result of the adverse publicity, the public believed that half of the defense budget was lost to waste and fraud.

The perception of misconduct on the part of defense contractors weakened public support for increased military expenditures and undercut efforts to strengthen U.S. defense capabilities. The depth of public sentiment and prospect of continuing tensions between government and industry were cause for concern.

The government began to tighten its surveillance and more actively investigate and prosecute cases where wrongdoing was detected. Where contractor managers did not exercise due care in charging and claiming costs under government contracts, the instances were no longer settled by negotiated financial restitution. Many companies were suspended or debarred.

THE PACKARD COMMISSION

Partly as a result of concerns about ethical misconduct in the defense industry, in 1985, President Reagan asked David Packard (a former secretary of defense) to chair the Blue Ribbon Commission on Defense Management. The Commission was directed to conduct a broad study of defense management, including the military-industrial procurement system and oversight of that system.

The Packard Commission's interim report stated that defense contractors must develop and enforce codes of ethics that address the unique problems and procedures involved in defense procurement. The final report from the Commission noted that managers and employees at defense contractors must apply the highest standards of business ethics and conduct, and that significant improvements in contractor self-governance were required. The report suggested that effective self-governance could help curb industry misconduct.

The Commission recommended that every defense contractor should develop and enforce written standards of ethical business conduct to address defense contracting problems and procedures. It stated that such standards of conduct (1) should include procedures for employees to report misconduct directly to senior management or to a committee responsible for oversight of ethical business conduct and (2) should protect employees who report instances of apparent misconduct. The Commission also urged contractors to develop training programs to insure that employees understand ethics policies and that ethical judgments are a regular part of the work experience.

The Packard Commission also recommended that contractors should develop and implement (1) an effective internal control system to monitor compliance with corporate ethics codes and standards of conduct and (2) an internal audit capacity to evaluate the internal control systems and to monitor compliance with contractual commitments and the requirements of law and regulations.

In addition, the Commission recommended that every major defense contractor should establish an effective oversight of the ethics and compliance process by an independent audit committee of its board of directors. This committee would have the ultimate responsibility to oversee corporate systems for monitoring and enforcing compliance with standards of conduct.

DEFENSE INDUSTRY INITIATIVE ON BUSINESS ETHICS AND CONDUCT

Defense industry contractors responded to the Packard Commission's recommendations by committing themselves to a series of ethics initiatives. In 1986, representatives of eighteen defense contractors drafted principles that became known as the Defense Industry Initiative (DII) on Business Ethics and Conduct. These principles pledge the signatory companies to promote ethical business conduct through the implementation of policies, procedures, and programs in six areas.

Each DII company agreed to have and adhere to a written code of business ethics and conduct. The written code includes a statement of the ethical standards that govern all employees in their relationships to the company as well as in their dealings with customers, suppliers, and consultants. The statement also includes an explanation of the consequences of violating the standards.

Each DII company agrees to train its employees covering their personal ethical responsibilities. Effective communication of ethics policies also includes dissemination of the code of conduct to all employees, informal discussions, new personnel orientation, group meetings and briefings, development programs, videotapes, and employee handbooks.

Each DII company will create an open atmosphere to encourage employees to report violations of its code without fear of retribution. To encourage employees to surface problems, companies create a confidential reporting mechanism (such as a telephone hotline). To receive and investigate employee allegations of violations, defense contractors can use an ombudsman, a corporate ethics office, the internal audit office, or similar mechanism.

Each DII company has the obligation to self-govern by monitoring compliance with federal procurement laws. Each company establishes procedures to voluntarily report violations of federal procurement laws and corrective actions to appropriate government authorities. Internal auditors are commonly used to identify and correct problems.

Each DII company has a responsibility to each of the other companies in the industry to live by standards of conduct that preserve the integrity of the defense industry. Strong self-governance programs are required. Each company's compliance with the DII principles will be reviewed by a Board of Directors committee composed of outside directors.

Each DII company must have public accountability for its commitment to these principles. Every year, each company submits answers to an ethics program questionnaire to an external independent audit firm. That audit firm reports the results for the industry as a whole and releases the data simultaneously to the companies and to the general public.

When the Packard Commission issued its final report, there were twenty-four signatory companies to the DII. That number had grown to sixty in 1994. Although the number of signatory companies seems small, the group includes twenty-one of the top defense contractors. Together, the group represents nearly half of the Department of Defense prime contract awards.

INTERNAL AUDIT AND BUSINESS ETHICS

As one of its tasks, the Packard Commission evaluated the role of internal audit and business ethics. It was clear from the Commission's comments that internal auditors are perceived as a crucial element in an effective company effort to maintain ethical business practices. The perception of internal auditing as a tool to validate compliance with business ethics policies goes beyond the traditional use of internal auditing. The Packard Commission recommended that contractors establish an internal audit capacity to monitor whether the controls they have put in place are effective. Internal auditing would help insure contractor compliance with standards of conduct and contractual requirements.

Internal auditors in most defense companies now find themselves active in this ethics effort recommended by the Packard Commission and implemented in the DII on Business Ethics and Conduct. They are involved in the DII business ethics program in two main ways. First, the auditors investigate allegations by employees who contact the corporate hotline or helpline telephone. Second, they perform internal audits of their company's ethics operations on a regular basis, as required by the DII initiatives.

ETHICS HOTLINE INVESTIGATIONS

Telephone hotlines or helplines are vital features in DII ethics programs. DII companies have established toll-free telephone numbers that employees may call to report suspected violations of a company's code of conduct or to obtain advice on what the code requires. Companies publicize the ethics hotline widely by posting numbers throughout corporate facilities, and some companies also distribute wallet cards with the number. Hotlines are generally equipped with answering machines so calls can be received twenty-four hours a day. Among the DII signatories, a variety of corporate managers staff hotlines or fulfill the function of ombudsman, including full-time ethics officers, internal auditors, corporate counsel, and senior executives.

While ethics officers or ombudsmen are usually responsible for receiving and investigating allegations of ethical violations, many ethics offices or ombudsmen have little or no staff to perform inquiries and follow-up work. Much of the time, companies use internal auditors or the legal staff to conduct investigations of reported or suspected violations of the company code of conduct or of laws. The time required to check out these matters takes time away from other work the internal auditors or lawyers must do.

At the conclusion of an investigation, the usual practice is to write a report to the corporate audit committee or ethics committee or to the board of director's group that oversees the company's ethics program. A written report states findings of fact and recommendations for appropriate action. The report can also include suggestions for any needed modifications to existing procedures.

DII signatories establish policies to insure confidentiality of hotline communications. The investigation only includes those individuals whose presence is clearly necessary to the investigative effort, and the findings are only reported to those individuals whose responsibility entails a need to know. Virtually all DII signatories inform employees that the subject matter and identity of the caller will be held in confidence if the caller so requests.

DII signatory companies also routinely guarantee that employees who report possible violations of a company's code of conduct will not be subject to adverse personnel actions. A typical policy states that no action will be taken or threatened against any employee as a reprisal for making a complaint or disclosing information.

AUDITS OF ETHICS PROGRAMS

Internal auditors at DII signatories perform regular evaluations of their ethics programs to monitor effectiveness, identify weaknesses, and recommend improvements. A number of signatories rely on the results of internal audits for program evaluation.

Internal audits serve a number of purposes including (1) to attest to the accuracy of the corporate responses to the annual DII ethics program questionnaire; (2) to verify the existence and the efficiency of a company's internal procedures; (3) to assess adherence to the company's code of conduct.

Typical objectives of an ethics program audit are (1) to measure employee knowledge of the standards of conduct, attitudes toward corporate ethics, ethical values, and skills for identifying and resolving ethics issues; (2) to assess the ethics training program's strengths and weaknesses; and (3) to assess perceptions and effectiveness of the ombudsman and hotline.

Auditors can also review all types of ethical practices throughout a company in order to assess compliance and search for problems. Examples of specific topics in which ethical practices could be evaluated include

1. standards of procurement;
2. conflicts of interest;
3. gifts and gratuities;
4. entertainment;
5. political activities;
6. fair trade activities;
7. antiboycott activities;
8. business travel and expense reporting;
9. patents and licenses;
10. use of the company name;
11. public announcements and speaking engagements;
12. antitrust activities;
13. customer relations;
14. minority businesses;
15. government relations; and
16. supplier relations.

CORPORATE AUDIT/ETHICS COMMITTEE

In addition to conducting hotline investigations or audits of ethics programs, internal auditors may find themselves involved in overall administration of a corporate ethics program. DII signatories have established varying internal structures for organizing their ethics, self-governance, and contract compliance activities. The typical organization includes a corporate audit or ethics committee. The chairman of the committee is usually a corporate officer or specifically appointed ethics program director. The membership of ethics committees is diverse, but includes personnel such as the corporate leader of internal audit, accounting or finance managers, training managers, corporate counsel, or senior executives. Although the membership of corporate ethics committees and the particular functions and relationships of each organization vary, the purpose of the organizations is essentially similar. Typically, the corporate ethics committee oversees the administration of the ethics program.

BOARD OF DIRECTORS AUDIT/ETHICS COMMITTEE

Corporate DII ethics programs regularly report to the companies' boards of directors. Most boards have established audit committees or ethics committees to supervise implementation of the companies' codes of conduct and ethics programs. These committees keep the complete boards apprised of the self-governance program through regular reports. By providing an oversight role on the actions of management, audit committees or ethics committees are an effective deterrent to improper ethical behavior. Audit or ethics committees of the boards of directors typically receive reports of DII activity. Reports made by outside, independent auditors are usually made to the same group as internal reports. Reports to boards of directors typically deal with the general status of the self-governance and ethics programs. They cover topics such as

1. compliance practice;
2. violations which have occurred and sanctions imposed;
3. reimbursements to the government;
4. alleged violations under investigation;
5. matters voluntarily disclosed to the Department of Defense;
6. general adherence to and progress of DII principles and responses to the DII questionnaire;
7. ethics training;
8. communications;
9. the annual DII audit;
10. disposition of hotline calls.

VOLUNTARY DISCLOSURE OF PROBLEMS

Another recommendation by the Packard Commission was also important to internal auditors. The report recommended that defense contractors voluntarily disclose irregularities or misconduct discovered as a result of self-review to government authorities. In response to the Packard Commission, one of the DII principles states that each company is required to review potential problems to determine if voluntary disclosure of a violation of federal procurement laws should be made. The DII commitment leaves with companies the discretion as to when to make a voluntary disclosure to the federal government. In general, these policies indicate that signatories will promptly and fully disclose to the responsible federal authorities substantiated violations of federal procurement law and instances of significant employee misconduct affecting or influencing the companies' government contracting activities.

Companies may choose to conduct their own internal investigation and to submit their own written report to the government summarizing the findings of an investigation. In that case, audit reports, audit work papers, supporting exhibits, and analytical documents are to be submitted with the report. The government may conduct an audit and investigation to verify the information submitted to the government, and it may initiate further independent audits or investigations.

SUSPENSION AND DEBARMENT OF CONTRACTORS

If the government conducts an investigation of a contractor and decides to penalize the contractor for violating federal procurement law, it can decide to suspend or debar the contractor from contracting with the government. Suspensions and debarments have become among the most important tactics used by the government to penalize a contractor. Until the 1980s, the government rarely used suspension and debarment sanctions to avoid doing business with a contractor. Since then, there has been a continued focus on procurement fraud, waste, and abuse; the ability of the government to detect and punish procurement fraud has been enhanced; the volume of criminal investigations and prosecutions has grown; and the number of suspended and debarred contractors has increased.

Temporary suspensions have been imposed on many major contractors. A typical suspension settlement requires a contractor

1. to maintain a corporate ethics and contract compliance program;
2. to revise and implement the corporate procedures related to ethics;
3. to provide the Department of Defense with copies of all internal audit reports, independent audit reports, and contract compliance reports, except those which are privileged or do not relate to defense contract operations;
4. to cooperate fully with any future investigation by the Department of Justice; and
5. to report periodically to the Department of Defense on the status of the implementation of the policies and resolution of the business disputes.

FEDERAL SENTENCING GUIDELINES

In 1991, the United States Sentencing Commission issued its Guidelines for the Sentencing of Organizations. Those guidelines add more emphasis to the role of internal audit for dealing with ethics and compliance issues. A main goal of the guidelines is to encourage companies to develop effective ethics and compliance programs. For those defense contractors participating in the DII on Business Ethics and Conduct, the new guidelines served to reemphasize the need to maintain the highest standards of business ethics and conduct.

The Sentencing Guidelines defined what an effective compliance program should be. A company must establish compliance standards and procedures that are reasonably capable of reducing the prospect of criminal conduct. Also, specific high-level personnel in the company must be assigned overall responsibility to oversee compliance with such standards and procedures. In addition, the company must take reasonable steps to achieve compliance with its standards (e.g., by using auditing systems reasonably designed to detect misconduct by its employees and other agents).

According to the Sentencing Guidelines (as well as the DII on Business Ethics and Conduct), one basic purpose of an auditing program is to verify compliance with the organization's published standards. The behavior of each part of the organization needs to be compared to the expected course of behavior. Another purpose of an auditing program is to help the firm prove that its compliance program is an effective one. Finally, an auditing program reinforces corporate standards by reminding employees that there is verification of compliance and correction of noncompliance.

CONCLUSION

More and more, defense contractors have a duty to take steps to prevent ethical violations from occurring, including all the steps associated with compliance programs. There is an increasing awareness by defense contractors that they need to comply with ethical, statutory, and regulatory requirements. Ethical and compliance programs have become vital to those companies engaged in government work.

To perform the required surveillance over defense contractors' ethical and compliance practices, the internal audit function is playing an ever-increasing role. Most government contractors now regard internal audit as an essential monitoring device, and the scope of the internal audit function has been significantly broadened. In the Federal Sentencing Guidelines, the term "auditing" is prominent; and it seems certain that the internal auditor will continue to have a significant responsibility in the enforcement of an organization's ethics and compliance program.

REFERENCES

Albrecht, Steve, and Kevin Stocks. (1993). "Ethical Dilemmas." *Internal Auditor* (June): 24–25.

Alpert, Stephen B. (1992). "Federal Sentencing Guidelines." *Internal Auditor* (October): 46–49.

Arthur Andersen & Company. (1986). *Study of Government Audit and Other Oversight Activities Related to Defense Contractors.* Houston, TX.

Bedingfield, James, and A. J. Stagliano. (1990). "The Defense Industry Initiative—Has It Made a Difference." *Contract Management* (November): 13–17.

Bureau of National Affairs and the American Corporate Counsel Association. (1993). *BNA/ACCA Compliance Manual—Prevention of Corporate Liability.* Washington, DC.

Dees, C. Stanley. (1986). "The New Morality Environment." Washington, DC: McKenna, Conner, and Cuneo.

Defense Industry Initiative on Business and Conduct. (1994). *1993 Annual Report to the Public and The Defense Industry.* Washington, DC.

Department of Defense. (1989). *Defense Management Review—Report to the President.* Washington, DC.

Ethics Resource Center, Inc. (1986). *Final Report and Recommendations on Voluntary Corporate Policies, Practices, and Procedures Relating to Ethical Business Conduct.* Washington, DC.

Gregory, William H. (1989). *The Defense Procurement Mess.* Lexington, MA: Lexington Books.

Madsen, Peter, and Jay Shafritz. (1990). *Essentials of Business Ethics.* New York: Meridian.

Packard, David. (1986). *A Quest for Excellence—Interim Report to the President by the President's Blue Ribbon Commission on Defense Management.* Washington, DC.

Peat, Marwick, Mitchell & Company. (1986). *Report on Survey of Defense Contractors' Internal Audit Processes.* Washington, DC.

Petry, Edward. (1992). "The Federal Sentencing Guidelines for Organizations." *Center for Business Ethics News* (Spring).

United States Sentencing Commission. (1991). *Sentencing Guidelines for Organizational Defendants.* Washington, DC.

13

The Critical Oversight Role of the Audit Committee

Curtis C. Verschoor

INTRODUCTION

The governance functions performed by independent members of the boards of directors of public U.S. corporations continue to gain significance. Greater attention is being paid to corporate governance issues in publicly held companies by institutional and other investors, by legislators and regulators, by financial analysts, and by the general public. The governance of charitable and other nonprofit organizations is being probed more frequently as well.

Typically, audit committees provide a focus and means for fuller review and analysis of matters relating to internal controls, auditing, and financial reporting. Audit committee oversight responsibilities for evaluating the adequacy of internal controls is gaining increased prominence. An important aspect of an effective system of internal controls is the presence of an appropriate ethical code of corporate conduct. Satisfactory implementation requires constant high-level oversight. In many cases, this function is provided by the audit committee, which may be renamed the audit and ethics committee.

The greater level of public expectations for better corporate accountability has not always been matched by improved performance. A number of unfortunate examples of breakdowns in effective internal control systems have occurred recently. In these cases, the control system was insufficient to prevent or detect large-scale fraud or mismanagement by senior executives. The inadequacy of audit committee oversight in these instances is

*This chapter includes the author's material previously published in *Audit Committee Guidance for the 1990's* (Washington, D.C.: National Association of Corporate Directors, 1994). Used with permission.

being challenged legally as often as is the detection failure of the affected auditing firms. Thus, the courts are becoming important determinants of what is expected from audit committees.

Although the SEC has recently mandated increased attention be given to the work of board compensation committees, most observers agree that board audit committees are still the most established and clearly defined standing committee. Thus, many audit committees find themselves directed by the full board to perform objective investigations of matters well beyond the usual scope of their responsibilities. Greater expectations from board oversight committees reflect the concerns of shareholders, other stakeholders, and the public that more accountability should be exercised over corporate actions of all types. The significance of an appropriate ethical environment in organizations is being increasingly recognized due to its pervasive effect on the effectiveness of the organization's overall system of internal control.

In view of these trends, it is hoped that boards of directors will recognize the critical importance of the functions audit committees perform so they may take the necessary steps to more nearly reach the level of public expectations.

DEVELOPMENT OF AUDIT COMMITTEES IN U.S. CORPORATIONS

Early Events

As long ago as 1940, the SEC endorsed the concept of nonofficer audit committees which had been suggested by the New York Stock Exchange (NYSE).[1] The committee responsibilities envisioned at that time were quite narrow, limited to nominating and arranging some of the parameters of the external auditor's engagement. The American Institute of Certified Public Accountants (AICPA) was also active in early discussions of audit committees and issued a policy statement in 1967, recommending that public corporations establish audit committees composed of outside directors.[2]

The SEC, in March 1972, again noted its long-standing interest in the oversight provided public companies by their audit committees and reaffirmed its support for the practice of naming only outside directors to audit committee membership. Two years later, the SEC required proxy statement disclosure of the existence and composition of audit committees in all public corporations where they were in place.[3] At approximately the same time, the NYSE issued a "white paper" on the subject of financial reporting to shareholders which strongly recommended that an audit committee be formed by each company listed on that exchange.

Several important developments concerning audit committees took place in the late 1970s. The AICPA Special Committee on Audit Committees renewed the support expressed earlier by that organization. In early 1977, the NYSE enacted a requirement that corporations appoint an audit committee of nonemployee directors as a condition of continuing their listing on the exchange. As of July 1978, NYSE-listed corporations were required to establish an audit committee consisting solely of directors "independent of management and free from any relationship that would interfere with the exercise of independent judgment as a committee member."[4] At about this same time, the American Stock Exchange also made a nonbinding recommendation to its listed companies that an independent audit committee be put into place. The National Association of Securities Dealers Automated Quotation (NASDAQ) system required its companies, in February 1989, to establish and maintain an audit committee, of which the majority are independent directors.

An early endorsement by the legal profession of the concept of audit committees in public corporations appeared in the 1978 edition of the *Corporate Director's Guidebook*, issued by the American Bar Association (ABA). Specific recommendations for the committee's primary and other responsibilities, who should serve, and potential legal liabilities of audit as well as other board oversight committees are contained in a report on *The Oversight Committees of the Board of Directors*. The report was prepared by the ABA Committee on Corporate Law Subcommittee on Functions and Responsibilities of Directors.[5]

Regulatory Guidance by the SEC

As the principal regulatory agency involved in matters of corporate accounting, auditing, internal control, and financial reporting, the SEC has occupied an important position affecting the development of audit committees of boards of directors. During the late 1970s, the SEC continued as an important force in supporting the need for effective audit committees and in articulating their responsibilities. Harold Williams, SEC chairman from 1977 to 1980, regularly championed the merits of audit committees in speeches and journal articles.

After 1980, however, the SEC was publicly silent on the subject of audit committees until July 1988. Then, the SEC circulated for public comment a proposal that a management report on internal controls and financial reporting be included in annual reports of public companies and their filings on Form 10-K. The contents of the proposed report differed from the SEC initiatives proposed ten years earlier. In this proposal, the focus was directed to the entire control structure in the organization, including the internal auditing function and the audit committee of the board of directors and not just internal controls relating to financial reporting. The proposal would have mandated a statement of:

- Management's responsibility for financial statement preparation, including determination of the estimates and judgments they contain.

- Management's responsibility for establishment and maintenance of a system of internal control adequate to provide integrity and reliability of financial reporting.

- Management's assessment of the effectiveness of internal control systems as of the fiscal year end.

- Management's responses to any significant recommendations made during the year by both internal and external auditors concerning internal control systems.[6]

Considering the costs of implementation, the SEC stated that it expected its proposal would cause only a minimal increase in the work of external auditors. Under existing professional auditing standards, external auditors are already required to determine whether disclosures similar to the proposed management report contain a material misstatement of fact or material omission.

However, the SEC received significant opposition to its proposal. Criticisms were based on a stated lack of generally accepted criteria for assessing internal control adequacy, cost considerations, and the lack of "safe harbor" provisions outlining what would be considered good-faith efforts at compliance. The SEC withdrew this proposed rule in 1992.

Work of the Treadway Commission

In its final report issued in October 1987, the Commission on Fraudulent Financial Reporting (also known as the Treadway Commission after its chairperson) highlighted its belief as to the importance of audit committees in preventing or detecting fraudulent financial reporting. Audit committee responsibilities were referred to in the section of the report containing discussions and recommendations concerning top management, internal auditing, and public accounting. The Treadway report offered eleven specific recommendations designed to clarify missions and processes involved in effective audit committees oversight. These were:

1. Annually, audit committees should review the program that management establishes to monitor compliance with the company's code of conduct.

2. Together with top management, the audit committee should ensure that the internal auditing involvement in the entire financial reporting process is appropriate and properly coordinated with the independent public accountant.

3. The SEC should mandate the establishment of an audit committee composed solely of independent directors in all public companies.

4. Audit committees should be informed, vigilant, and effective overseers of the company's financial reporting process and its internal control system.

5. A written charter for the committee should be developed. The full board should approve, review, and revise it when necessary.

6. Audit committees should have adequate resources and authority to discharge their responsibilities.

7. Audit committees should review management's evaluation of the independence of the company's public accountant.

8. Before the beginning of each year, audit committees should review management's plans to engage the company's independent public accountant to perform management advisory services.

9. The SEC should require audit committees to issue a report describing their responsibilities and activities during the year in the company's annual report to the shareholders.

10. Management should inform audit committees of any second opinions sought on significant accounting issues.

11. Audit committees should oversee the quarterly as well as the annual reporting process.[7]

In another section of its report, the Treadway Commission recommended that the SEC require management to annually report publicly as to its responsibilities for preparing financial statements and for maintaining an adequate system of internal control. Also recommended was a discussion as to how each of these responsibilities was fulfilled, as well as management's assessment of the effectiveness of the company's internal controls. Management's internal control opinion was intended to encompass the entire internal control system, not just the narrow definition of internal accounting control that is contained in the Foreign Corrupt Practices Act.[8]

Audit Committees in the Defense Industry

The President's Blue Ribbon Commission on Defense Management, also known as the Packard Commission after its chairperson, David Packard, made, in 1987, numerous recommendations designed to give prompt attention to an increasing public perception of a loss of confidence in the defense industry's integrity. In its Interim Report issued in 1986, the Commission suggested that an effective system of self-governance rather than more extensive federal regulation might prove helpful in preventing and detecting misconduct in the defense industry.

The strategies recommended by the Packard Commission to accomplish these goals included:

• Develop a code of business conduct.

• Promulgate and enforce an internal control system which will be effective in en-

suring compliance with this code and other sensitive aspects of government contracting.

- Establish sufficient internal auditing capability to monitor compliance with the
  code of conduct as well as the efficacy of the internal control system.
- Establish effective oversight of the entire process by an independent committee,
  such as the audit committee of the board of directors.[9]

Thus, two independent national public commissions have both arrived at
very similar means of achieving goals which on the surface appear to be
quite different.

Informed Commentary

Many books, monographs, and articles in professional journals have expressed opinions and indicated guidance about the growing and changing
role of audit committees and how they can become more effective. Causes
of pressures for increased corporate accountability and greater board of
director influence include the significant number of corporate bankruptcies,
a perceived "expectation gap" in the performance of external auditors, the
increasing influence of large institutional investors, the number of un-
friendly corporate takeovers and business combinations, and the greater
professionalism of internal auditing.

A 1987 booklet by the Institute of Internal Auditors: *Internal Auditing
and the Audit Committee: Working Together Toward Common Goals*, expressed support for audit committees in not-for-profit and government organizations as well as public corporations. Most large CPA firms have
published booklets or brochures describing their thoughts as to the importance of audit committees to their clients and the practice of public accounting.

Details of the trend toward increased audit committee involvement in
areas of auditing, internal control, and financial reporting are discussed in
a 1988 report published by the Conference Board.[10] A mail survey of the
3,600 members of the American Society of Corporate Secretaries resulted
in a response rate of only 23 percent. The very heterogeneous group of
companies surveyed included very small, private as well as large, publicly
held enterprises. These factors make generalization of the results to all public corporations difficult.

Indications of the importance being accorded audit committees are found
in surveys of compensation and meeting frequency. A 1988 survey sponsored by the National Association of Corporate Directors shows that in
spite of their increasing responsibilities and public visibility, audit committee members on average are not the highest paid nonemployee directors.
This report states that for all industry groups as a whole, the compensation
for committee members ranks fourth.[11] The highest compensation for com-

mittee membership as a percentage of regular board members' compensation is paid to members of the executive, finance, and investment committees, respectively. These are management committees rather than oversight committees. The relationship for audit committees is only 18 percent.

A 1989 survey of board practices by a large firm of executive recruiters shows that audit committees met an average of four times per year, whereas executive and finance committees met an average of five and six times, respectively.[12] The same survey reports that the average committee fee paid to outside directors is lowest for audit committee members, at $719 per meeting and highest for finance committee members, at $744 per meeting.[13]

A 1993 research study sponsored by the Institute of Management Accountants outlined responsibilities recommended for audit committees, described the evolution of audit committees, and presented the results of a survey of audit committee members, external auditors, and internal auditors. The conclusion reached in the research is that the individuals selected for such responsibilities as audit committees and their training and perceived authority are important determinants of their effectiveness.[14]

An audit committee monograph was also prepared by Price Waterhouse in 1993, from the perspective of the external auditing profession: *Improving Audit Committee Performance: What Works Best*.[15] It emphasizes the importance of audit committee independence from management influence.

The presence of private sector initiatives motivating public reporting on internal controls and the involvement of audit committees in maintaining an effective control system has been a strong factor influencing the SEC's continuing decisions to refrain from making such reports mandatory. A 1993 research study shows that almost 80 percent of the 250 largest U.S. publicly held corporations include in their annual report to shareholders some kind of report affirming management's responsibilities for designing and implementing an effective system of internal controls. Virtually all of these reports mention the activities performed by the audit committee.[16]

LEGAL ASPECTS OF AUDIT COMMITTEES

The corporation statutes of only one state, Connecticut, specifically require the appointment of an audit committee. However, as noted below, the 1991 bank reform act sets forth a requirement for the board of directors to designate an audit committee consisting entirely of independent directors in all insured banks and savings institutions having assets of more than $500 million.

Audit Committee Performance Standard

Other than the Treadway Commission "Good Practice Guidelines for the Audit Committee" and the American Law Institute "Principles of Corporate

Governance," no generally accepted procedural direction has yet emerged as a recognized standard for assessment and evaluation of audit committee performance. However, a considerable body of corporate law and court decisions has developed over the years to guide all members of the boards of directors of for-profit and not-for-profit corporations. These articulate a duty of care and a duty of loyalty both to the corporation and to the shareholders whom they represent.

The duty of due care involves discharging the duties as a director in good faith, with the care an ordinarily prudent person in a like position would exercise under similar circumstances, and in a manner he/she reasonably believes to be in the best interests of the corporation. The duty of loyalty means that a director must not act as a director with respect to a matter in which he or she has a personal interest.

The Business Judgment Rule

Under the duty of care, all directors are required to be diligent and prudent in overseeing the corporation's affairs. In exercising their judgment, courts will not overturn or second-guess directors' decisions made in good faith unless the business judgment was unintelligent or unadvised and not based on adequate information.

Before making decisions, directors must inform themselves of all material information reasonably available to them and proceed with a critical eye in assessing corporate information. The caveat requiring directors to be well-informed about the affairs of the corporation is especially applicable to the work of the audit committee.

In what appears to be a very significant court decision in the field of corporate governance, the Delaware Supreme Court in the 1985 Trans-Union case, *Smith v. Van Gorkom*, narrowed the business judgment rule. Previously, this rule had protected directors from having their decisions second-guessed by the courts as long as they adhered to standards of good faith and fairness. The court's action in this case extends the responsibilities of directors and mandates additional prudence, greater investigation of issues, and requires an independent evaluation process which must support decisions made by nonmanagement directors.[17]

Additionally, due to the emergence of the standard of differential liability, audit committee members have the possibility of increased legal liability beyond the exposure of a director without specific oversight committee responsibilities. Under this standard, a director assuming special duties is obliged to inquire, learn, and act affirmatively upon matters within the purview of those duties. The directors who are most vulnerable to increased liability are those who fail to effectively discharge their responsibilities. Most observers postulate that those who fail to learn and act upon that which they reasonably could have learned and acted upon are the most susceptible.[18] The leading case applying the differential liability standard under the federal securities laws is *Escott v. BarChris Construction Corp.*[19] In the MiniScribe Corporation case decided in 1992, the audit committee chairperson was personally assessed damages amounting to more than $20 million.[20]

Cases of Breach of Duty of Care

The source of director civil liability is usually the Securities Act of 1933. Under Section 11 of this act, directors and others are held civilly liable for any untrue statement of a material fact in an effective registration statement and also for any failure to state a material fact or needed information to make other statements not misleading. The defense against such liability can be based on the directors' exercise of due diligence.

A 1992 case, *Brane v. Roth*, alleged inadequate internal controls in a grain cooperative. It was decided by the Supreme Court of Indiana and assessed liability to the directors under that state's corporation law. The directors failed to properly hedge the economic exposure represented by the inventory on hand and were found to have breached their duty of care.[21] A similar subsequent case has been filed alleging that the directors of Compaq Computer Co. had not maintained adequate hedges of its foreign exchange exposure.

Effects of Banking Reform Legislation on Audit Committees

Noting the record number of bank failures, a 1991 General Accounting Office (GAO) study indicated a major cause was internal control breakdowns, which contributed to improper loans, outright fraud, and insider dealings. The report contained the results of GAO's survey of the audit committees in forty of the largest U.S. banks. The objective was to determine whether audit committees had the necessary independence, expertise, and information on bank operations to effectively perform their important corporate governance functions. The findings indicated that the audit committees in these large banks were not sufficiently independent, lacked the expertise to accomplish their responsibilities, and did not receive assessments of key bank operations.[22]

The conclusions in the report provided further support for GAO recommendations for a strengthened role for audit committees in insured banks and savings institutions. Through the legislative process, many of these recommendations were embodied in the FDIC Improvement Act of 1991 (FDICIA).[23] Among its provisions, the FDICIA mandates that the approximately 1,000 insured bank and savings institutions having at least $500 million in assets must each appoint an audit committee consisting entirely of directors who are independent of management. Although the published regulatory guidelines state a $500 million threshold, the FDIC had previously issued a formal policy suggesting that every insured depository institution, regardless of size, should establish an audit committee comprised entirely of outside directors.

Principal functions the FDICIA requires the audit committee to perform include oversight of management's discharge of its responsibilities for maintenance of effective internal controls and compliance with relevant laws and regulations, for reliable financial reporting, and assurance that internal and external auditing functions are effective. The specific duties are enumerated as follows:

1. Review the scope of the external audit.
2. Review assessments of the adequacy of internal controls.
3. Review compliance with laws and regulations.
4. Discuss the selection and termination of the external auditing firm and any significant disagreements.
5. Oversee the internal auditing function.[24]

FDICIA requirements include the presentation by management of an annual public report stating its responsibility for maintaining proper internal control systems designed to foster the continued safety and soundness of the institution. The FDICIA also contains a requirement for the annual evaluation and public report as to the effectiveness of these systems. Also required is an annual public report by management declaring compliance with the designated laws and regulations affecting the safety and soundness of the institution. Both of these public management assertions must be attested to by the institution's external auditing firm. The audit committee is required to oversee all of the auditing, financial, internal control, and compliance reporting done pursuant to the statute.

In bank and savings institutions having assets over $3 billion, the FDICIA outlines additional requirements for audit committees. In these institutions, the audit committee must include members having relevant banking or financial experience and expertise and should have access to its own outside counsel. Also, the audit committees of these large banks may not include any members who are also large customers of the institution.

ALI Corporate Governance Project

For most of the decade of the 1980s, the legal profession has been involved in deliberations with affected groups concerning corporate governance, including the appropriate role of board of director audit committees. The American Law Institute (ALI) is a professional organization of prominent practicing attorneys, judges, law school deans, and senior professors.

The primary objective of the group is "the clarification and simplification of the law and its better adaptation to social needs." The ALI has spent more than twelve years on its corporate governance project to analyze and make recommendations concerning the law governing the structure and governance of the business corporation. Earlier works by the ALI have included restatements of the Federal Securities Code, the Model Penal Code, and many others.

The final report was approved by the members of the Institute in May 1992, by the Council of the Institute in May 1993, and was published in 1994. It contains potentially sweeping revisions to the legal governance and structure of U.S. business corporations. Some of the recommendations will require statutory revision to be implemented. Others are set forth as "good corporate practice" and will depend on voluntary compliance. Important aspects of the proposals include dividing for-profit corporations into three tiers based on size and degree of public ownership with a different legal structure for each. According to the ALI principles, every large, publicly held corporation:

should have an audit committee to implement and support the oversight function of the board by reviewing on a periodic basis the corporation's processes for producing financial data, its internal controls, and the independence of the corporation's external auditor. The audit committee should consist of at least three members, and should be composed exclusively of directors who are neither employed by the corporation nor were so employed within the two preceding years, including at least a majority of members who have no significant relationship with the corporation's senior executives.[25]

The ALI report recommends significant powers and duties be delegated to the audit committees of all publicly held corporations. These are:

a. Recommend the firm to be employed as the corporation's external auditor and review the proposed discharge of such firm.

b. Review the external auditor's compensation, the proposed terms of its engagement, and its independence.

c. Review the appointment and replacement of the senior internal auditing executive, if any.

d. Serve as the channel of communication between the external auditor and the board and between senior internal auditing executive, if any, and the board.

e. Review the results of each external audit of the corporation, the report of the audit, any related management letter, management's responses to recommendations made by the external audit in connection with the audit, reports of the internal auditing department that are material to the corporation as a whole, and management's responses to those reports.

f. Review the corporation's annual financial statements, any certification, report, opinion, or review rendered by the external auditor in connection with those financial statements, and any significant disputes between management and the external auditor that arose in connection with the preparation of those financial statements.

g. Consider, in consultation with the external auditor and the senior internal auditing executive, if any, the adequacy of the corporation's internal controls.

h. Consider major changes and other major questions of choice respecting the appropriate auditing and accounting principles and practices to be used in the preparation of the corporation's financial statements, when presented by the external auditor, a principal senior executive, or otherwise.[26]

SIGNIFICANT AUDIT COMMITTEE FUNCTIONS

Relevant Literature

In addition to the ALI listing of recommended duties for audit committees, a few published listings show suggested functions audit committees should perform on behalf of the board. An SEC release in 1978 set forth eight "customary functions" of audit committees:

- Recommend engagement or discharge of the independent auditors.
- Direct and supervise investigations into matters within the scope of its duties.
- Review with the independent auditors the plan and results of the auditing engagement.
- Review the scope and result of internal auditing activities.
- Approve each professional service provided by the independent auditors prior to its performance.
- Review the independence of the independent auditors.
- Consider the range of audit and nonaudit fees.
- Review the adequacy of the system of internal controls.[27]

However, rules to require disclosure of whether audit committees actually did perform these functions were not adopted.

Table 13.1 is a survey of the largest publicly held U.S. corporations making public disclosure of selected audit committee functions.

The 1993 Price Waterhouse monograph published by the Institute of Internal Auditors has an extensive listing of audit committee functions. It also contains a self-assessment guide of audit committee practices.[29]

Suggested audit committee charters and other descriptions of appropriate functions have appeared in issues of professional journals, including *Financial Executive, Journal of Accountancy*, and *CPA Journal*. One model audit committee charter aptly contrasts the oversight authority of the audit com-

Table 13.1
Public Disclosure of Selected Audit Committee Functions
(Largest Publicly Held U.S. Corporations)

Oversight of External Auditing	Banks	Other Industry
Recommended appointment or retention of firm *	81.8%	83.8%
Review annual audit plans *	54.5	70.7
Review results of annual audit *	54.5	58.1
Approve fee arrangements *	18.2	31.9
Review services other than auditing *	18.2	32.3
Evaluate firm independence *	13.6	14.4
Determine whether responsibilities are properly discharged	13.6	21.4
Determine whether firm partner has unrestricted access without management presence	45.5	53.1

Oversight of Internal Auditing

Review scope of annual audit plan *	63.6	38.9
Review reports of audit performance *	45.5	27.9
Determine whether responsibilities are properly discharged	13.6	24.9

Oversight of Internal Control System

Generally evaluate adequacy of system	40.9	57.5

Oversight of Financial Reporting

Review annual financial statements	27.3	29.7
Discuss accounting practices	13.6	32.8

*Identified as one of the customary functions of audit committees by the SEC in 1978 (Ver-
schoor, *Journal of Accountancy*.)

mittee with management's primary responsibility for internal operating controls and financial reporting. It also notes that the committee should have
unrestricted access to company personnel and documents and also the necessary resources to properly discharge its functions and responsibilities.

A recent example of the interest being expressed in strong corporate governance has been issued by TIAA/CREF, the largest U.S. institutional investment group, with assets in excess of $130 billion. The policy statement
by TIAA/CREF acknowledges a responsibility for being an advocate for

improved governance. Therefore, it recommends that the boards of the corporations in which it has investment positions should exercise their fiduciary responsibility to "ensure that corporate resources are used only for appropriate business purposes" and also to "foster and encourage a corporate environment of strong internal controls, fiscal accountability, high ethical standards, and compliance with applicable laws and regulations."[30] The statement also recommends the audit committee be composed exclusively of independent outside directors.

Definition of Internal Control

The concept of internal control in an organization has been described in many ways. It has been called the glue that holds an organization together and also the safety net that insures risks are kept within acceptable limits. Internal controls encompasses more than concerns about accounting, auditing, and financial reporting. Internal control also involves business, operational, and administrative factors, including an organization's control of its internal environment.

A committee of the five sponsoring organizations of the Treadway Commission (also known as COSO) initiated a study to harmonize and integrate existing internal control concepts. The COSO report, *Internal Control: Integrated Framework*, was issued in September 1992, and is designed to be helpful to corporate directors and officers as well as legislators and the general public.

The COSO report suggests that internal controls should be viewed broadly, and apply to everything management must do to achieve the organization's objectives. The overall premise of internal control concepts is the management perspective, which is much broader than just the controls over matters of accounting. The Executive Summary of the COSO report contains the following definition of internal control:

Internal control is broadly defined as a process, effected by an entity's board of directors, management, and other personnel, designed to provide reasonable assurance regarding the achievement of objectives in the following categories:

Effectiveness and efficiency of operations
Reliability of financial reporting
Compliance with applicable laws and regulations.[31]

The COSO report also describes internal controls in terms of five interrelated components. The components are integrated into the management process. All organizations, small as well as large, make use of these components, although they may implement them in differing ways. The components are:

Control Environment—the tone or control consciousness of the organization overall.

Risk Assessment—the identification and analysis of risks to the achievement of the organization's objectives which forms the basis of determination of how they can be kept within appropriate limits.

Control Activities—the policies and procedures that help ensure that management's directives are carried out.

Information and Communication—recognition of the need for methods of communicating vital information to all levels of the organization.

Monitoring—the process of assessing the quality of the internal control system's performance over time.[32]

The COSO report notes that an entity's objectives and the way they are achieved are based on preferences, value judgments, and management styles. Those preferences and value judgments, which are translated into standards of behavior, reflect management's integrity and its commitment to ethical value. The effectiveness of internal controls cannot rise above the integrity and ethical values of the people who create, administer, and monitor them.[33]

The control environment represents the collective effect of many factors. These include management's underlying philosophy, operating style, and ethical orientation. The entity's organization structure, the functioning of the board of directors and its audit committee, methods of communicating and implementing the assignment of authority and responsibility, and practices of monitoring and following up on performance are also components. The control environment includes activities of top management and the board of directors and also their responsiveness to the control structure as well as the activities of employees at all levels.

Audit Committee Oversight of Internal Control

Audit committee activities relating to the organization's internal controls primarily involves a review of the assessments and evaluations of the adequacy of all of these components of the internal control systems. The assessments and evaluations may have been performed by management itself or by the internal and external auditors. A periodic review of actions taken by each of those groups to test the validity of their assessments together with an objective analysis of results of their tests should enable the audit committee to fully understand and then evaluate the basis supporting each of the evaluations.

Careful review of any trends in the numbers and types of internal control system deviations and inadequacies discovered or other findings should be helpful in determining progress or its lack. Careful liaisons with internal and external auditors are important in assuring that the audit committee remains in touch with current developments. Audit committee oversight should direct particular attention toward controls maintained over computer systems, businesses in foreign locations, and any operations in high-risk businesses.

CONCLUSIONS

The role of audit committees has changed rapidly in recent years, reflecting the increasing demands of corporate stakeholders and the litigious environment in which corporations find themselves. Increased emphasis on effective internal controls as important to proper corporate governance has been noted recently in other countries. In the United Kingdom, the Cadbury Committee report on financial aspects of corporate governance was issued in 1992. As is happening in the United States, this report places great emphasis on the need for strong, independent audit committees. The Toronto Stock Exchange report on corporate governance is expected in 1996. The failure of internal controls in the Metallgesellschaft, A.G. case has led to calls for consideration of augmenting corporate governance practices in Germany by adding board of director audit committees similar to the Anglo-American model.

The changing business environment is also the source of more extensive challenges for audit committees. Empowering individual employees to work with less supervision may tend to increase business risks. The concurrent trend toward restructuring of operations to reduce costs and provide a greater focus on customer concerns leads to actions that are at variance with traditional methods for achieving strong internal controls.

Recognition of the importance of the role of the audit committee in achieving an effective control environment that results from emphasis on appropriate ethical conduct will result in significant benefit to U.S. corporations. It will allow mutual trust at all organizational levels to function as a more efficient control mechanism than was thought possible only a few years ago. Audit committee members must be selected with great care and provided the information and support they need to accomplish their very important functions.

NOTES

1. SEC Accounting Series Release No. 19.
2. Statement by Executive Committee of American Institute of CPAs.
3. SEC Accounting Series Release No. 165.
4. NYSE Listed Company Manual, Section 303.00, Corporate Responsibility, Audit Committee.
5. American Bar Association, "The Oversight Committees of the Board of Directors," *Business Lawyer* (April 1980), pp. 1355–1364.

6. SEC 1934 Act Release No. 25925

7. James C. Treadway, Jr., *Report of the National Commission on Fraudulent Financial Reporting (Treadway Report)* (Washington, DC: National Commission on Fraudulent Financial Reporting, 1987), pp. 31–48.

8. *Treadway Report*, p. 46.

9. David Packard, *A Quest for Excellence: Interim Report to the President* (Washington, DC, President's Blue Ribbon Commission on Defense Management, 1985), pp. 76–77.

10. Jeremy Bacon, *The Audit Committee: A Broader Mandate*, Research Report No. 914 (New York: The Conference Board, 1988).

11. James A. Giardina and Thomas S. Teighman, *Organization & Composition of Boards of Directors* (New York: Arthur Young, 1988).

12. Korn/Ferry International, *Board of Directors Sixteenth Annual Study* (New York: Korn/Ferry International, 1989), p. 16.

13. Ibid., p. 19.

14. Larry E. Rittenberg and R. D. Nair, *Improving the Effectiveness of Audit Committees* (Montvale, NJ: Institute of Management Accountants, 1993).

15. Price Waterhouse, *Improving Audit Committee Performance: What Works Best* (Altamonte Springs, FL: Institute of Internal Auditors Research Foundation, 1993).

16. Curtis C. Verschoor, "Status of Internal Control Reporting: COSO Ignored," *Accounting Today*, October 18, 1993, pp. 10–13.

17. *Smith v. Van Gorkom*, Del. Supr. 448 A. 2nd 858 (1985).

18. Leech & Mundheim, "The Outside Director of the Publicly Held Corporations," *Business Lawyer*, 1975, p. 1814.

19. *Escott v. BarChris Construction Corp.*, 283 Federal Supplement, pp. 688–692.

20. *U.S. National Bank of Galveston v. Coopers & Lybrand.*

21. *Brane v. Roth*, 590 North Eastern Reporter, 2nd Series, 587.

22. U.S. General Accounting Office, *Audit Committees: Legislation Needed to Strengthen Bank Oversight*, GAO/AFMD 92-19 (Washington, DC: General Accounting Office, 1991).

23. P.L. 102–42.

24. 12 CFR Part 363.

25. American Law Institute, *Principles of Corporate Governance: Analysis and Recommendations* (Philadelphia: American Law Institute, 1994).

26. Ibid.

27. SEC 1934 Act Release No. 14970.

28. Verschoor, *Journal of Accountancy*.

29. Price Waterhouse, *Improving Audit Committee Performance*.

30. Teachers Insurance and Annuity Association/College Retirement Equity Fund, *Policy Statement on Corporate Governance*, 1993.

31. Committee of Sponsoring Organizations of the Treadway Commission (COSO), *Internal Control: Integrated Framework—Executive Summary* (New York: Committee of Sponsoring Organizations, 1992), p. 1.

32. Ibid., p. 3.

33. Ibid., p. 19.

14

Why Banks Fail

Mark Cheffers

THE PROBLEM OF BANK FAILURES

Buried deep within the federal government's $4 trillion debt are hundreds of billions of tax dollars paid to bail out failed financial institutions. According to some estimates the cost of bailing out these institutions has added $2,000 to the effective debt load of every person in this country. Will the failures occur again? Could we sustain another round of failures? Have we earned the right to demand a higher level of competence and ethical standards from the financial service industry? In order to address these questions, we must first seek to understand the core reasons why bank failures have occurred.

In contemplating the problems associated with the massive bank failures of the 1980s and early 1990s, two questions are particularly relevant:

1. What were the true causes of the failures?
2. Have we taken the necessary steps to prevent a recurrence of such failures?

In addressing these questions, it may be helpful to apply the "Five Why" technique. It is known in management advisory circles that many Japanese companies have been successful in solving problems using a technique called "The Five Whys." The technique is relatively simple. One must ask the question, "why" (to seek casual links), at least five times at successively deeper levels. The method's objective is to identify the true sources of problems. Clearly, if one can find the true sources of problems, the probability of finding appropriate solutions is higher. Certainly, any analysis that seeks to identify weaknesses in the current internal/external control mechanisms responsible for preventing a repeat of the massive failures should be looked at seriously.

ANALYSIS OF BANK FAILURES, THE FIVE WHYS

1. Why did our financial system experience such incredible financial institution failure rates during 1980s and early 1990s?
2. Why are external factors most often blamed for failures and why is such blame inappropriate?
3. Why are there so many poor management decisions and why is it inappropriate to claim that existing internal and external controls are sufficient to prevent future failures?
4. Why have management teams so often failed in their efforts to keep banks from failing?
5. Why would manager/management desire to be dishonest, hire incompetent people, or refuse to acknowledge their inadequacies?

The First Why—Why did our financial system experience such incredible financial institution failure rates during 1980s and early 1990s? Many experts have addressed this question. Generally, the discussion has focused on the following:

1. Anomalies and/or changes in the industry structure including deposit insurance, interstate banking regulation, increased competition from nonbanks, and increase in the underlying risks of borrowers.
2. Incompetent, overly aggressive or corrupt management.
3. Overzealous regulation, tax law changes, deregulation and/or abrupt removal of tax incentives.
4. External forces such as oil price shocks, sharp interest rate changes, real estate market collapses, and foreign government instability.

Of note in the above list is that the four items relate to external influences, including several items which mandate internal bank compliance. Before discussing why these items cannot be associated directly with failures, it is important to understand why failures are attributed to them.

The Second Why—Why are external factors most often blamed for failures and why is such blame inappropriate?

INDUSTRY STRUCTURAL ANOMALIES

Deposit insurance anomalies are the most often-cited in the financial marketplace, and there are good reasons for this claim. Deposit insurance anomalies are best understood by considering the depositor. In a nondeposit insurance community, individuals have to evaluate the safety and soundness of financial institutions prior to depositing money. Such investigations reward safer banks.[1] This allows safer institutions, within certain boundaries, to pay lower savings rates, thereby bettering their competitive position.

On the flip side, deposit insurance equalizes the risks (and consequently savings rates) associated with nearly all deposits. This effectively takes away an entire profit center for the institution leaving the asset side of the balance sheet as the only substantial area for achieving profitability.

Further, it takes away incentives to build surplus (beyond statutory levels), as owners gain little advantage from tying up such funds. As a result of such a structure, owners are more likely to take higher risks with their investments because they can leverage them highly, utilizing essentially risk-free capital (in the form of insured deposits).

Consider, for example, an investment opportunity that will require a $10 million loan at 10 percent interest and a 5 percent cost of capital. Further, it will either result in $5 million in interest earnings over 5 years or a $2 million principal loss after 5 years. If an institution with a 5 percent capital ration makes this loan, it will be effectively investing $500,000 of the owners' funds and $9,500,000 of its depositors' money. In the case of the first option, the owners will net approximately $2.5 million in net earnings (5%/ 10% * $5,000,000 net earnings). This amounts to an approximately 100 percent annual return on investment. In the second option, the owners will lose approximately $4.5 million (principal loss plus $2,500,000 cost of funds). While this would seem to indicate that the owners were taking significant risks, the $4.5 million loss would only be incurred up to the extent of their investment in the capital of the company. Therefore, if the institution had only $1 million in capital and had invested in two such projects as above, that would represent the extent of its loss. Such a circumstance would have been betting $1 million in order to try to make $5 million ($2.5 million + $2.5 million) in distributable profits. Alternatively, the owners' loss would be capped at $1 million while the federal government would be forced to pick up the tab on $8 million in losses ($4.5 million + $4.5 million − $1 million).

While the above is significantly simplified, it exemplifies the profit incentive that an institution has in a deposit insurance system. This differs from a nondeposit insurance system, which would, according to risk/return theories, set the amount of interest paid to depositors at this institution at a level sufficient to properly remunerate the depositors for the real risk of the institution's investment. In such a market system it is unlikely that the proposed investment would be significantly reduced. For example, if the owners of this imaginary bank had to pay 9 percent for their deposits, their potential return would have been approximately $500,000 (1%/10% * 5,000,000) over a 5-year period. Their downside would still have been their entire investment of $1 million. This paints a dramatically different financial picture than under deposit insurance.

In short, the existence of federally insured deposit insurance creates an incentive for owners of financial institutions to take higher risks than they might otherwise take. The profit for this kind of statement is only too evident. Consider the massive loans granted to Third World countries in the 1970s at near-usury rates, without a proper understanding of where repayment was going to come from. Or more recently, billions of dollars of loans to build office space in cities with high vacancy rates were granted, simply because of tax advantages.

And yet, is this structural incentive the root problem causing bank failures? It certainly is a factor. The system currently rewards in the short term those owners that take higher risks. It is not at all clear, however, that such a strategy is either good for owners financially or good for the key officers professionally over the long term.

Consider the following example. I could leave a $100 bill on my desk at work. Arguably, that represents a structural problem in terms of my protecting my money. However, it would be inappropriate to say that the problem is the $100 on the table. The real problem, the failure of the system, only occurs if someone takes the $100. The failure occurs when someone gets greedy and commits an unethical act.

In a similar way, it is inappropriate to consider deposit insurance anomalies in the marketplace to be the true cause of bank failures. The problem is that key bank personnel have often taken advantage of such structural anomalies in inappropriate ways: They get greedy and they roll the dice. They realize that by investing in risky assets or refinancing bad debt with more bad debt, they can in the short term positively affect their remuneration, prestige, and/or power. Certainly, neither the institution nor the taxpayer benefits from this kind of risk taking. A number of other structural effects exist within the banking industry which adversely influence failures/viability. These include:

1. Shortening of product life cycles.

2. Differentiation and commodization of certain bank loan products.

3. Increased competition from nonbanks, financial markets, and foreign banks.

Shortened Product Life Cycles

Shortened product life cycles are increasing business failure risk of institutional borrowers. This is particularly apparent in the real estate and high technology industries. The Real Estate Owned and troubled loan portfolios of most major banks are still littered with such problematic entities. And yet, could we attribute bank failures to this external influence? Isn't the root cause of the problem management's decision to invest heavily in particular industries or its failure to adequately monitor the performance of those credits.

Differentiation of Bank Product Lines

As competition increases, differentiation of the bank product lines is a natural response. Banks that become "experts" at certain types of lending can expect to draw a certain concentration of those certain types of lending. While initially profitability may increase, an adverse effect on the overall viability of the bank can result if these loans cannot be participated or sold.

Commodization of Bank Product Lines

In addition to differentiation, commodization of bank product lines is also a major structural factor affecting financial institutions. Few bankers would deny that profitability in the industry has been adversely affected from the commodization of formerly bread-and-butter lines of business. The loan market for single-family residential loans and short-term lines of credit has been turned into commodities. As commodities, banks cannot make anywhere near the same profit margin as in the past.

Competition from Nonbanks

In terms of competition from nonbanks (insurance companies, trust funds, etc.) and financial markets (commercial paper, financial futures, bonds, etc.), the real adverse effect derives from these competitors taking away a bank's best customers. A natural selection occurs in banking. When a company obtains a certain bond rating level, it can raise both short- and long-term funds at lower rates than bank financing. This situation obviously puts banks in the position where their pool of potential borrowers is becoming riskier. Nevertheless, this factor is manageable.

OVERZEALOUS REGULATION, TAX LAW CHANGES, AND OTHER

Without going into much detail, it seems that the same analysis which was done without regarding the structural influences above can also be applied to these other external influences. External factors such as reduced depreciation write-offs, overzealous regulation, and so on, usually affect an industry equally. In this respect, they represent challenges to management, not causes of failures. Further, the institutions most adversely affected are often the ones which had put themselves at risk prior to the changes.

So what then can we conclude about structural and external problems?

Table 14.1
Banking Controls

Internal Controls	External Controls
1. By-laws and loan/investment policies	1. Legislative requirements
2. Loan review committees, etc.	2. Regulatory requirements and examinations
3. Employment screening procedures	3. Outside GAAP audits
4. Employee review and development procedures	4. Depositor insurer examinations
5. Supervision and review procedures	5. D&O and Fidelity Bond Company examinations
6. Segregation of duties	6. Liquidity provider analysis
7. Loan closing procedures	7. Certification requirements for appraisers
8. Internal ethics procedures	8. Outside counsel advice and activities
9. Budgets/targets	9. External board member input
10. Loan limit and borrower limit restrictions	10. Member or shareholder input

We can conclude that they are factors, but inappropriate management decisions and inappropriate internal/external controls within banking organizations are more critical factors in that they can be directly linked to failures.

Third Level "Why"—Why have so many failures occurred in the area of management decision making and why is it inappropriate to claim that existing internal and external controls are sufficient to prevent failures?

Failures in management decision making can derive from several distinct sources. First, management control (internal and external) and information processing framework in which decisions are made can be somehow deficient. Second, management may not be sufficiently competent or experienced to either recognize major problems and/or react to problems. Third, management has a different agenda than the long-term betterment of the corporation. And fourth, some combination of all of the above exists.

The first item is the subject of analysis in this section. The control system (internal and external) that exists in banking is comprehensive and exhaustive. It would seem after evaluating this system of controls that it would succeed in preventing the vast majority of bank failures (see Table 14.1). While this list is far from exhaustive, a quick review would seem to indicate that a vast array of controls over poor banking practices and hence, poor/imprudent management decisions exists. One would think that it would be almost impossible for a bank to fail considering these controls. And yet, the massive failures of the last fifteen years is self-evident proof of the ineffectiveness of such controls.

My own experience in investigating the failure of numerous financial institutions and lecturing on control systems tells me the following:

1. External controls often come into play too late. The old adage that auditors/ examiners are the ones to go onto the battlefield after the battle is over to bayonet the wounded is basically true.

   a. Banking laws are thought of by some as unjustified shackles on an otherwise ethical free market system. Such thoughts create a counterproductive environment where stretching a law's intent becomes heroic in a Robin Hood–like sense.

   b. External accountants are often more interested in selling additional services to clients than putting their best accountants on evaluating the loan loss reserve.

   c. Potentially effective external controls such as independent board reviews are ineffective because such people are subject to significant influence by management.

   d. Outside counsel is so closely wed to management that it is more likely to find ways for management to justify what it is doing, as opposed to counseling it to stay within its authority levels.

2. Internal controls seem to be easily manipulated. A great deal depends on the management culture. When key management people want internal controls to be ineffective, they generally are ineffective. In a management culture that wants internal controls to be effective, they generally are effective. However, even in such cultures, the commercial loan department and sometimes other departments (arbitrage, foreign currency dealings, and related) are treated differently.

THE WEAKNESSES OF INTERNAL CONTROLS

Internal control systems are rendered ineffective by several factors extant in many banking organizations. First, the nature of bank decision making is that it is highly dependent on the honesty and competence of a few individuals. Most banks have a narrow band of authority in management, which is responsible for practically all the risks undertaken. For example, the success or failure of a $10 million loan is highly dependent on the competence, integrity, and sometimes courage of a commercial loan officer and his immediate supervisors. This makes banks susceptible to dramatic and swift changes in loan/investment philosophy which can affect likelihood of failures.

Second, management does not often have a proper understanding of what makes up internal controls within organizations and how these controls need to be managed. Unlike textbook discussions of internal controls, internal controls can be broadly defined as those forces or influences which can restrict or guide human conduct within organizations. This definition does not limit the scope of internal controls to things like separation of duties or compliance procedure. Some of the most important and powerful internal controls exist in the form of hiring procedures, budgets, production incentives, and cultural incentives. For example, a cultural norm that promotes the "highest ethical standards" is potentially a powerful control tool.

Alternatively, a cultural norm that believes in being the "most aggressive" financial institution in town can also be a powerful control tool in terms of behavior. Obviously, these two different control tools can take the respective organizations in different directions. Internal controls can be divided into the following areas:

1. Organizational behavioral controls,

2. Organizational attitudinal controls,

3. Organizational accountability controls.

Organizational behavioral controls include things like security restrictions, lending limits, and supervision. These restrict what people might otherwise do if left to their own discretion.

Organizational attitudinal controls relate more to hiring, training, corporate cultural development, and so forth. These are much more powerful controls that go to a person's core beliefs. For example, if a key bank officer is secure in his understanding and belief about the importance of prudent underwriting standards, it is not likely that he will become involved in imprudent lending activities.

Organizational accountability controls can fall in either or both of the above two categories, but are best evaluated separately. These controls may consist of items like budgets, targets, incentives, and so on. A good example of the potential effect of controls such as these was Walter Wriston's famous (or infamous) demand for a 15 percent after-tax return from his managers at Citibank in the mid-1970s. The problem with that goal, however, was that the only place to get such a return was in foreign government lending. In an effort to achieve this performance goal, some of his managers almost led the entire U.S. financial system into disaster. For his efforts, Wriston was given the "Banker of the Decade Award."

I have mentioned these different internal control mechanisms to indicate both the positive and negative aspects of internal control systems when it comes to considering failures. Behavioral controls are often not significant factors in preventing bank failures. The reason is that they are often looked at as not being progressive, not taking into account the experience of the individual, and too restrictive. Further, obeying orders within some institutions is demanded. Dissent or any hint of disloyalty is punished.

It could be further argued that violation of behavioral controls (like house limits for foreign currency trading) is an all-or-nothing situation for senior management. There is a tendency to shy away from confronting certain key officers within organizations. Certainly, the head of audit may not want to take on certain personnel because of their power and ability to bully their way to what they want. How many times have we read in the last ten years about a senior executive in a financial institution losing a substantial amount of money from inappropriate house trading or flawed arbitrage deals.

It must be said, however, that strong behavioral controls can lead to positive attitudinal controls. For example, if lending limits are strictly adhered to and properly established, the lending officer begins to believe in their importance. This in turn can lead to better underwriting standards. Attitudinal controls can be the most effective in preventing failures. The reason is that such controls are the closest to the heart of individual conduct. It is difficult to override a key bank officer's disapproval of a transaction if he believes the loan/investment is not in the interests of an institution that he cares about and has a relatively high view of its reputation. Alternatively, it seems to be the area where most failures are likely to be originated. A culture of "aggressive, pompous, and prideful" attitudes can lead to financial disaster if not directed properly.

Accountability controls seem to fall in between the behavioral and attitudinal controls in their potential impact. In a culture of "prudence" in underwriting, aggressive goals are not likely to have a major negative effect. Alternatively, a culture of aggressive lending in a system of soft goals is likely to be much riskier.

I believe the above analysis leads the search for the real reasons for failures in the direction of management: its competence and honesty. The vast majority of financial institutions have sufficient internal controls in place and external controls present to promote appropriate conduct. The extent to which these controls are ignored, however, depends on a small band of authority in management. In particular, the overall culture established by top management can have a dramatic effect on failures.

WHY INTERNAL CONTROLS ARE SO EASILY BYPASSED

From the above analysis, it should be evident why internal controls are so easily influenced by management. The reason is that the most powerful internal controls, attitudinal and accountability, are the controls most influenced by senior management. Hiring, training, financial and nonfinancial incentives, cultural activities, kudos, and related items are the areas most focused on by management. Alternatively, behavioral controls such as policies and procedures are heavily affected by the above controls, which in turn are controlled by management.

Fourth level "Why"—Why have management teams so often failed in their efforts to keep banks from failing?

COMPETENCE OF KEY BANK OFFICERS

A strong case can be made that to be an effective banker one must have a significant wealth of knowledge about a number of industries in addition to financial services itself. The kind of loans/investment that can sink a bank are not commodities like house or car loans. These circumstances are always different. Anyone who has ever appraised properties knows that no two properties or commercial loans are alike. What this translates to is that "green" M.B.A. students or newly promoted consumer loan officers just cannot be expected to have the seasoning and experience necessary to know what is right for the bank and the potential borrower in the long term.

The same problems can be evident in bank officers who have been moved into positions they do not have the capacity to handle. I'll never forget the deposition of an individual who had been a board member for twenty years, a special loan committee member for ten years, and an executive committee member who had approved hundreds of millions of dollars in loans; he went into a near-catatonic state when asked what his primary responsibilities were as a director. When asked to describe the three basic methods used by appraisers in appraising commercial properties, he broke into a sweat and called for a recess.

Clearly, the above individual had no idea what he was supposed to know and may not have had the ability to learn. He had been looking the part for years. While this sort of incompetence may not be common in organizations, too often key loan officers are more like salespeople. They are capable of understanding the most complicated incentive systems even if they are not capable of understanding the underlying loan risks. They understand well what they have to do to get ahead in an organization and please senior management: If aggressiveness is demanded, it will be produced.

In summary, it is nothing more than common sense to assert that institutions with incompetent people in key positions are much more prone to failure than others.

DISHONESTY OF KEY BANK OFFICERS

The inherent structure of the industry, the limited band of authority and the ability to dramatically change bank cultures inherently makes banks targets for dishonest people. Dishonesty at the top levels of an institution can permeate an organization in a very short period of time. The best and most ethical cultures can be changed dramatically with a few key personnel replacements. Clearly, the honesty of key bank personnel is critical to the potential failure of an institution.

Fifth level "Why"—Why would managers/management desire to be dishonest, hire incompetent people, or refuse to acknowledge their inadequacies?

I know that many people in the industry and in regulation will not like where this analysis ends up. However, whether the results are likeable or not is irrelevant. Banks fail because human beings with flawed human natures, egos, and desires run them. Human nature is such that loan applicants take the rejection of loan applications very personally. This makes for a difficult interaction. This situation is made much worse if the person is a high-profile borrower, community business person, or developer. Human nature is such that it is difficult to pull out of a deal once it has been verbally agreed to, even if the terms change and/or the due diligence does not work out. In a recent case, a key bank officer had sought approval for a multimillion dollar commercial real estate loan. From the time of commitment to closing, information was obtained which indicated that the building could not even remotely operate in a viable manner. The bank officer was in awe of the "reputation" of the borrower and the loan closed anyway.

Human nature is such that key bank officers tend to believe they can do more (judge character, financial conditions, financial capacity, etc.) with less time, effort, and investment. Recent testimony was taken in a case where one key loan officer lent over $1 million in unsecured loan funds to a deeply troubled borrower because, "I felt like we had to help him." This officer lost sight of his position as a representative of a bank and acted more like a benefactor. Human nature is such that it is easier to follow a trend or perception than to buck same. If someone in the institution knows the customers and he is a good borrower or has a "strong" financial condition, that assessment is often accepted. If a competitor decided that lending on condominiums is a great idea, he is often followed into the market by other financial institutions. Human nature is such that people tend to first deny objective negative evidence or news which contradicts a key officer's perception of a situation. I can remember one circumstance where a loan officer testified to being told by the president to wash out his mouth with soap because he raised a question about the financial viability of a "favored" borrower. Human nature is such that business professionals push to earn more money, receive accolades, and build a reputation. A deep disparity often exists between the financial status of borrowers and lenders. A significant temptation exists for key bank officers to start believing that they should be living a similar lifestyle and in similar circles as that of many borrowers. I have seen this situation many times in the cases investigated.

CONCLUSION AND RECOMMENDATION

To some, this conclusion may seem like common sense but it isn't what financial institutions or bank regulators want to hear. It is also not a situation which the current failure prevention system handles well. Financial institution executives have steadfastly maintained that the primary problems causing failures are regulatory and systematic factors including the deposit structure, interstate banking regulations, external economic influences, and so on. When the argument is pressed, however, they acknowledge that these external factors have not been the real proximate cause of most bank failures.

Bank regulators also do not like to hear character-rooted explanations because they highlight their inability to keep institutions from failing. Elaborate and extensive control measures have been set up to give the appearance of greater control and protection from failure. Nevertheless, the one area which is almost impossible to regulate, in real time, is management competence and honesty. It is also difficult to regulate away failings of human nature, some of which do not manifest themselves until crises occur. If you remain unconvinced, ask yourself how many bankers and/or regulators adapted well to deregulation of the industry a decade ago. Failures to adapt were not a function of poor internal or external controls, but individual desires and bank-specific management cultures.

DOES A REFOCUSING OF REGULATION EFFORTS NEED TO BE MADE?

If the above assertions are correct, a different approach to bank regulation—one that addressed the primary problem at the point of greatest risk to a financial institution—needs to be considered. That point is at the time of initial underwriting and approval of large commercial loans or nonstandard investments.

The "five why" analysis reveals that banks fail primarily because of failure of key bank officers to conduct themselves in a prudent manner. The system that we currently have in place does not provide the one control it needs to put in place the most. That is an objective, comprehensive, and effective program of certification and ethics training. An analysis of the pros and cons of such a proposal would have to be the subject of a completely separate paper. The objections are substantial and need to be addressed one at a time. In short, however, one must ask whether a key bank officer is accountable in part as a fiduciary of the public trust. Further, one must ask whether lending/investing should be considered a highly skilled profession and treated like other professions. My simple answer to these questions is yes. As a result, any regulatory effort must be appropriate to the profession and related responsibilities.

Such a program, over the long term, will provide what similar programs in law, auditing, and other professions are beginning to achieve. Such a program could provide a safety valve for key bank officers being pressured by aggressive management or management cultures. It could also establish a minimum level of demonstrable competence over a broad area of banking knowledge. It can provide key officers with a downside for massaging loan deals to get them through and an upside by becoming certifiably qualified. In addition, special programs could be put in place for directors and senior banking officials.

NOTE

1. By safer banks, I am referring to those that have a high surplus ratio, invest in lower risk loans of appropriate size and diversity, and show a history of steady growth and performance.

IV

Lessons from the Past and a Look toward the Future

15

The Ethics of Financial Derivatives in the History of Economic Thought

Jay C. Lacke

INTRODUCTION

A recent *Wall Street Journal* editorial, "Geeks Versus Physiocrats" (Anon. [a], 1994) expressed concern over the prospect of federal regulators "tinkering" with the complex financial products called derivatives, instruments that the financial "techno-geeks," or "quants," seem to be introducing and altering at a dizzying pace. While financial innovation is said to serve valuable functions, such as enabling the pooling of risks, spreading of risks over time and across wider markets, and increasing liquidity, the *Journal* fears that derivatives will be viewed primarily as destabilizers of both the product and financial sectors of the economy (i.e., they are bad from a consequentialist perspective), as well as deceptive vehicles that further enrich the few "lords of finance" at the expense of the less-sophisticated (i.e., they are bad from a justice perspective).

The concern over derivatives escalated in 1994, due, in part, to huge losses, such as Proctor & Gamble's $100-million-plus write-off owed to interest rate swaps. According to Saul Hansell (1994a):

It is eyecatching, of course, when speculators like George Soros, or banks like Bankers Trust, acknowledge that they have lost millions of dollars by trading in the bond and currency markets, but that is the business they are in . . . it was far more surprising that the Procter & Gamble Company [would suffer such losses since] it is not a Wall Street firm, and its investors do not expect the volatility in its earnings due to trading positions that they would, say, for a firm like Salomon Brothers.

Hansell (1994b) has noted, furthermore, that hedge funds have come under particular scrutiny, raising the question, "Do the funds, with their sheer size and leverage and ability to flit from one market to another . . . , [sharply add] to the instability in global financial markets?"

In appraising the concerns about financial derivatives, and making suggestions about how to handle the issue, the *Journal* (Anon [a], 1994) cites Nobel laureate Merton Miller, who developed an argument using an analogy found in the history of economic thought:

Some of the complaints about the harmful social consequences of the financial innovations appear to be little more than updated versions of a once-popular 18th century doctrine known as Physiocracy, which located the ultimate source of national wealth in the production of physical commodities, especially agricultural commodities [where man's ability to "add value" was particularly significant]. Occupations other than commodity production were non-productive. Modern-day Physiocrats . . . automatically and enthusiastically consign to that nonproductive class all the many thousands on Wall Street and LaSalle Street now using the new instruments.

The issue of productive-versus-nonproductive labor, and, with it, productive-versus-nonproductive goods and services, has a long and substantial history in economic thought, and is not an issue limited to inquiry by the French physiocrats. Among other works, this issue represented a major theme the *Wealth of Nations* (Smith, 1776/1937). Adam Smith, who was strongly affected by the doctrines of the physiocrats, attacked the alleged premise of mercantilism, that value and wealth arose in exchange. Smith emphasized the importance of the production (value-added activity) of "vendible" commodities; services, which implied only the transfer of existing value from one party to another, were deemed nonproductive, though often necessary to the functioning of the productive sector of the economy and the consequent accumulation of surplus. In this sense, "good" services would be viewed as those that supported the growth and maintenance of productive (commodities-producing) capital, while "bad" service (e.g., household servants) would cause the wasting away of productive capital.

In this chapter, I will take a more extensive look at how the ideas of the historians of economic thought relate to the use and the ethics of modern financial derivatives. It will be seen that the consequences of speculation for the real economy of consumption and production, and the ethical issue of the fairness or justice of exchange, have long permeated the thought of economists with regard to finance, generally, and financial speculation, specifically. Moreover, financial speculation and derivatives, along with the speculators, have been viewed as providing valuable service to the real sectors of the economy. Contrary to what might be concluded from Miller's aforementioned quote, nonproductive workers and services were not necessarily considered to be economic noncontributors or, worse, wastrels.

ARISTOTLE'S FINANCIAL ETHICS

In a recent work on financial derivatives and ethics, Patrick Raines and Charles Leathers (1994: 201) state, "According to economic philosophy rooted in ethical considerations of the nature of market prices tracing back to Aristotle, prices play a socially legitimate role by reflecting true values and efficiently allocating resources." To the extent that economic institutions can help to get the prices right, and communicate accurate information about true values, such institutions play valuable roles in market economies.

For Aristotle (Polanyi, 1957: 100), "The economy, then, consisted in the necessaries of life—grain, oil, wine, and the like—on which the community subsisted [and commodity] prices should be such as to strengthen the bond of community; otherwise exchange will not continue to take place and the community will cease to exist." Like the physiocrats, Aristotle focused on the "real" economy, that is the product sector, and the effects that things like trade and prices had on the production and "just" distribution of commodities. Aristotle's treatment of finance, including its relation to commodity production, has been described by Amartya Sen (1993: 209):

He discussed a number of related issues together, including the following: the distinction between making profits from the production of [physical] output (at constant prices) and making profits by arbitrage (with constant quantities); the lower level of art involved in making financial gains in comparison with the science of commodity production; the evil effects—in generating monopoly and inequality—of the relentless pursuit of profits.

Sen (p. 211) continues on to make the point that,

It is clear that Aristotle is much concerned that, in some types of financial or business activities, there may be little social gain—in fact, considerable social loss—even though the activities yield handsome profits. . . . In the *Nicomachean Ethics*, Aristotle is concerned with the exploitive aspects [of finance and] points to considerations underlying the need for behavioral constraints in dealing with acceptable business and finance activities.

Early on, then, there was an explicit recognition of the idea that individuals pursuing their own rational self-interest may not be consistent with societal, or "community" welfare maximization, or with the norms of justice.

The concern over the exploitative nature of finance, especially as it relates to speculative instruments, has woven its way into most of the works of the major economists, carrying forward to the present. The theme is poignantly captured by Harry Markowitz (1991), who suggests that "The moral question is this: Suppose you can legally gain the reward and stick other people with the risk?" With regard to that question, Markowitz explains:

I now hold the hypothesis that excesses in [junk bonds] were primarily due to the availability of large pools of money whose ultimate owners or guarantors could be stuck with risk with little or none of the reward, without their knowledge or consent. Without those pools the junk bonds would mostly be a vehicle for bringing together those who need funds but do not have an investment grade rating with those who seek higher returns understanding the risk [i.e., they would serve a legitimate economic function].

Markowitz's statements raise, at least implicitly, two social issues regarding finance. One issue deals with the duty-based ethics, in the sense of justice or fairness, of certain dealings. The second issue is consequentialist in nature, having to do with the enhancement or degradation of economic efficiency. Both of these issues are apparent in Aristotle's thought as well.

ADAM SMITH AND PRODUCTIVE CAPITAL

Adam Smith (1776/1937) was likewise concerned that the individual pursuit of profits, especially through projects that seemed to promise high and quick profits, could be costly to society in general, as "Every injudicious and unsuccessful project in agriculture, mines, fisheries, trade, or manufactures, tends in the same manner [as prodigality] to diminish the funds destined for the maintenance of productive labour" (p. 324). Smith believed, however, that imprudent and unsuccessful projects, leading to a waste of capital, were relatively few compared to "prudent and successful" ventures, and it is interesting to recall his expressed logic for this circumstance (p. 325): "Bankruptcy is perhaps the greatest and most humiliating calamity which can befall an innocent man. The greater part of men, therefore, are sufficiently careful to avoid it." Of course, Smith was writing prior to the widespread development of limited liability through incorporation of Chapter Eleven of the bankruptcy code, and of an apparently greatly diminished social stigma associated with bankruptcy. But the main idea expressed here is that Smith, like many other historical economists, perceived some natural process(es) that tended to alleviate the danger presented by speculation.

Smith's concern over the potential waste of capital affected his position on limiting the legal rate of interest. With too high a rate of interest, according to Smith (p. 339):

the greater part of the money which was to be lent, would be lent to prodigals and projectors, who alone would be willing to give this high interest. . . . A great part of the capital of the country would thus be kept out of the hands which were most likely to make a profitable and advantageous use of it, and thrown into those which were most likely to waste and destroy it.

Again, the issues of finance were important not just in and of themselves, but because of their effects on society's real output and the accumulation of real wealth. In this sense, Smith's ethical precepts of virtue, as presented in *The Theory of Moral Sentiments*, were consonant with what was economically beneficial.

JOHN STUART MILL ON THE BENEFITS OF SPECULATION

John Stuart Mill (1848: 705), the world's leading economic theorist for most of the second half of the nineteenth century prior to Alfred Marshall, argued that speculation involved the purchasing of goods, by "speculative merchants" employing their "large capitals," in order to resell them at higher price, an action which tended to "equalize price, or at least to moderate its inequalities." For Mill (p. 705), the utilitarian consequentialist, speculation's societal effects were positive:

Speculators, therefore, have a highly useful office in the economy of society; and (contrary to common opinion) the most useful portion of the class are those who speculate in commodities affected by the vicissitudes of the seasons. If there were no corn-dealers, not only would the price of corn be liable to variations much more extreme than at present, but in a deficient season the necessary supplies might not be forthcoming at all.

Mill also attacked the premise that a speculator could profit by creating an artificial scarcity, driving up prices by his own purchasing activity and then unloading his goods at the higher prices. If a speculator had the power to raise prices by bringing his demand to the market, he would also cause prices to decline by bringing his supply back to the market. Moreover, Mill (p. 707) argued, just as the individual speculator could not benefit from a price bubble of his own doing, "neither can a number of speculators gain collectively by a rise which their operations have artificially produced." His argument in the latter regard proceeded as follows (p. 707):

Some among a number of speculators may gain, by superior judgment or good fortune in selecting the time for realizing, but they make this gain at the expense, not of the consumer, but of other speculators who are less judicious . . . it is not to be denied, therefore, that speculators may enrich themselves by other people's loss. But it is by the losses of other speculators.

In Mill, speculation plays a key role in stabilizing the real economy, while the financial cost of this speculation is, quite justly, absorbed by the speculators (who supposedly understand the risks) themselves. This line of argument, supporting speculation as ethical on both consequentialist and justice-based grounds, would be continued on, by others, to the present day—as long as speculators are using their money, not other peoples' money.

Mill (p. 707) further argues that speculator actions do not cause price volatility, and tend to graduate inflation (minimizing big price spikes) that does occur in the economy:

When speculation in a commodity proves profitable to the speculators as a body, it is because, in the interval between their buying and reselling, the price rises from some cause independent of them, their only connexion with it consisting in having foreseen it. In this case, their purchases make the price begin to rise sooner than it otherwise would do, thus spreading the privation of the consumers over a longer period, but mitigating it at the time of its greatest height: evidently to the general advantage.

Furthermore, it can be deduced that actions in the speculative market, representing speculators as a body, would give critical indications as to future price expectations, allowing economic agents to make appropriate and efficient adjustments which would further graduate the inflation.

Of course, something can go wrong when agents speculate, and Mill (p. 707) recognized that: If speculator expectations are "overrated," speculation will not moderate price fluctuations but, rather, will cause "a fluctuation of price which otherwise would not have happened, or aggravated one which would have." Under such circumstances, speculation would indeed be destabilizing. However, in response to this possibility, Mill (p. 707) offers a just and rational solution:

The operations, therefore, of speculative dealers, are useful to the public whenever profitable to themselves; and though they are sometimes injurious to the public, by heightening the fluctuations which their more usual office is to alleviate, yet whenever this happens the speculators are the greatest losers. The interest, in short, of the speculators as a body, coincides with the interest of the public; and as they can only fail to serve the public interest in proportion as they miss their own, the best way to promote the one is to leave them to pursue the other in perfect freedom.

Since the speculators' interest is in making a profit, and the speculators' success coincides with a benefit to society, society should allow the speculators to pursue their own, rational self-interest (their self-interest and ability will reduce failure, and they will, as if led by the Smithean Invisible Hand, benefit the society).

Mill also allows that some speculators will occasionally make very large, seemingly unjust, profits. However, Mill (p. 709) argues, this is appropriate as the "chances of failure, in this most precarious trade, are a set-off against great occasional profits." Moreover, looked at on average, "the chances of profit in a business in which there is so much competition, cannot on the whole be greater than in other employments" (p. 708), and as long as the markets in which financial speculation occurs are competitive, they will, according to Mill, serve to benefit the public even while generating a profit for the average speculator. From Mill's utilitarian perspective, speculation is ethical.

ALFRED MARSHALL'S ETHICS OF SPECULATION

As Raines and Leathers have pointed out (p. 197), "relatively unsophisticated derivative instruments" existed in the late 1800s and early 1900s, and that:

By the ethical precepts then in vogue, speculative trading in commodities futures and options and transactions at bucket shops (mock brokerage houses) were construed as forms of gambling . . . we note that if those ethical precepts still prevailed today, modern financial derivatives would be subject to a similar indictment.

With such instruments, the underlying asset was never exchanged, nor was it intended to be, and settlements were strictly in cash; the full intent of the parties was to profit through price changes. Moreover, according to Carol Loomis (1994: 41), such derivatives could be considered "to be gambling bets, in the sense that the outcome of the transaction is not under the control of either party to it."

In the early 1900s, bucket shops became outlawed, based on this premise that their deals were really wagers as opposed to a form of indirect insurance, and that such gambling was not socially beneficial. Based on the concept of the diminishing marginal utility of wealth, Marshall (1920: 112n) provided an economic rationale for this conclusion: "gambling involves an economic loss, even when conducted on perfectly and even terms [and that as a direct converse] a theoretically fair insurance against risks is always an economic gain." Again, economic outcomes (or consequences) were used to assess the ethics of derivatives.

Of course, speculation in futures occurred on the organized commodities exchanges of the late 1800s–early 1900s, and then, as today, most positions were closed out before the expiration dates of the future contracts. As Marshall stated (1921: 257):

Comparatively few transactions in futures lead to the actual delivery of the produce. . . . Either side may insist on completion: but that is generally effected through the organization of the exchange, by bringing together those who wish actually to deliver with those who actually wish to receive; the rest are "rung out." The practical effect of this is that anyone can as a rule buy a future, without being called upon to pay its price either at the time of making the contract [margins and margin calls existed], or afterwards.

Nevertheless, as Raines and Leathers (p. 198) indicate, "the right to require delivery of the underlying commodity established a legitimate intent, in contrast to the bucket shop deals; and the fact that the intent was so infrequently carried out was considered to be immaterial." Furthermore, state Raines and Leathers (p. 200), "speculation on organized exchanges was defended as being necessary to the efficient functioning of the real economy of production and distribution," a consequentialist defense to which Marshall also contributed.

Marshall (1921:253) invoked Aristotle's thesis that neither party to a trade can benefit except at the expense of the other party, but proffered that this conclusion "is true only of that particular form of trade which is classed as gambling, a class to which many varieties of trade speculation belong." Marshall (p. 253) continued on to explain how trade speculation provided benefits to both consumers and producers:

When a man, having superior knowledge as to horses, lays a wager about them on advantageous terms to himself, he effects an immediate increase in his property; but without advantage to the world. [But] when a man has superior knowledge that the supply of anything is likely to run short . . . and buys it either outright or for future delivery; then, on the assumption that his judgment is right, his action is to be regarded as constructive speculation. Such work adds to the world's wealth . . . for it tends to increase the supply of things where and when they are likely to be most wanted, and to check the supply of things where and when they are likely to be in less urgent demand. This is its most conspicuous service.

Marshall (p. 269) recognized that while there were business (e.g., commercial construction) where the firm "works only on contract under precise specifications, and contracts in advance for [its] chief supplies at fixed prices," most businesses involved the production of goods in anticipation of demand and the purchasing of inputs at variable prices. In this sense, production itself was a noble yet speculative undertaking. Marshall (p. 262) believed that the professional speculators in commodities futures were "generally alert, well-informed, and capable . . . [and that their] influence certainly tends to lessen the amplitude of price variations from place to place and from year to year," thus mitigating uncertainty associated with the inherent speculation in the real economy.

Marshall (p. 253) also explained "[a] less conspicuous [but] not much less important" service of constructive speculation, that being the producer's ability "to insure himself against the risk that the materials which he will need in his business will not need to be purchased at an enhanced price." Conversely, producers want to insure against the price of their output falling. Since these risks of price fluctuation, according to Marshall (p. 253), are "governed by broad causes over which [the producer] has scarcely any control, and the study of which requires knowledge and faculties other than his own," the speculative agent can play a valuable, specialized role. First, the speculator specializes in the "knowledge and faculties" needed to minimize the risks of speculation. Second, according to Marshall (p. 254), speculators specialize in pooling compensating risks:

the two sets of risks [regarding fluctuations in the prices of inputs and outputs] are in opposite directions, and it is obvious that much economy might be affected by setting these to neutralize one another. In spite of the abuses connected with them, organized markets [in futures] render many services to business men and to the world at large; and perhaps the chief, though not the most prominent of these is their indirect effect in so concentrating risks [which] will tend to extinguish each other.

Marshall (p. 255) observed that by providing this function of "indirect insurance," speculators could "take many grievous risks off the shoulders of others, [earning] a goodly profit for themselves [while bearing] little net risk [since] opposite risks would have partly extinguished one another." For Marshall (p. 256), the specialization of certain economic agents in financial speculation was clearly a beneficial division of labor in society, whereby "professional dealers [often rendered] great public services by carrying risks that would otherwise be borne by people whose special aptitudes lie in other directions."

Nonetheless, while Marshall (p. 255) argued that the "chief function of organized [commodity] markets is to accomplish what is in effect [an insurance]," he admitted that this function was conducted in a "manner [that] is rather that of wagering than insurance." He (p. 257) remained clearly aware of excesses and exploitation in the organized commodity exchanges:

It is true that this beneficent work is often marred, and sometimes overborne, by evil practices which intensify fluctuations and mislead honest dealers; but, for now, that evil has to be taken with the good. An organized market generally gives scope . . . for dealings in "futures."

In the preceding quote, Marshall obviously alludes to the idea that pure speculation has the benefit of increasing market liquidity, perhaps compensating for some of the unavoidable deception and fraud that occurs along with it. But he is not willing to simply accept the evil. He (p. 258) further comments that "by far the greater part of the [futures] transactions are in substance merely wagers to the effect that the price of produce will rise or fall, [and are sometimes] parts of large manipulative policy, which is in the main evil economically and morally," and goes on (p. 262) to discuss the evil, or abuse, thusly:

Manipulative speculation has many forms and many degrees. Its chief method is to create false opinions as to the general conditions of supply and demand. . . . False suggestion is a chief weapon; and it has so many shades, some of which seem trivial, that men of fairly upright character are apt to be drawn on insensibly to condoning and even practicing it.

Marshall (p. 263) notes that other, competing professional speculators are about as canny as the would-be manipulators, and, given "the forces of the modern Money-market and modern means of communication," these counterforces would tend to negate the manipulators. However, in their efforts, these manipulators "reckon on obtaining great, though willing assistance, from the folly of amateur speculators" (Marshall, p. 263) who wind up being "to their own great loss, a powerful force on the side of evil manipulations of the market" (Marshall, p. 264). If "the folly" of such amateur speculators could be overcome, then "the power of selling the future command of a thing [would come to be controlled by] honest and able men" (p. 264), with beneficial results for the society.

In this latter sense, Marshall is very close to Nobel laureate William F. Sharpe, who has claimed (Anon. [b], 1994): "In general, financial systems are self-governing. Given time, participants learn to use new instruments and procedures to improve overall welfare, not just to re-allocate wealth from one set of hands to another." With regard to the issue of the effects of "amateur speculators," Marshall is also close to the current thinking, per Hansell (1994a):

The [P&G] incident underscores the warnings that derivatives experts have been raising for some time: that the biggest potential problems in derivatives lie not with the banks and brokers who specialize in them, but in the [relatively unsophisticated and uninformed] corporations and investors that use them.

Marshall was, indeed, concerned about the dangers of speculation for the real economy and society generally, but he also recognized the difficulty with attempts to constrain it and cautioned against ill-conceived efforts to regulate or ban speculation. Sounding very much like Alan Greenspan (Harlan, 1994), who has suggested to Congress that legislation regulating derivatives could "have unintended consequences" and wind up being more hurtful than helpful, Marshall stated (1920: 598):

It is true that many of the largest fortunes are made by speculation rather than by truly constructive work: and much of this speculation is associated with anti-social strategy, and even with evil manipulation of the sources from which ordinary investors derive their guidance. A remedy is not easy, and may never be perfect. Hasty attempts to control speculation by simple enactments have invariably proved either futile or mischievous: but this is one of the matters in which the rapidly increasing force of economic studies may be expected to render great service to the world in the course of this century.

Marshall was cautious about intervention in the financial market, and felt that the natural forces of competition would effect the best outcome. In this, Marshall sounded very much like some of today's theorists, such as Sen, who feels that the complexity, cost, and problems of enforceability constrain effective regulation of derivatives. Sen (1993: 220) suggests, instead, that "an important part could be played by self-regulating rules and behavioral ethics." Likewise, comparison to Marshall is conjured up by Markowitz's (1991) statement:

In short, I take the story of mortgage properties at Salomon [Brothers] as an example of Adam Smith's thesis that individuals seeking their own self-interest through the marketplace will promote the common good, even if some of them are crude.

THE CONCERN OF W. STANLEY JEVONS

Jevons, one of the key theoreticians associated with the "marginalist revolution" in economics (using concepts like marginal utility and marginal costs, the "marginalists" ushered in an era of intense mathematization in economic theory), was ambivalent about speculation. He (1931: 87) believed that "knowledge of the real state of supply and demand [is so essential] to the smooth procedure of trade and the real good of the community . . . [and] the welfare of millions, both of consumers and producers, depends upon an accurate knowledge of the stocks [of important products]." As a result, Jevons supported many actions to gather and disseminate market information, and he claimed (p. 88), "Publicity, whenever it can thus be enforced on markets by public authority, tends almost always to the advantage of everybody except perhaps a few speculators and financiers."

Obviously, the last segment of the preceding quote attests to Jevons's distaste for speculators in commodities (or other real assets) or financial assets, though he recognized a benefit from speculation (p. 87):

Secrecy can only conduce to the profit of speculators who gain from great fluctuations of prices. Speculation is advantageous to the public only in so far as it tends to equalize prices; and it is, therefore, against the public good to allow speculators to foster artificially the inequalities of prices by which they profit.

As with certain analysts today, Jevons's primary solution to manipulation and deception in the derivatives market, and the negative effects that such activity has on the real economy, would be regulation that forced fuller, more timely disclosure. The effective disclosure solution would have also been preferred by the other major figures of economic thought up to and including Jevons, except where financial speculation was perceived to represent pure gambling (as in the bucket shops).

SUMMARY AND CONCLUSIONS

The history of economic thought has been permeated with a concern over not only Pareto efficiency but also by what Hersh Shefrin and Meir Statman (in James Ang, 1993: 48) label "informational efficiency [which] is achieved when prices are set as if all [economic agents] hold objective beliefs and information in common." Efficient prices are deemed to provide valid decision-making guidance to investors in both real and financial assets, reducing the risk of making bad investments, which waste society's capital. Asymmetric information can destroy informational efficiency. Furthermore, asymmetric information can destroy trust, with negative impacts on economic affairs and ethical behavior, as Kenneth Arrow (1973: 163) has observed:

the differential ease of communication when allied to self-interested behavior can lead to exploitation and mistrust. [Agents] with a perceived informational disadvantage fear manipulation and resist cooperating with persons or groups perceived to have an informational advantage.

The historians of economic thought would not have been quick to support federal regulation of the speculative markets, in part based on their liberal philosophy but also, and I think mostly, on their doubt over regulation's efficacy. These historical theorists, however, would support better disclosure and other efforts aimed at reducing informational and communications asymmetries in financial markets. Thus, they would pretty much concur with Michael Schrage's (1994) belief that:

The real issue surrounding derivatives today isn't their sophistication and complexity; it's the openness and honesty of the institutions that trade them. The truth is that it's easy to lie with derivatives. So some people do. Complexity isn't a reason, it's an excuse. . . . If your intention is to disguise and deceive, you can do that. . . . The greatest risk derivatives bring to the marketplace is not their complexity or volatility; it's the shadowy way in which they can be used by companies that would rather not tell the marketplace the truth about their investment intentions. The antiseptic for that infection is not more regulation; it's better and fuller disclosure.

Of course, "openness and honesty" is not one word. Disclosure—more openness—may help without being adequate, as remaining imperfections leave opportunities for self-interest seeking with guile. The "exchanges" still must be run by Marshall's "honest and able men." In this light, Ang (1993: 34) has cited the argument that financial managers should "recognize that—should a conflict arise—their duty to shareholders may be overridden by their duty to uphold the moral standards of professionals as servants of society." As such, the duty of financial managers to their principals lies within their duty as professionals, per R. F. Duska (1992: 163):

Professionals are expected to practice in ways that conform to prescribed ethical standards. To be a professional means, in part, to be committed to using professional skills and knowledge, in morally acceptable ways, for the benefit of society. There are several interrelated reasons, centering on the need for trust and protection against the abuse of power, that justify this interpretation.

Robert G. Ruland (in Ang, p. 35) has argued that "The duty [of financial executives] is derived from the general information providing nature of the reporting function and from the specific role the financial executive assumes vis-à-vis that function." Mr. Ruland suggests that all providers of information are bound by a duty to be truthful. However, Ruland concludes (Ang, p. 41):

I think that the financial executives may feel they have a conflict of duties with regard to public financial representation (disclosure) about their companies. They have a duty to the company to try to advance the corporate interests. This presumably includes making the company look as good as possible while complying with the letter of any disclosure regulations. At the same time, financial executives have a duty to the public to communicate the substance of financial transactions as clearly as possible.

Ruland then observes that the financial executive's duty to the firm may be seen as overriding the duty to the society "unless there is fraud or serious misrepresentation," and that the financial executive will fulfill his duty to the community by complying with accounting disclosure rules and regulations. Ruland (Ang, p. 41) challenges this assumption, arguing that "the duty to the public is paramount when accounting information is of concern." He further argues (Ang, p. 42) that accounting is an "objective-oriented activity" whose "rules are instrumental rules and should neither be always necessary . . . nor sufficient . . . for right behavior." To be honest, professional financial managers must, at times, either violate the established disclosure rules or go beyond the letter of the rules to fully inform the public, avoiding, therefore, any material misrepresentation or manipulation of the public.

Arrow (1973: 24) has argued that markets cannot function without some degree of trust, and has been interested in trust-enhancing social mechanisms that go beyond "private ordering instruments which support confidence in exchange." Regulation, disclosure rules, and the like represent institutions that monitor, sanction, and reward professional behavior that can enhance confidence, but these instruments are imperfect substitutes for trust. Derivatives, for example, frequently enable a user to get around a regulation or standard. In addition to fuller disclosure, or the informational efficiency that economists have long promoted, we must still deal with the issue of integrity, an issue which consumed, especially, Mill and Marshall. The "geeks" who generate these financial innovations, the dealers who market them, and the derivative users all share the burden of creating and maintaining trust.

REFERENCES

Ang, James S. (1993). "On Financial Ethics." *Financial Management* 32 (3) (Autumn): 32–59.

Anon. (1991). "Nobel Lessons in Finance." *Wall Street Journal*, May 14, p. A14.

———. (1994). "Geeks Vs. Physiocrats." *Wall Street Journal*, April 13, p. A12.

Arrow, Kenneth J. (1992). "The Division of Labor in the Economy, the Polity, and Society." In G. P. O'Driscoll (ed.), *Adam Smith and Modern Political Economy: Bicentennial Essays on the Wealth of Nations*. Ames, IA: Iowa State University Press, pp. 153–64.

———. (1973). "Information and Economic Behavior." Lecture to the Federation of Swedish Industries.

Duska, R. F. (1992). "Why Be a Loyal Agent? A Systematic Ethical Analysis." In N. E. Bowie and R. E. Freeman (eds.), *Ethics and Agency Theory*. New York: Oxford University Press, pp. 143–68.

Hansell, Saul. (1994a). "For P. & G., a Bet that Backfired." *New York Times*, April 14.

———. (1994b). "Huge, Secretive and for the Rich: Hedge Funds Under Scrutiny." *New York Times*, April 13, p. D.

Harlan, Christi. (1994). "Greenspan Suggests Derivatives Require Wholly Different Kind of Regulation." *Wall Street Journal*, May 26, p. A4.

Jevons, W. Stanley. (1931) *The Theory of Political Economy*. London: MacMillan.

Loomis, Carol. (1994). "The Risk That Won't Go Away." *Fortune*, March 7, pp. 40–52.

Markowitz, Harry M. (1991) "Markets and Morality: Or Arbitragers Get No Respect." *Wall Street Journal*, May 14, p. A14.

Marshall, Alfred. (1920). *Principles of Economics*. Philadelphia: Porcupine Press.

———. (1921). *Industry and Trade*. London: MacMillan and Co.

Mill, John Stuart. (1848/1987). *Principles of Political Economy*. New York: Augustus M. Kelley.

Polanyi, Karl. (1957). "Aristotle Discovers the Economy." In Karl Polanyi, Conrad M. Arensberg, and Harry W. Pearson (eds.), *Trade and the Market in Early Empires*. Glencoe, NY: The Free Press, pp. 64–94.

Raines, J. Patrick, and Charles G. Leathers. (1994). "Financial Derivative Instruments and Social Ethics." *Journal of Business Ethics* 13 (3) (March): 197–204.

Schrage, Michael. (1994). "Disclosure Key in Easing Derivatives," *The Boston Sunday Globe*, May 8, p. 80.

Sen, Amartya. (1993). "Money and Value: On The Ethics and Economics of Finance." *Economics and Philosophy* 9: 203–227.

Smith, Adam. (1776/1937). *An Inquiry into the Nature and Causes of the Wealth of Nations.* New York: The Modern Library.

———. (1971). *The Theory of Moral Sentiments.* New York: Garland Publishers.

16

Accounting Ethics and the Traditional Jewish Perspective

Rabbi Gordon M. Cohn

INTRODUCTION

Considerable research has focused on whether investors are fooled by mis-leading corporate earnings information (Watts and Zimmerman, 1986).[1] However, there has been less investigation of the ethical implications of such reporting. This chapter represents such an examination. It focuses on ethical dilemmas that result from the economic harm caused by reporting misleading accounting earnings. Talmudic[2] sources are used as a framework to analyze ethical issues.

The chapter does not present definitive opinions as to the ethically correct behavior in specific situations. Rather, it conveys a feeling for the Talmudic view of business conduct. An exposure to the traditional Jewish approach can benefit a wide range of readers. Gaining a familiarity with other cultural positions provides improved understanding of societal norms. The tradi-tional Jewish view is particularly informative due to the Judeo-Christian influence on Western societal mores. In addition to discussing the Talmudic view, the chapter uses Rabbinical teachings to identify and reflect on general ethical issues which are connected to earnings manipulations and misrep-resentations.

The American Heritage Dictionary defines ethics as a theory or system of moral values. According to this definition, in order to determine if a behavior is ethical it must be held up to a system of moral values. There is considerable theoretical debate about whether a religious perspective is use-ful for examining secular problems (see Appendix II). There have been only minimal attempts to actually use a religious approach.[3] This chapter rep-resents such an effort.

Talmudic law (*halakhah*) and its derivatives offer a well-articulated and thorough approach to proper business behavior. The observant Jew is required to follow these statutes. However, the universality and Biblical derivation of these laws enables the *halakhah* to provide the Jewish and non-Jewish, religious and nonreligious with insights regarding appropriate business demeanor.

Before beginning this discussion, it is important to understand the actual process of a Talmudic legal analysis. The analysis involves a Rabbinical authority analyzing particular actions to determine if they violate specific religious laws. There are several Jewish legal codes which present an overall legal framework. (Rabbis Caro and Asher's are the two principal codes). If the exact case being analyzed is not explicitly discussed, the Rabbinical analyst combines the codes' frameworks with his general knowledge of Talmudic principles. The multifaceted legal analysis of a law's applicability also elucidates fundamental ethical quandaries.

This discussion assumes the following scenario. An observant Jewish person works as a company's certified public accountant. This company has just adopted a new accounting procedure which will increase accounting earnings without affecting future cash flows.[4] The accountant is troubled by a possibility that the new earnings report might inappropriately increase the company's stock market price. The company is about to issue new stock and would directly benefit by an increased stock market price. The accountant suspects that the sudden decision to make an accounting change is related to the new stock issue. He goes to a Rabbinical authority and asks if his approval of the reported accounting earnings is a violation of any *halakhic* (Jewish legal) principals. The nature of accounting earnings and their correlation to stock market performance is explained to the Rabbi. The following is a possible description of the Rabbi's analysis.

After hearing the accountant's concern the Rabbi decided that laws related to overcharging are a logical place to begin an investigation. There is a Talmudic prohibition of overcharging based on the verse from Leviticus 25:14. The verse says, "When you buy or sell to your people you should not afflict your brother." From this verse the Talmud derives regulations about *ona'ah* (overcharging).[5] The ordinances are expanded upon in Chapter 227 of the *Choshen Mishpat* section of the *Shulchan Arukh* (the business section of the *Code of Jewish Laws*).

THE PHILOSOPHY UNDERLYING THE *ONA'AH* PROHIBITION

The analysis could being by reflecting on the general characteristic of the overcharging transgression. Rabbi Asher explains that *ona'ah* is a type of stealing since it extracts an unfair price. Furthermore, the word *ona'ah* used in the Pentateuch literally means afflict. Overcharging, besides causing financial loss, also precipitates psychological distress.[6] The anguish is caused by the victim's awareness that he foolishly and willingly gave the "thief" his money. The verse thus teaches that when someone is unexpectedly injured by a trusted merchant, he is both psychologically and financially abused.

It is important for accountants to realize that there are similar feelings of betrayal and loss of confidence when, for example, bankers and investors are duped as a result of an audit which allows misleading information on a company prospectus. These feelings can be as significant as the accompanying financial loss.

Supported by the above mentioned verse, the *halakhah* stresses the importance of merchants upholding public trust.[7] A merchant can be guilty of fraud even though the victim suffers no loss and does not realize he is being deceived. An example would be a customer being made to think that he received a bargain when he actually paid a fair price.[8] Rabbi Epstein[9] explains how, even if no mispricing occurs, it is forbidden for a businessman to artificially improve an item's appearance for the purpose of implying that is of a higher quality. He says that, for example, a slave's hair cannot be dyed in order for him to appear younger and that an animal can not be fed bran-water to look fatter.

An accountant who comprehends his Pentateuchal responsibility to prevent fraud will perform his duties with an increased carefulness. As indicated above, accountants can be violating their ethical responsibilities even if no scandal or loss results from their negligence. A financial statement which misleads investors to think that they are receiving a bargain for a fairly priced stock is an example of such a transgression. Thus, according to the Pentateuchal position, the Generally Accepted Accounting Principles (GAAP) charge for faithful representation is an ethical requirement even if no mispricing occurs.

Chief Justice Burger has expressed a similar view of the auditor's responsibility to insure accurate reporting.

By certifying the public reports that collectively depict a corporation's financial status, the independent auditor assumes a public responsibility transcending any employment relationship with the client. The independent public accountant performing this special function owes ultimate allegiance to the corporation's creditors and stockholders, as well as to the investing public. This "public watchdog" function demands that the accountant maintain total independence from the client at all times and requires complete fidelity and public trust.[10]

In contrast to the Pentateuchal position, Benston (1985) presents another approach to accounting ethics. He asserts that the accountant's expected diminished profits due to exposure of wrongdoings is greater than potential profits from such activities. Benston uses fear of lawsuits and loss of clients as sufficient motivations for insuring ethical behaviors. However, the above discussion has emphasized that the *halakhah* requires accountants to avoid endorsing misleading financial statements even if they know that no monetary loss will occur and that no negligence will be uncovered. It is obvious that such high standards of behavior cannot be established through fear of law suits and loss of reputation. Thus, it can be seen that Benston's notion of automatic regulation has only limited potential to insure ethical standards which are in accordance with *halakhic* opinions.

THE TALMUDIC LEGALITY OF EARNINGS MISREPRESENTATIONS

After the above attempt to gain a philosophical perspective, the Rabbinical authority would focus on the legality of earnings misrepresentation. His goal is to determine if earnings misrepresentation violates the *ona'ah* prohibition. The Rabbi examines all aspects of the potential infraction with the same precision as a secular judge. The Rabbi's examination could probe four independent issues.

The first is the issue of corporate versus individual corporate responsibility. There is broad discussion in both the secular and Talmudic literature as to the extent that corporate entities are bound by the same moral statutes as individuals. Schweiker (1993) asserts that even if the corporations have more limited ethical responsibilities, they are no less than an aggregate of managers, each socially obligated to the larger public.

However, evaluating an individual corporate manager's community obligation is problematic. Since single corporate activities can be performed by numerous individuals, it is difficult to allocate responsibility. Each person may claim that another member was the culprit. For example, suppose a corporate accountant misrepresents earnings while someone else in the corporation sells the company's stock at an inflated price. The accountant might claim that only the actual seller of the new issue is guilty of the *ona'ah* prohibition.[11]

The Rabbinic literature provides a framework for exploring the culpability of each of the above individuals. However, the complexity of analysis creates another obstacle. Due to the lack of straightforward guidelines, a corporate actor who is confronted by a subtle ethical dilemma may easily succumb to the less ethical alternative.

The second issue deals with indirect damages. While the Rabbinic law is strict with respect to direct damage, it is more lenient in terms of indirect damages. For example, if someone cuts a hole in a fence through which an animal escapes, there is a requirement to pay for the value of the lost animal.[12] The hole only indirectly caused the animal's disappearance, since the animal ran through the hole on its own volition. However, even though the courts cannot legally obligate payment, such action is forbidden and there is a moral obligation to pay for indirect damages.

Recapitulating, the legal standards for indirect damages are lower than for direct damages. If this logic is applied to earnings misrepresentations it mitigates the *ona'ah* prohibition. Assume that as a result of the misrepresentation the stock price increased. However, the accountant did not personally set the higher price. Rather, his earnings misrepresentation only caused the stock market to wrongly conclude that the company was financially strong. The stock market then independently raised the price. When the company sells additional corporate shares at an increased price, it is only a passive price taker. It did not fix the inflated price. Thus, the accountant has limited culpability for the higher price. The accountant's earnings misrepresentation is comparable to making the hole in the fence. In summary, although the accountant is prohibited from causing damages, ex post facto, he is only morally, but not legally, responsible.

Third, the prohibition of *ona'ah* implies that an article was sold for more than fair value (Rabbi Caro, Chapter 227). In the classic case, value is determined by examining the competitive market price.[13] For homogeneous goods, such as a bushel of wheat, the market price is readily available. However, corporations have unique stock market prices which are not directly comparable.[14] Thus, since a company's stock price has no readily available benchmark, its fair price cannot be established. An increase due to misleading information is not a violation of the *ona'ah* prohibition.

Fourth, *ona'ah* implies that the buyer was hurt by the merchant's actions. One can argue the stock purchaser's dominant interest is not whether a share of the company is worth what she is paying, rather, her consideration is if her investment will be profitable. The buyer wants to estimate the "true" value of the company only to the extent that true value is a predictor of shares' appreciation. The investor may be indifferent to misrepresented accounting earnings increasing the stock price as long as the price will not collapse to its "true" value.

Kaplan and Roll (1972) and Hand (1990), for example, claim that stock prices rise as a result of misleading accounting earnings. However, according to the analysis, only if the artificially inflated price eventually falls is there a transgression of the *ona'ah* prohibition. To this writer's knowledge, there has been no research which examines the ethically significant point of whether prices return to their nonmanipulated levels. Thus, the lack of evidence on investors being damaged by earnings misrepresentations is another source of leniency in terms of a violation of the *ona'ah* prohibition.

Nevertheless, one might speculate that the artificially induced price changes must eventually reverse. If a company in one period uses all its income increasing accruals, in the next period, having expended these accruals, ceteris paribus it should report a lower income. Just as announcing higher income increased the stock price, reporting lower income in the subsequent period should decrease it.

Second, assume that manipulating accounting procedures causes unsophisticated investors to inflate the stock price. One would expect that prices eventually return to a level which is commensurate with the company's true value. Further analysis is required to determine if the above conjectures are sufficient to establish a potential *ona'ah* transgression.

CONCLUSION

In conclusion, this chapter explored whether someone who misrepresents earnings has violated the Pentateuchal transgression of *ona'ah*. It found four reasons for leniency. They included the difficulty of pinpointing the transgressor in the corporate context, indirectness of the damages, the lack of a standard market price for a share of stock, and the problem of proving that investors are actually damaged. These reasons for leniency also represent general ethical issues involving the culpability of someone who misrepresents earnings.

This discussion could be expanded to analyze the applicability of other Talmudic business-related laws. Furthermore, there would be value in comparing the issues raised by the Talmudic approach with those examined by both secular and religious theorists. It is hoped that this chapter's examination demonstrates the possibilities of using Talmudic analysis to illuminate accounting ethical issues.

APPENDIX 1: ACCOUNTING THEORY RELEVANT TO ETHICAL ISSUES

1. It is well-known that researchers have shown a relationship between earnings and stock market prices. Thus, misleading accounting earnings can be expected to result in mispriced stocks. In order to help insure that buyers receive fair value, managers have a responsibility to issue earnings statements that are representationally faithful (Statement of Financial Accounting Standards #2). In other words, accounting numbers are expected to convey the actual substance of transactions, not just surface appearances. They should report to users the economic reality in a particular company. Unfortunately, due to the abstractness of the representational faithfulness concept, combined with flexibility of the GAAP guidelines, managers have sizable latitude in presenting their company's financial picture.[15] This latitude can allow managers to report misleading earnings which do not technically violate the present accounting regulations (Briloff, 1993).

2. Accounting earnings levels are not objectively determined. In particular, the size and timing of accruals directs this amount.[16] Beaver (1991) explains how the process of recognizing these accruals is a subjective process. It requires estimation, judgment, and discretion. Faithful representation should be used in determining accruals; however, it is not uncommon that the accruals become vehicles for pro-

moting both corporate and management's personal ambitions. For example, Healy (1985) has shown that managers manipulate accruals in order to increase their level of compensation.

3. Accounting and finance researchers have investigated a number of issues whose resolution could help resolve the ethical issues related to earnings manipulations and misrepresentations. They have concerns such as:

A. Are the stock prices set by the sophisticated or naive investors (Hand 1990)? The sophisticated investor discerns the "true" implications of earnings changes. If the sophisticated investor dominates, then accounting earnings are appropriately understood and stock prices are not distorted due to changing accounting procedures.

B. Does the stock market show a reaction to changes in earnings levels which are driven only by accounting earnings procedural changes which have no cash flow implications (Kaplan and Roll 1972)? Only those changes with such ramifications should influence stock market prices.

C. Is there a strong form of market efficiency (Fama 1970)? When this efficiency exists, stock prices incorporate all private information. According to this assumption, prices reflect the underlying implications of accounting procedural changes.

If researchers who investigated the above questions had concluded that the market can see through procedural changes, there would have been fewer ethical problems connected to earnings manipulations. Since investors are properly interpreting earnings levels, the reported earnings do not cause mispricing. The fear of fooling investors would not be raison d'être for requiring corporations to make greater efforts to clearly depict their financial position. However, Watts and Zimmerman (1986) claim that there have been no conclusive resolutions as to what extent investors are misled. In this writer's opinion, the situation has not changed since Watts and Zimmerman's assessment.

APPENDIX 2: AN INTRODUCTION TO THE RANGE OF VIEWS ON THE USEFULNESS OF THE RELIGIOUS PERSPECTIVE

Camenish (1986), Hauerwas (1981), and Rossouw (1994) question whether religion can provide society with a system of moral values. They claim that religious moral values cannot be separated from religious dogmas such as a prior acceptance of a supreme being, the righteousness of Biblical figures such as Moses or Abraham, and the existence of an eternal reward and punishment based on one's worldly deeds. If a secular society does not accept religion's basic precepts, it will be unable to utilize religion's morality code.

On the other hand, others have suggested that it is appropriate to employ a religious framework for examining even a secular society's business problems. Hus and Patterson (1993) recommend that educators searching for values to impart can derive them from doctrines espoused by religious institutions. They say that a description of a religious perspective can provide general guidance.

Furman (1990) describes a first-hand experience of religious idealogy positively influencing ethical values. She reports a college class reading *A Man For All Seasons* in order to become acquainted with Thomas More as a role model for withstanding temptations. While More's moral stance stems from Christian imagery, Furman argues that More's fortitude was inspirational for even her non-Christian students.

Cottell and Perlin (1990), in their accounting ethics textbook, call for more efforts to present religious views. They claim that such opinions can offer specific recommendations to those who would appreciate clerical counseling on specific ethical dilemmas. They observe that while there are many religious accountants, unfortunately there have been limited attempts to introduce theologically oriented ethics into the general accounting literature.[17]

Noreen (1988) uses the agency theory model for demonstrating the value of agent and principal adopting religious values. In agency theory, conflicts are lessened by a series of carefully constructed contracts which insure that the agent behaves according to the interest of the principal.[18] Noreen explains that in many instances designing a system of rewards and punishments which efficiently insure that agents engage in promised behaviors is infeasible. This is particularly problematic in situations where activities and their outcomes are nonobservable. Noreen uses the prisoner's dilemma case to show that the optimal solution can be reached more quickly when there is mutual trust among the participants.[19] He says that adoption of religious values is a mechanism for establishing trust.

Noreen's suggestion that the adoption of religious values would help to alleviate agency problems has particular relevance to the issues discussed in this paper. Earnings misrepresentation can be thought of as an agency false-signaling problem. The manager has an incentive to present misleading earnings in order to raise the stock price. The stock prices should be automatically lowered by the market in order to compensate for those companies with undetected inflated earnings levels. In a similar fashion to Akerlof's (1970) market for lemons argument, those companies whose earnings are appropriately conveyed are penalized by suspicious investors who automatically discount all managerial presentations. Thus, adoption of an ethical code could lessen indiscriminate discounting of earnings and generate more optimal outcomes.

NOTES

1. It is assumed that investors are nonsophisticated (Hand 1990) and that there is not a strongly efficient market (Fama 1970). Appendix 1 presents a description of relevant accounting theory concepts.

2. Talmudic law is a highly intertextual literature. It was written and developed over a 2,000-year period. The Talmud exists in two versions. The first version is the shorter, Jerusalem edition. The second version is the more extensive, Babylonian edition. The Talmud was written between 300 B.C.E. and 500 C.E. It records and synthesizes previous centuries of Rabbinical discourse. The contents of these volumes were later categorized and catalogued into easier-to-understand legal guides. These guides also expanded on the Talmudic discussions in order to consider a broad range of contemporary issues.

3. Cottell and Perlin (1990).

4. This chapter makes two assumptions concerning public disclosures of these procedural changes. First, there is an inefficient capital market such that many investors are not aware of these changes. For example, footnotes in financial statements may not be examined. Second, the disclosures are not publicized until after the initial earnings announcement. As a result of the second assumption, the reason for an earnings increase can be initially misunderstood. A topic for future discussion is the extent that the above-mentioned types of disclosures fulfill a company's ethical obligations. Perhaps it can be claimed that it is an investor's responsibility to utilize all publicly available information or to wait until an explanation of earnings changes is released before she purchases stock.

5. Babylonian Talmud Tractate Bava Mezia folios 50–59. Although the Hebrew word *ona'ah* literally means afflict, for the purpose of this discussion it is used in its legalistic sense to mean overcharging.

6. This psychological interpretation of the term *ona'ah* in a nonfinancial context is explicit in verse #17, which refers to exclusively emotional damage.

7. See Rabbi Epstein, chapter 228. There is presented extensive discussions concerning the importance of conducting business without deceptions.

8. Rabbi Caro, chapter 228. The laws in chapter 228 are derived from Leviticus 25:14 as well as 25:17. As mentioned in endnote #6, verse 25:17 provides a general prohibition against afflicting another individual.

9. Rabbi Epstein, chapter 228.

10. *The United States v. Arthur Young & Co. et al.*, 104 S. Ct. 1495, 465 U.S. 805 (1984), p. 1503

11. The hierarchical design of a corporation necessitates that many positions have extensive support personnel. An analysis could examine the degree of liability of passive supervisory personnel. A more subtle question is ascertaining the culpability of a person in the organization who is not directly involved, but could have prevented the earnings misrepresentation.

12. The Babylonian Talmud, Tractate Bava Kammah, folio 57.

13. Rabbi Epstein, *Arukh Halshulchan, Choshen Misphat*, chapter 227.

14. It might be possible to develop a mathematical model which uses Betas, returns, ratios, and so on, to determine a standard price for each corporation. This price might be used as a benchmark for measuring the amount of overcharges.

15. Briloff (1993) has suggested that requiring companies to all use identical accounting procedures would eliminate manipulations. However, Leftwich (1980) presents a strong argument against such a plan. He demonstrates that stockholders benefit from the GAAP's flexibility in accounting procedure requirements.

16. For example, choosing a more rapid method of depreciating assets increases expenses and lowers income.

17. A search of *Journal for Business Ethics*, 1989–1993, located only one Rabbinical opinion on business ethics.

18. Many of the GAAP guidelines can be considered as contractual limitations established to insure that the preparation of financial statements done by the accountant, the public's agent, is performed according to the best interests of the principal.

19. Below is a payoff table for the prisoner's dilemma problem.

		Player 1	
		C¹	D¹
Player 2	C²	10,10	−10,15
	D²	15,−10	−5,−5

The highest overall payoffs occur in situations where both players trust each other and choose {C¹C²}. If they do not trust each other, each one chooses strategy D, and they end up at {D₁D₂}. In this case, both lose.

REFERENCES

Note: In those cases where the exact date of publication for Rabbinical works is not available, the life span and birthplace of the author is presented for reference.

Akerlof, G. A. (1970). "The Market for Lemons: Quality Uncertainty and the Market Mechanism." *Quarterly Journal of Economics 84*: 488–500.

Arrington, C. E., and J. E. Francis. (1993). "Giving Economic Accountants." *Accounting, Organizations and Society 18* (2/3): 107–124.

Asher, Rabbi Jacob B. (Germany, 1270–1343). *Tur, Choshen Mishpat,* chapter 227.

Ball, R. J. (1972). "Changes in Accounting Techniques and Stock Prices." *Empirical Research in Accounting: Selected Studies 1972.* Supplement to vol. 10 of *Journal of Accounting Research*: 1–38.

Ball, R. J., and P. Brown. (1968). "An Empirical Evaluation of Accounting Numbers." *Journal of Accounting Research*: 159–178.

Beaver, W. B. (1991). "Problems and Paradoxes in the Financial Reporting of Future Events." *Accounting Horizons* (December): 122–134.

Benston, G. J. (1985). "The Market For Public Accounting Services: Demand, Supply, and Regulation." *Journal of Accounting and Public Policy 4*: 33–79.

Briloff, A. J. (1993). "Unaccountable Accounting Revisited." *Critical Perspectives on Accounting 4*: 301–335.

Camenish, P. (1986). "On Monopoly in Business Ethics: Can Philosophy Do It All?" *Journal of Business Ethics 5* (6): 433–444.

Caro, Rabbi Joseph. (Safed, 1488–1575). *Shulchan Arukh, Choshen Mishpat,* chapter 227.

Collins, D. W., and S. P. Kothari. (1989). "An Analysis of Intertemporal and Cross-Sectional Determinants of Earnings Response Coefficients." *Journal of Accounting and Economics 11*: 143–181.

Cottell, P. G., and T. M. Perlin. (1990). *Accounting Ethics: A Practical Guide for Professionals.* New York: Quorum Books.

DeAngelo, L. E. (1981). "Auditor Independence, 'Low Balling,' and Disclosure Regulation." *Journal of Accounting and Economics 3*: 113–127.

Epstein, Rabbi Yechiel Michel. (Belorussia, 1829–1908). *Arukh ha-Shulchan, Choshen Mishpat.*

Fama, E. F. (1970). "Efficient Capital Markets: A Review of Theory and Empirical Work." *Journal of Finance 25*: 383–417.

Furman, F. F. (1990). "Teaching Business Ethics." *Journal of Business Ethics 9*: 31–38.

Hand, J. R. M. (1990). "A Test of the Extended Functional Fixation Hypothesis." *Accounting Review* 65 (4): 740–763.

Hauerwas, S. (1981). *A Community of Character: Toward a Constructive Christian Social Ethic.* Notre Dame, IN: University of Notre Dame Press.

Healy, P. (1985). "The Impact of Bonus Schemes on the Selection of Accounting Principles." *Journal of Accounting and Economics* 7: 86–107.

Hus, H. F., and D. M. Patterson. (1993). "Ethics in Accounting: Values Education Without Indoctrination." *Journal of Business Ethics* 12: 235–243.

Jensen, M. C. (1978). "Some Anomalous Evidence Regarding Market Efficiency." *Journal of Financial Economics* 6: 95–102.

Kaplan, R. S., and R. Roll. (1972). "Investor Evaluation of Accounting Information; Some Empirical Evidence." *Journal of Business* 45: 225–257.

Leftwich, R. (1980). "Market Failure Fallacies and Accounting Information." *Journal of Accounting and Economics* 2: 193–211.

Noreen, E. (1988). "The Economics of Ethics: A New Perspective in Agency Theory." *Accounting, Organization, and Society* 13 (4): 359–369.

Rossouw, G. J. (1994). "Business Ethics: Where Have All the Christians Gone?" *Journal of Business Ethics* 13: 557–570.

Schweiker, W. (1993). "Accounting for Ourselves: Accounting and the Discourse of Ethics." *Accounting, Organizations, and Society* (Spring): 231–253.

Watts, R., and J. Zimmerman. (1986). *Positive Accounting Theory.* Englewood Cliffs, NJ: Prentice-Hall.

17

The Development of Moral Reasoning and Professional Judgment of Auditors in Public Practice

Daniel Brugman and Marcelle E. W. Weisfelt

In the professional judgment of auditors,[1] moral values such as independence, trust, responsibility, and integrity play an important role, implicitly and explicitly. Whether, and if so, how, individuals acquire these values and what role they play in the accomplishment of a professional judgment can be studied from the perspective of the cognitive developmental theory of Kohlberg (1981, 1984). This paper focuses on the personal, situational, and demographic characteristics that influence auditors' reasoning and decision making in professional moral dilemmas, that is, the professional moral performance.[2]

MORAL DEVELOPMENT

Moral norms and principles govern the social relationships between people. They define which social agreements, laws, practices, and customs are permitted, which rights and responsibilities belong to certain social roles, and which are applicable to all members of society. In this sense, morality refers to the governing of social interactions and not to individual values that do not pertain to social intercourse (Rest, 1979b).

The interests of one person or party can conflict with those of another. This is the case in a moral dilemma. In a moral dilemma, moral norms and principles have to be applied in order for a fair agreement to be reached between persons or parties. The considerations building up to a decision are referred to as moral reasoning.

Kohlberg's theory has, in particular, generated research into the reasons and considerations people use in making a decision in hypothetical moral dilemmas. According to Kohlberg, hypothetical dilemmas tap the highest stage of moral reasoning persons are capable of; this is called the moral competence. In hypothetical dilemmas, practical concerns to execute what is considered to be an ideal decision are of minor importance. Little attention is paid to the decision itself; rather, it is the reason or consideration with which the decision is justified which is of major importance.

Kohlberg's theory describes the development of the moral reasoning competence as a stage-like process. The development takes place in three levels: the preconventional, conventional, and postconventional or principled level. Each level consists of two stages. A higher stage of moral reasoning means that one is able to solve moral dilemmas more adequately, taking into account the different claims, needs, and interests. It indicates a more differentiated, more integrated, and more universal way of thinking than a lower stage. More differentiated means that individuals discriminate between different moral values and perspectives in a dilemma. More integrated means that they rank different moral values in a hierarchy and take into account more interrelated issues. More universal means more abstract ethical principles. Particular laws or social agreements are usually valid because they rest on such principles; when laws violate these principles, individuals can act morally in accordance with the principle and violate the law (Colby and Kohlberg, 1987).

The importance of Kohlberg's stages of moral reasoning for the auditing profession is demonstrated in the following example: Independent professional judgment means that one is not motivated in one's judgments by one's own interests (stage 2), nor by the interests of one's family and friends (stage 3), those of one's own firm (between stages 3 and 4), or by rules and laws only. Rather, it means that one is motivated by the ethical principles underlying the professional performance within the constellation of values and normative regulations within our society (stage 5/6). Auditors are, so to speak, contractually obliged to the society at large to "assure the integrity of the financial information on which our economy is based." (Wood, cited in Armstrong, 1989).

The Relationship Between Moral Competence and Moral Performance

Within the framework of the cognitive developmental theory, studies have been made on the moral reasoning of dentists (Bebeau, 1993; Rest, 1985), medical doctors in training (Candee, 1985), teachers (Oser, 1991), managers (Elm and Nichols, 1993; Weber, 1990), administrators (Stewart & Sprinthall, 1991) and auditors (Armstrong, 1987; Ponemon and Glazer, 1990). Some of these studies, however, pertain to the moral competence only.

Walker, De Vries, and Trevethan (1987) have reviewed the research on the relationship between moral reasoning competence and moral reasoning performance. They found a strong relationship ($r = .83$) between the moral reasoning competence and the moral reasoning performance of adolescents and adults in personal-life situations, which is higher than that reported by other researchers. In most studies, the moral reasons used in real-life or practical dilemmas were of a somewhat lower stage than in hypothetical dilemmas. In the work situation these results were confirmed by, for example, Weber (1990).

Several factors have been proposed that may account for lowering the relationship between moral competence and performance, one of these being the moral atmosphere of the institution in which the practical dilemma is embedded (Higgins, Power, and Kohlberg, 1984). This might be of importance for this study because several situational variables are used that are related to the workplace of the auditor.

A positive relationship between the level of moral judgment and clinical performance of medical interns is reviewed by Thoma, Rest, and Davison (1991). They proposed an index (U-index) indicating the degree of consistency of respondents in using moral reasonings that logically support their decisions in a dilemma. They found that the moral behavior of persons that are highly consistent in using reasons that support their decisions is easier to predict than the behavior of persons who are relatively inconsistent in the utilization of the reasons for their decisions. The effect of this variable will be tested in this study on the relationship between moral reasoning competence and performance.

According to Blasi (1980: 37), a clear relationship has been found between stages of moral judgment competence and independence of judgment. This is of special interest to this study because an auditor's role is to provide independent opinions. Blasi (1980) also made clear that the higher the stage of moral reasoning competence, the stronger the relationship between moral reasoning competence and moral behavioral performance. According to Kohlberg and Candee (1984), higher-stage subjects accept a greater responsibility in order to act consistently on their own judgment. In this study we will distinguish several audiences to which an auditor may feel some responsibility when making a decision and investigate the effects of the senses of responsibility on moral performance.

RESEARCH QUESTIONS

The research questions which we address in this study are:

1. Is moral reasoning as applied in hypothetical moral dilemmas related to moral reasoning applied in professional dilemmas among auditors?

2. Which personal, situational, and demographic characteristics influence professional moral reasoning?

METHOD

Sample

A sample of 200 subjects was randomly chosen from a population of approximately 2,000 auditors having at least two years' working experience in public practice, registered with the Netherlands Institute for Registered Accountants (NIVRA). The sample was stratified according to the size of the firm (seven large, international firms versus the rest) and to the subject's position within the firm (partner versus manager). The sample was considered to be representative for auditors working in the Netherlands. The 200 chosen auditors were asked by letter to participate in the study. One hundred and twenty-one subjects complied with our request, of which 7 were women and 114 were men. The average age of the respondents was 42. The youngest participant was 29 years of age and the oldest was 62. There was no selective attendance for size of firm, position within the firm, or region of the country. One hundred and five subjects complied with the criteria which Rest gives for completing the forms in a careful way.

Instruments

We presented the subjects with three paper-and-pencil instruments: (1) a questionnaire to obtain some background information on the respondents such as age, education, and size of the firm; (2) the Defining Issues Test (DIT, Rest, 1979a, 1979b, 1986), an instrument to assess the level of moral reasoning in hypothetical dilemmas (moral competence, Dutch translation by Hoeks, Dudink, and Wouters, 1984); and (3) the Defining Issues Test for Auditors (DITA, Brugman and Weisfelt, 1992; see Appendix), an instrument to assess the level of moral reasoning in professional dilemmas (moral performance).

The DIT contains six hypothetical moral dilemmas. For each dilemma the subject has to choose from three possible courses of action. After selecting one of these options, subjects have to evaluate moral reasonings: in each dilemma 12 statements are rated according to the degree of importance on a 5-point Likert scale. These will be called the importance ratings. Each of these statements reflects the kind of reasoning characteristic associated with one of the stages of moral development. Of these statements, 21 refer to the principled level. Finally, the subjects have to rank four statements which they regard as being the most important in relation to their decision about what action to take in each dilemma. These will be called the preference ratings.

The most widely used index from the DIT is the so-called Principled (P)-score. The P-score indicates the percentage of a subject's preference for considerations at a principled level when making a decision. (Thus, the P-score is based on the preference ratings). We also used the "humanitarian-liberal" score (hum-lib, in Rest, 1979b), which reflects the total number of decisions in the dilemmas that coincide with the decisions taken by students in moral philosophy with a high P-score. Finally, we used the Utilization (U)-score which reflects the degree to which subjects use reasonings which are consistent with their decision taken in each case (Thoma et al., 1991).

The Defining Issues Test for Auditors (DITA) contains 5 professional dilemmas and 73 statements, of which 17 refer to the principled level. The dilemmas are partly derived from Armstrong (1989). The instrument has the same format as the DIT. In addition, subjects are asked to score the degree of confidence they have in relation to the decision reached in each case on a 5-point Likert scale and the extent to which they feel a sense of responsibility toward different stakeholders: the client; the employees of the client; the code of responsible conduct[3]; society as a whole; and, their own firm. For the DITA, indices similar to that for the DIT were calculated.

On the DIT, subjects are asked as to what the protagonist in the dilemma ought to do, while on the DITA they are asked to consider what they themselves should do. While the DIT is constructed with the aim of tapping the highest stage of moral reasoning, the DITA is constructed with the aim of tapping the reasoning and behavior of auditors which closely resemble their actual behavior in professional situations.

The instruments were presented in random order, in one session, under the supervision of an experimenter. The sessions took place locally in small groups in one of the offices of an international firm of auditors.

RESULTS

The Relationship Between Moral Reasoning Competence and Performance

The P-score on the DIT ranges theoretically from 0–95. In our group of 105 subjects the minimum score was 12 and the maximum score was 63. The average P-score on the DIT was 36.5, which is in line with the P-score reported for CPAs in the United States by Armstrong. According to Armstrong, this P-score has to be considered as lower than might be expected because of their level of education. This seems to be the same for our group of auditors if the results in the Netherlands with other groups are taken into account (Table 17.1).

There was a low positive relationship between the principled moral reasoning (P-score) in hypothetical dilemmas and that applied in professional dilemmas (the preference ratings, $r = .24$, $p < .01$). The relationship on the principled level was much stronger, however, when all principled items were used (the importance ratings, $r = .62$, $p < .001$). That is, the more often principled reasoning in hypothetical dilemmas was rated as important,

Table 17.1

Average P-score in Hypothetical Moral Dilemmas (DIT)

Studies conducted in The Netherlands

Brugman & Weisfelt 1992, auditors	N = 19	Pscore = 38.2	sd = 12.5
Brugman & Weisfelt 1993, auditors	N = 105	Pscore = 36.5	sd = 12.1
Emanuels 1993 pers.comm, auditors	N = 50	Pscore = 33	
Van Holland 1986, psychology students	N = 96	Pscore = 43.2	sd = 11.8
Van Holland 1986, psycology students	N = 85	Pscore = 44.0	sd = 11.1
Boom Molenaar1989, high school students	N = 84	Pscore = 29.3	

Studies conducted in the United States

Armstrong 1987, auditors	N = 119	Pscore = 38.5	sd = 15.1
Armstrong 1989, auditors	N = 55	Pscore = 37.1	sd = 15.7
Rest 1979a(1), adults	N = 1149	Pscore = 40.0	sd = 16.7
Rest 1979a(2), college students	N = 2479	Pscore = 42.3	sd = 13.2
Rest 1979a(3), graduate students	N = 183	Pscore = 53.3	sd = 10.9
Elm & Nichols (1993), managers	N = 243	Pscore = 41	

the more this kind of reasoning was also considered important in professional dilemmas. When it comes to a decision to be taken and justified (preference ratings), however, the relationship weakened. The average P-score on the principled level was substantially lower for the professional dilemmas ($M = 22.2$) than for the hypothetical dilemmas ($M = 36.5$), even when taking the number of items and dilemmas into account. We will refer to this difference in principled moral reasoning as the "gap" between moral competence and moral performance.

A positive relationship was found between the principled stage of moral reasoning and hum-lib, in the DIT ($r = .43$, $p < .001$) as well as in the DITA ($r = .24$, $p < .01$). The P-score on professional dilemmas appeared to be a better predictor for the decisions taken in each professional dilemma than the P-score on the hypothetical dilemmas (Rest, 1986b).

The U-score on the professional dilemmas is higher than that on the hypothetical dilemmas. This means that the reasoning has been rated in a more consistent way with the decision taken on the professional dilemmas than with the decision taken on the hypothetical dilemmas. The correlation between principled moral reasoning in hypothetical and professional moral dilemmas was higher in the case of 80 more consistent auditors ($r = .33$; $p < .001$) than the average correlation in the case of the whole group of 105 auditors; there was no correlation at all in the case of 23 more inconsistent auditors ($r = -.05$). This confirms the hypothesis of Thoma et al. (1991) that the behavior of consistent persons is more predictable by means of the DIT than that of inconsistent persons.

The Effects of Personal, Situational, and Demographic Characteristics on the P-scores for Hypothetical and Professional Dilemmas

To investigate the effects of background characteristics on the P-scores, one-way analyses of variance were carried out, that is, the effect of each variable on the level of moral competence and moral performance was separately investigated. Table 17.2 provides an overview of the independent variables and their effects on the P-scores; where appropriate, reference is made to the category of the independent variable which related to the higher P-score.

By combining the effects of the independent variables on both P-scores, this provides an insight into the gap between moral competence and moral performance. The following variables were found to be most important: (a) the size of the firm (number of auditors), (b) differences in the sense of responsibility, (c) the region of the country.

(a) Table 17.2 shows that the "size of the firm" had no effect on the use of principled reasonings in hypothetical dilemmas, while it had a strong effect on the reasonings applied in professional dilemmas. The average P-score for the use of principled reasonings in professional dilemmas was, in the case of small firms (number of accountants < 10) about 30, and, in the case of large firms, 20. Given that there were no differences in the P-score of the DIT, the result is that the gap between moral competence and performance is smaller in the case of auditors working in small firms ($N < 10$) than compared to those working in larger firms (see Figure 17.1).

(b) A stronger sense of responsibility toward society and toward the client's employees contributed to a higher P-score on professional dilemmas, whereas a stronger sense of responsibility toward the firm had the opposite effect. The sense of responsibility had no effect on the P-score in the hypothetical dilemmas; consequently, the "backsliding" in principled moral

Table 17.2

Effects of Background Characteristics on Hypothetical and Professional
Principled Reasoning (univariate analyses)

Independent variables	Dependent variables	
	Pscore DIT	PrPscore DITA

personal characteristics

	Pscore DIT	PrPscore DITA
age younger than 50 years	*	-
time of registration as an auditor: less than 20 years	-	*
gender	-	-
qualifications for auditor	-	-
working at the university	*	*
current position (partner or manager)	-	-
membership of a board or professional society	-	-
religious background	-	-

characteristics of the work environment

	Pscore DIT	PrPscore DITA
size of firm (small firms with less than 10 auditors)	-	**
size of the place of business	-	*
region of the country (north)	-	**

client characteristics

	Pscore DIT	PrPscore DITA
percentage (non) profit clients: high nonprofit	-	*
specialization in a particular field: no specialization	*	-
annual turnover of the biggest client:<1 milliard	*	-
having clients listed at the stock exchange: none	-	-

sense of responsibility of the auditor toward

	Pscore DIT	PrPscore DITA
the client	-	-
the employees of the client: relatively high	-	**
code of responsible conduct	-	-
society: relatively high	-	**
firm: relatively low	-	*

Note: * indicates the probability of $p < .05$, ** $p < .01$. The number of * indicates the
strength of the effects.

reasoning was relatively small in the case of auditors who attached great
importance to their responsibility toward society (see Figure 17.2). These
results confirm the finding of Blasi (1980) that the higher the moral reasoning competence, the smaller the gap, and the hypothesis of Kohlberg

and Candee (1984) that higher-stage subjects have a stronger sense of responsibility than lower-stage subjects. However, the backsliding was bigger in the case of auditors who attached great importance to their responsibility toward their own firm. Auditors working in large firms attached greater importance to the sense of responsibility toward their own firm than auditors working in small firms.

(c) Due to the lack of effect of the region of the country on principled reasoning in hypothetical moral dilemmas, and a strong effect on professional moral dilemmas, the gap between moral competence and moral performance was smaller in the northern region than in the three other areas (see Figure 17.3).

These results are consistent with earlier research reported by Armstrong (1987, 1989) with CPAs, and by Weber (1990) with business managers. Armstrong (1989) reported the same relatively low P-score for CPAs in the United States. We support her conclusion that the P-score is lower than one might expect because of their educational level. Armstrong also reported that the P-score levelled off in older CPAs which she attributed to the education older CPAs had received. In our opinion, a different explanation should be considered. We not only found a negative correlation between moral reasoning competence and age, as did Armstrong; a stronger negative correlation was found between moral reasoning performance and the time of registration as an auditor (Figure 17.4). Consequently, the practice of auditing itself might have a negative influence. Some support for this interpretation can be found in the change in the sense of responsibility that was observed in auditors who had been registered for at least twenty years. They valued their responsibility toward their own firm more highly than any other kind of responsibility.

Weber (1990) found that the size of the organization had a negative effect on the moral reasoning of business managers in professional dilemmas. We found a comparable effect on the principled moral reasoning of auditors. Weber's hypothesis, that loyalty toward the organization has a depressive effect on the stage of moral reasoning in a professional judgment, was confirmed in our study of auditors. Of course, one has to accept that the sense of responsibility toward the firm is a good operationalization of this kind of loyalty. The results of our study also show that auditors employed in large firms scored higher in their sense of responsibility toward their own firms than auditors employed in smaller firms. Conversely, the opposite effect was observed in relation to the sense of responsibility toward the employees of the client. In our view, these results give credence to Weber's speculations about cultural differences between large and small firms.

Figure 17.3
Principled Level of Moral Reasoning by Region of the Country

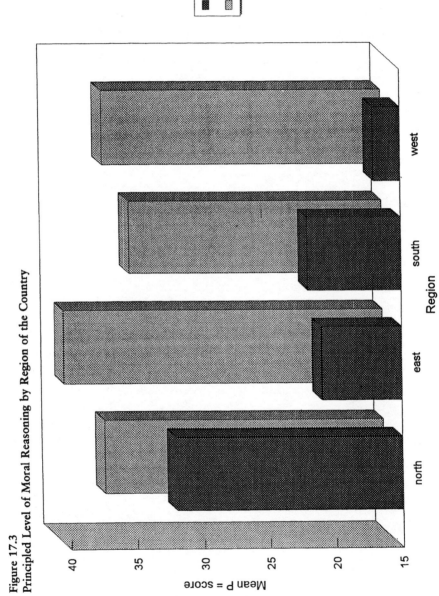

Figure 17.4
Principled Level of Moral Reasoning and Duration of Registration

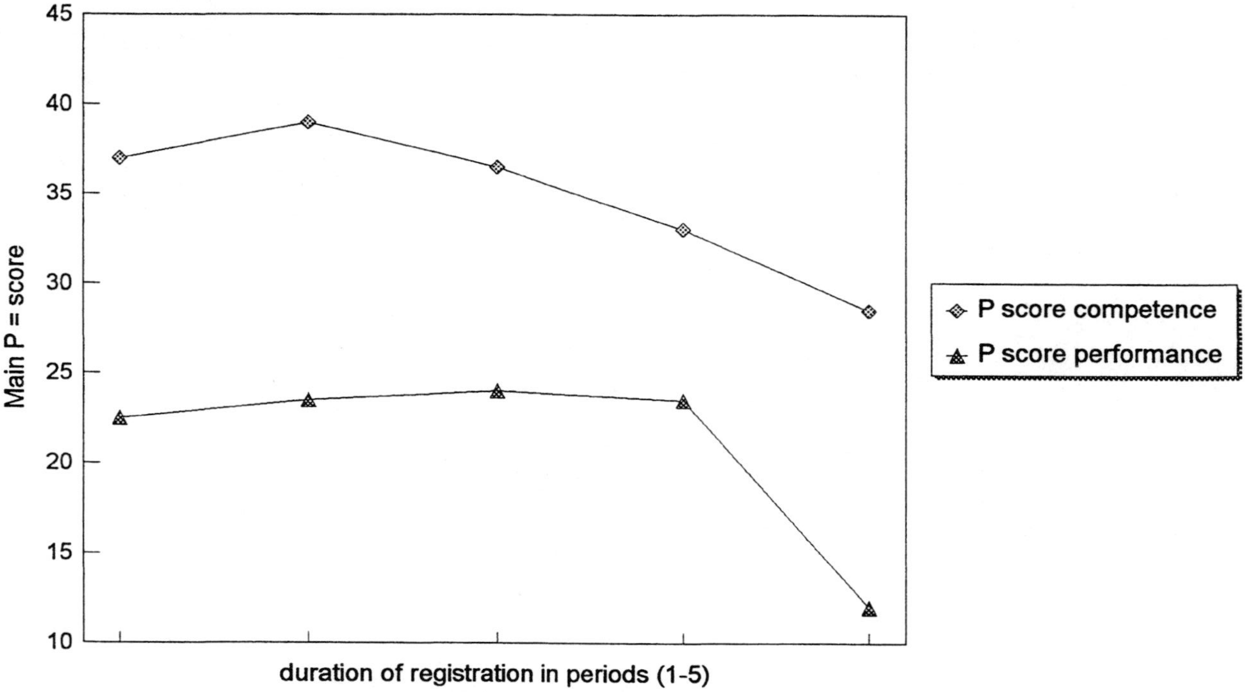

Note: 1 = up to 5 years, 2 = 6–10, 3 = 11–15, 4 = 16–20, 5 = > 20 years registered.

Predictors of Principled Moral Reasoning in Professional Dilemmas

In addition to the separate effects of each variable, the combined effects of various factors on principled moral reasoning in professional dilemmas were investigated by means of a stepwise multiple regression analysis. Important predictors of principled moral reasoning (P-score) in these dilemmas were: a higher score for moral competence; working in a small firm ($N < 10$); a high percentage of not-for-profit clients; being situated in the northern part of the country; a relatively strong sense of responsibility toward society and the employees of the client; a relatively low sense of responsibility toward one's own firm; and, a higher sense of certainty about the decisions taken in the dilemmas. These variables together explained 50 percent of the variance.

DISCUSSION

These results call for an explanation to be given to at least the following questions:

1. How can we explain backsliding within a theory about stage-by-stage development of moral reasoning?
2. What are the consequences of a relatively large backsliding in principled moral reasoning with regard to the confidence society places in the auditing profession?
3. Would an educational program to stimulate moral reasoning be the most effective method for decreasing this gap?

The *first* question concerns how we can understand the backsliding between moral competence and moral performance. The following explanations for this difference could be suggested.

Rest (1983) is of the opinion that as people pass through the different stages of moral development, they retain these different stages. Accordingly, the DIT shows the profile of all moral stages. Depending on the circumstances, a certain way of reasoning is appropriate. For example, one can imagine that a certain minimum stage, for example, stage 3, provides a satisfactory answer to a dilemma from daily life; higher stages provide no better insights. In that case, the need to develop considerations of a higher stage for this problem does not exist (Krebs, Vermeulen, Carpendale, and Denton, 1991). This explanation does not apply to professional dilemmas when considering the relationship between the use of principled reasoning and the decision taken in each dilemma.

Another explanation suggests that self-interest can activate a lower stage of moral reasoning. In attempting to explain the results of our study, it could be suggested that an auditor's sense of responsibility toward his own firm will bring greater rewards in terms of the auditor's own career in large firms than in the case of small firms. However, auditors working in large firms do not seem to have a higher stage 2-score, which corresponds with self-interest, than their colleagues, but a higher stage 4-score, which corresponds with the interest of the organization. It seems to be more obvious that large firms stress a formal attitude that is stronger than small firms and have a more extensive set of regulations. As Weber (1990) has pointed out, bureaucratic structures of large organizations might have a depressing effect on the higher stages of moral thinking. Working in a small firm seems to offer more opportunities in social practice, enhancing the use of principled moral reasoning in professional dilemmas.

The variables related to the working environment have a stronger effect on the principled professional moral reasoning than on the principled moral reasoning competence. In our opinion, these variables cannot directly influence professional judgment. Rather, we believe that they do so by virtue of the moral atmosphere within the firm and a specific local business culture in which the auditor operates (Power, Higgins, and Kohlberg, 1989).

The *second* question concerns the consequences of a relatively large "gap" in principled moral reasoning with regard to the level of confidence society places in the auditing profession. An appeal is made to the moral values as applied in the so-called "humanitarian-liberal" index. A positive relationship was found between the application of principled considerations and the hum-lib score. The results indicated that a large gap in the application of principled considerations was consistent with a different decision in one of the five professional dilemmas.

Like Armstrong, we also found a negative correlation between moral competence and age. However, moral competence decreases more strongly in relation to time of registration than to age. As far as there exists a crisis of confidence in the independent judgment of the auditor, in our view this cannot be explained by the emergence of an egoistic morality in a *new* generation of auditors. However, a morality in the present, older generation of auditors, which is influenced by the moral culture existing within the auditor's own firm, cannot be excluded.

The *third* question asks for an advice about the education and schooling of auditors based on these results. The above analysis suggests that the auditing profession should stimulate the use of the moral reasonings which auditors already have at their disposal in a professional judgment during education and schooling. In our opinion, the first priority should not be to improve the moral judgment in hypothetical dilemmas, as Armstrong (1987) has proposed, because of the relatively low average P-score for auditors' moral competence. When the negative correlation between the use of principled reasonings and years of registration is taken into account, these findings suggest that improvement should be undertaken not only or primarily during college years, but as an integral part of the continuing professional education of auditors. This education should also include stimulating auditors to become aware of cultural effects.

An intervention aimed at stimulating the moral reasoning in professional judgment must use professional moral dilemmas. As these cases are often already part of an auditor's training, the moral component should be more explicitly dealt with than has been the case hitherto. (See Rest, 1986). One of the assumptions of a stage-like development is that moral reasoning—characteristic for a certain stage—cannot be learned theoretically, even if the necessary logical operations are acquired. Specific experience is gained in social situations in which the auditor is asked to place himself in the position of different stakeholders and/or different roles. Experiencing moral conflict and being confronted by a colleague's considerations belonging to a higher stage provide the auditor with the experience needed to be able to formulate moral considerations of a higher stage.

When an intervention program for auditors is set up, it may be helpful to focus on weighing their different responsibilities. In our view, such an intervention program can only succeed with respect to the professional performance if it results in simultaneous changes in the workplace.

Appendix: An Example of the DITA Instrument Adapted to Practical Professional Dilemmas

You are approached by a potential client who is still an employee of a client corporation of yours, in which company he holds an important position. The employee discloses—unasked—that he wants to form his own company in competition with his employer and that he is in the final stages of negotiation with other key personnel of your client organization. Although the corporation operates in a growing market, continuity might be endangered if the plans of this employee materialize.

Question 1:

Would you reveal this scheme to your client?

_____ Yes, I would reveal or would give a hint to the client
_____ does not know, cannot decide
_____ No, I would give no information at all to the client

How sure are you of your opinion?

1	2	3	4	5
fairly unsure	somewhat unsure	somewhat sure	fairly sure	very sure

Question 2:

How important for taking your decision is each of the considerations mentioned below?
It is not a matter of a "yes" or "no" answer to each question: you need to ask yourself whether it is important to have an answer to the question before making your decision. (Note: of the total of 17 questions we list only a few by way of example.)

Appendix (continued)

Importance:

great	much	some	little	no
—	—	—	—	—
—	—	—	—	—
—	—	—	—	—
—	—	—	—	—

1. Whether, after the event, the client would reproach you that you had said nothing, although you had been informed?

2. Whether impartiality would be expected from you in this case?

3. Whether the client always behaved in an irreproachable manner toward his employees?

4. Whether you are obliged to maintain confidentiality with respect to unsolicited information?

Question 3:

From the list of questions above, select the four most important:

Most important ____   Second most important ____   Third most important ____   Fourth most important ____

Question 4:

How would you consider your responsibility in this case?

	much	some	little	none
a. with respect to your present client	—	—	—	—
b. with respect to the possible future client	—	—	—	—
c. with respect to the employees of your client	—	—	—	—
d. with respect to the code of responsible conduct	—	—	—	—
e. with respect to society as a whole	—	—	—	—
f. with respect to your firm	—	—	—	—

Note: This example is partially derived from one of Armstrong's dilemmas (1989).

NOTES

1. The word "auditor" as used in this chapter means "Certified Public Accountant" (U.S.) or "Chartered Accountant" (U.K.).

2. This chapter is written for a broad public and is a shortened version of a scientific manuscript. Readers interested in the extended scientific manuscript are invited to contact the authors.

3. As defined in Article 5 of the Dutch code of ethics: "The auditor refrains from any action that would be considered detrimental to the standing of the profession." (unofficial English translation)

REFERENCES

Armstrong, M. B. (1987). "Moral Development and Accounting Education." *Journal of Accounting Education* 5: 27–43.

———. (1989). *Internalization of Professional Ethics by Certified Public Accountants*. Unpublished manuscript.

Bebeau, M. (1993). *Influencing the Moral Dimensions of Practice*. Paper presented at the AME conference "From Moral Judgment to Moral Action," Tallahassee, FL, November.

Blasi, A. (1980). "Bridging Moral Cognition and Moral Action: A Critical Review of the Literature." *Psychological Bulletin* 88: 1–45.

Boom, J., and P. C. M. Molenaar. (1989). "A Developmental Model of Hierarchical Stage Structure in Objective Moral Judgments." *Developmental Review* 9: 133–145.

Brugman, D., and M. E. W. Weisfelt. (1992). *Overwegingen bij vraagstukken voor accountants in de openbare beroepspraktijk*. Vragenlijst. [Defining Issues Test for Accountants. Questionnaire.] Utrecht/Amsterdam: Department of Developmental Psychology, Utrecht University/Limperg Instituut.

———. (1993). "The Development of Moral Reasoning and Professional Judgement." *De Accountant* 100: 66–71.

Candee, D. (1985). "Classical Ethics and Live Patient Simulation in the Moral Education of Health Care Professionals." In M. W. Berkowitz and F. Oser (eds.), *Moral Education: Theory and Application*. Hillsdale, NJ: Lawrence Erlbaum, pp. 297–318.

Colby, A., & L. Kohlberg. (1987). *The Measurement of Moral Judgement. Vol. 1: Theoretical Foundations and Research Validation*. Cambridge: Cambridge University Press.

Elm, D. R., and M. L. Nichols. (1993). "An Investigation of the Moral Reasoning of Managers." *Journal of Business Ethics* 12: 817–833.

Higgins, A., C. Power, and L. Kohlberg. (1984). "The Relationship of Moral Atmosphere to Judgments of Responsibility." In W. M. Kurtines and J. L. Gewirtz (eds.), *Morality, Moral Behavior and Moral Development*. New York: Wiley, pp. 74–106.

Hoeks, C., (1984). *Overwegingen bij sociale beslissingen*. Vragenlijst. [Defining Issues Test. Questionnaire]. Universiteit van Amsterdam: Dudink and Wouters.

Holland, G. A. van. (1986). *DIT-onderzoek, betreft een speurtocht naar de validiteit en correlationele verbanden van de Defining Issues Test.* [DIT research, a quest into the validity of the Defining Issues Test]. Unpublished doctoral thesis. Amsterdam: UvA.

Kohlberg, L. (1981, 1984). *Essays in Moral Development* (2 vols.). San Francisco: Harper & Row.

Kohlberg, L., and D. Candee. (1984). "The Relationship of Moral Judgment to Moral Action." In W. M. Kurtines and J. L. Gewirtz (eds.), *Morality, Moral Behavior and Moral Development.* New York: Wiley, pp. 52–73.

Krebs, D. L., S. C. A. Vermeulen, J. I. Carpendale, and K. Denton. (1991). "Structural and Situational Influences on Moral Judgment: The Interaction between Stage and Dilemma." In W. M. Kurtines and J. L. Gewirtz (eds.), *Handbook of Moral Behavior and Development. Vol. 2: Research.* Hillsdale, NJ: Lawrence Erlbaum, pp. 139–169.

Oser, F. K. (1991). "Professional Morality: A Discourse Approach (The case of the teaching profession)." In W. M. Kurtines and J. L. Gewirtz (eds.), *Handbook of Moral Behavior and Development, Vol. 2: Research.* Hillsdale, NJ: Lawrence Erlbaum, pp. 191–228.

Ponemon, L., and A. Glazer. (1990). "Accounting Education and Ethical Development: The Influence of Liberal Learning on Students and Alumni in Accounting Practice." *Issues in Accounting Education* 5: 195–208.

Power, C., A. Higgins, and L. Kohlberg. (1989). *Lawrence Kohlberg's Approach to Moral Education.* New York: Columbia University Press.

Rest, J. R. (1979a). *Manual DIT.* Minneapolis: University of Minnesota Press.

———. (1979b). *Development in Judging Moral Issues.* Minneapolis: University of Minnesota Press.

———. (1983). *"Morality."* In J. H. Flavell and E. Markman (eds.), *Manual of Child Psychology: Vol. 3. Cognitive Development.* New York: Wiley, pp. 555–629.

———. (1985). "An Interdisciplinary Approach to Moral Education." In M. W. Berkowitz and F. Oser (eds.), *Moral Education: Theory and Application.* Hillsdale, NJ: Lawrence Erlbaum, pp. 9–26.

———. (1986a). *Moral Development. Advances in Research and Theory.* New York: Praeger.

———. (1986b). "Moral Research Methodology." In S. Modgil and C. Modgil (eds.), *Lawrence Kohlberg: Consensus and Controversy.* London: Falmer, pp. 455–469.

Stewart, D. W., and N. A. Sprinthall. (1991). "Strengthening Ethical Judgment in Public Administration." In J. S. Bowman (ed.)., *Ethical Frontiers in Public Management: Seeking New Strategies for Resolving Ethical Dilemmas.* San Francisco: Jossey-Bass.

Thoma, S. J., J. R. Rest, and M. L. Davison. (1991). "Describing and Testing a Moderator of the Moral Judgment and Action Relationship." *Journal of Personality and Social Psychology* 61: 659–669.

Walker, L. J., B. J. De Vries, and S. D. Trevethan. (1987). "Moral Stages and Moral Orientations in Real-life and Hypothetical Dilemmas." *Child Development* 58: 842–858.

Weber, J. (1990). "Managers' Moral Reasoning: Assessing Their Responses to Three Moral Dilemmas." *Human Relations* 43: 687–702.

18

Trust Is Good Business

Christopher S. Eklund

My career on Wall Street has led me to observe that successful firms put the financial success of their clients ahead of maximizing their own short-term income. This prescription is founded on three basic observations, each of which is developed in one of three parts of this chapter:

1. *The Myth of Cheating and Self-Dealing as the Best Source of Profit.* In this section, I argue that maximizing client welfare is the most reliable, long-term source of revenues and profits on Wall Street.
2. *The Economic Value of Principles.* This economic "best practice" is best governed by a set of principles that establish a link between the altruistic notion of "putting customer first" and business profits.
3. *The Need to Address Conflict.* Conflicts sometimes occur when a firm tries to serve different types of customers at once. Managers can get to the "meat" of these challenging issues by posing a few questions.

THE MYTH OF CHEATING AND SELF-DEALING AS THE BEST SOURCE OF PROFITS

In his 1863 essay *Utilitarianism*, John Stuart Mill argued that a man's own happiness is closely tied to the happiness of his fellow men: Individuals prosper chiefly by promoting the welfare of others.[1]

I think that were he alive today and challenged by ABC's Sam Donaldson to defend his philosophy, Mill would have called the "general happiness" principle not a noble virtue, but a self-evident and indisputable fact of life. I agree. Individuals *do* succeed by truly helping others fulfill their needs and desires. Nowhere is it more applicable than in the bare-knuckled world of capitalism, where favors are typically returned in kind: good for good, and eye for eye. Most of the time, however, the former is a far more profitable exchange for all parties involved.

People assume that Mill was referring to *spiritual* prosperity in his famous work. The fact is, the doctrine of utility applies equally to *financial* prosperity. Helping others pays on Wall Street. *Doing well by customers is more than soft-minded, feel-good lip service to moral values: it is good business practice.*[2] This may come as a surprise to people who believe that cheating the other guy is and always has been the ticket to long-term economic prosperity. In practice, however, Mill's "high-minded" moral principle happily coincides with the most exacting measures of financial success.[3]

Proof is in the numbers. Banks, securities firms, and mutual funds establish trust with their clients by helping them to achieve or surpass their long-term financial objectives. For a financial firm, this "trust" is really an intangible asset—a pervasive favorable reputation with customers based on many positive experiences they have had with both product and personnel. The impact on the firm's bottom line is quite measurable: Greater trust usually means greater customer assets in custody, which in turn generates greater earnings. Greater earnings are capitalized as a form of customer goodwill, which in turn perpetuates the cycle. This goodwill can be so strong that *customers may at times be willing to suffer lower investment returns and short-term declines in the values of their portfolios.* Unlike corporate restructurings or investments in productivity-enhancing equipment, the return on investment associated with a client-first orientation is nearly infinite.[4] As a result, a company should focus its efforts on serving customers rather than boosting reported earnings, ROE, or its stock price— if customers are happy, the rest will follow.[5] These institutional economics apply equally at the individual level.

That Mill's principle operates in reverse is well documented. The financial services industry depends on public confidence for its very survival. A run on the bank occurs when management abuses the public trust either through ineptitude or by putting its own interests ahead of customers'. Financial institutions are fragile things, held together not by marble columns and steel girders but a lot of faith in people and a few capital rules to prevent things from getting really bad. Even people who have never experienced a bank failure can vividly recall George Bailey, played by Jimmy Stewart in Frank Capra's 1946 movie *It's a Wonderful Life*, pleading with the people of Bedford Falls *not* to withdraw their money from the bank. "You're thinking of this place all wrong, as if I had the money back in a safe. The money's not here! Why your money's in Joe's house and in the Kennedy house and Mrs. Macklin's house and a hundred others. . . . We can get through this thing all right, we've got to stick together though, we've got to have faith in each other!"[6] As poor George learned, trust is

Table 18.1
A Question of Trust

A Question of Trust		
Americans' mistrust of Wall Street increases with their income level		
Do you think manipulation of the stock and bond markets is typical of what happens on Wall Street?		
By Household Income	Percentage Answering "Typical"	
Under $20,000	60%	
$20,000-$50,000	70%	
Over $50,000	78%	
THE WALL STREET JOURNAL / NBC NEWS POLL		

the only thing that ultimately matters in businesses built on other people's money.

While the old spectacle of a bank run is rare today,[7] the phenomenon is very much alive in several different forms. Large-scale mutual fund redemptions are commonplace whenever shareholders discover that their holdings are suddenly not worth what they thought they were, or that supposedly "risk-free" portfolios are in fact laden with speculative securities.[8] Salomon Brothers was nearly forced to close its doors in 1993, *not* when the U.S. government charged it with wrongful action, but when nervous creditors refused to extend any more credit.[9] Loss of public confidence, moreover, need not be rapid, news of scandal, corruption, insider trading, or self-dealing can cause "slow leaks" within the industry, resulting in slower account growth and declining assets under management.

Mill's principle, however, should not be misconstrued. Evidence suggests that helping customers is rewarding, while a loss of trust is certainly unrewarding. Yet it does not follow that self-dealing is always unprofitable (fortunes have been built on cheating and deception) or that all financial institutions put their customers' interests first. If that were so, the securities industry would enjoy a better public image than shown by a 1991 poll.[10]

Unfortunately, the criminal actions of Ivan Boesky and Michael Milken promote public confusion about the legitimate economics of Wall Street (See Table 18.1). Mutual fund pioneer John Templeton laments that religious professionals are relatively ignorant about the workaday world and how business operates. "They become caught up in the concept that if someone becomes rich, it's because he stepped on someone else," he says. "That's not true. You become rich by helping people."[11] With few exceptions, financial institutions that have enjoyed *long-standing* prosperity do exactly that.

THE ECONOMIC VALUE OF PRINCIPLES

Successful firms have put the financial success of their clients ahead of maximizing their own short-term income. This economic "best practice," however, is better governed by a set of principles than by hard-and-fast rules. The financial markets are far too complex to be incorporated into rules and formulas (anybody who's ever tried to beat the S&P 500 by watching P/E ratios and dividend yields knows that). In 1993, Merrill Lynch articulated five "Principles for Performance":

- *Client Focus*: "Our clients come first. They are the driving force behind everything we do."
- *Respect for the Individual*: "We believe in treating everyone with dignity, whether an employee, shareholder, client, or member of the general public."
- *Teamwork*: "We strive for seamless integration of services because in our clients' eyes there is only one Merrill Lynch."
- *Responsible Citizenship*: "We seek to improve the quality of life in the communities where we live and work."
- *Integrity*: "No one's personal bottom line is more important than the reputation of our company."

What's noteworthy is that all five principles *are* really embodied in the first, client focus. Respect for the individual requires that clients, members of the general public (i.e., potential clients), and employees be treated with dignity. Employees who are treated with dignity within the firm are likely to treat customers in that manner. Teamwork is a "best business practice" that has to do with serving all of customers' financial needs across a range of products and services in a noncontradictory way.[12] Responsible citizenship serves the communities of both employees *and* clients. Integrity puts the firm, whose primary focus is the customer, ahead of the individual. There is some similarity, I think, between the mission statements of successful firms. Three basic principles successfully guided IBM for seventy years— excellence; customer service; and respect for the individual. When customers stopped buying its mainframes,[13] however, new management replaced the original principles with a new set more directly focused on the customer.[14]

Watson Principles	New Principles
• Pursue Excellence	• The marketplace is the driving force behind everything we do
• Provide the Best Customer Service	• At our core, we are a technology company with an overriding commitment to quality

- Respect the Individual

- Our primary measures of success are customer satisfaction and shareholder value

- We operate as an entrepreneurial organization with a minimum of bureaucracy and a never-ending focus on productivity

- We never lose sight of our strategic vision

- We think and act with a sense of urgency

- Outstanding, dedicated people make it all happen, particularly when they work together as a team

- We are sensitive to the needs of all employees and to the communities in which we operate

Thomas J. Watson, Jr., son of IBM's founder, once said that to succeed, IBM must be willing to change everything—"except these basic beliefs."[15] Apparently this guidance worked: For decades, IBM stood virtually alone as the most respected, profitable, and imitated company in the world. Only after the company lost sight of its original mission—serving the customer— were the principles reexamined. The biggest difference between the old and new sets of principles is that the new more closely resemble a detailed set of rules—a prescription for behavior in an uncertain business environment. Beyond that, however, the most striking difference is the location and articulation of the "customer first" concept. The original second principle, "Provide the best customer service," has been elevated to first place and reworded to "The marketplace (i.e., customer) is the driving force behind everything we do." The corollary, "Our primary measures of success are customer satisfaction and shareholder value," follows closely behind. Wall Street analysts disagree about IBM's future prospects. What's clear, however, is that new management strongly believes there is a close correlation between a "customer first" strategy and business profits.[16]

THE NEED TO ADDRESS CONFLICT

Serving customers would be easier were there no potential conflicts of interest within the capitalist system. Unfortunately, that is not the case. Well aware of the potential for self-dealing, Alexander Hamilton restricted America's first national bank to borrowing and lending money: Shareholders and customers might be hurt, he argued, if the bank was allowed to

deal in government bonds for its own account.[17] The term "conflict" was
sharply defined in the banking scandals of the 1920s and 1930s prior to
Glass-Steagall. In one case, an investment affiliate of Continental Illinois
Bank & Trust Co. used public investment funds to purchase Continental
Bank stock, supporting the price.[18] In another case, Goldman Sachs Trading
Co., a closed-end mutual fund, bought controlling blocks of stock in large
banks, causing them to buy large amounts of Goldman-underwritten bonds.
Making matters worse, customer cash in the mutual fund was relent to the
banks at rates up to 20 percent.[19]

Resolution of internal conflicts is the first order of business for customer-
focused financial firms. Conflicts fall into several categories:

Illegal Conflicts

—Mutual funds buying stock underwritten or owned by their own firms[20]

—Banks owning securities firms, and vice versa[21]

—Using bank deposits or public investment funds to enrich the firm principals[22]

—Mutual fund portfolio managers buying stock in companies they are associated
with[23]

—"Front running" or buying/selling securities before executing customer orders

—Mutual fund portfolio managers using fund purchases to support personal investments

Structural Conflicts

—The combination of an investment bank and a brokerage house

Can research analysts and brokers be objective about securities underwritten by
their own firms?[24]

—Investment banks and brokerage houses engaging in merchant banking

By buying and selling companies for their own accounts, are they competing with
their customers?

Compensation-Related Conflicts

—Commission-based broker compensation

Can establish trading versus investing mentality, or encourage account churning

—Performance incentive bonuses

Paying fund managers to outperform the competition may encourage risk taking

—Underwriting fees

Large, up-front fees may encourage firms to underwrite risky or overpriced securities, and favor issuers over investors

Transactions-Related Conflicts

—Principal trading (the firm trading for its own account) in competition with clients

—Selling customers unsuitable securities (i.e., too risky or illiquid)

This incomplete list of potential conflicts underscores the challenge of operating ethically in the financial markets. The financial services industry *does* serve legitimate economic interests by moving capital from where it is plentiful to where it is needed, raising funds for expanding businesses, and providing liquidity to markets. At the same time, Wall Street professionals need to be constantly alert to inherent biases, client suitability issues, and structural inconsistencies. Brokerage firms that decide to enter the merchant banking arena, for example, must juggle the desire to create great wealth for themselves with the need to provide objective service to clients. Firms wishing to market new, high-margined products must put themselves in customers' shoes and do their best to honestly assess the solidity of their "chinese walls" to avoid public perception of bias in their research reports and broker recommendations. Finally, securities firms must ask whether broker payouts on assets under management, rather than transactions-based commissions, better serve the customer.

As difficult as they are, however, most of these questions can be answered by asking a second, simpler question: *In each case, is the financial success of our clients our primary consideration?* If not, the firm may be headed for trouble. When a firm subordinates the interests of clients to whom they have fiduciary responsibilities, the resulting loss of trust has a tendency to affect not only the firm itself, but also the financial markets as a whole. Merrill Lynch chairman Daniel P. Tully asks Merrill employees to take the "New York Times" test: As an employee, is there anything you do that you would not want displayed on the front page of the *New York Times*?[25] The idea of personal integrity on public display usually elicits the right kind of discussions.

A customer-focused corporate culture does *not* protect a firm against all misdeeds. On Wall Street, particularly within large firms, it is impossible to prescribe—let alone *observe*—the behavior of all individuals, nor is it desirable to do so. But such a culture does reduce the frequency of self-dealing relative to the opportunity for it to occur. Extensive media coverage of Wall Street scandals often makes immorality in business seem to be a historical high. That may not be the case, however, when put in the perspective of trading volume that is one hundred times as great as it was fifty years ago. The ratio of number of scandals—the amount of money lost in dishonest dealings—is probably smaller today in relation to the size of the total operation.[26]

It is nice when marketplace realities happen to fall in line with a moral code of conduct. But this is not just a coincidence on Wall Street, where the practical economics of long-term success and the principle of treating people right are one and the same thing.

NOTES

1. "Each person's happiness is a good to that person, and the general happiness, therefore, (is) a good to the aggregate of all persons," he argued. Helping other people leads to the general happiness of the population at large, which in turn leads to the happiness of the individual. Q.E.D. J. S. Mill, *Utilitarianism*, 1863. Reprinted in 1987 by Prometheus Books, Buffalo, NY, p. 50.

2. For the sake of clarity, this chapter will not focus on institutional traders. Although ultimately governed by the same economic forces as the firm, they are expected to be both greedy and opportunistic in taking advantage of market inefficiencies, a role that promotes liquidity and efficiency of the markets as a whole.

3. I see Mill's principle as complementary, not contradictory, with Adam Smith's notion of maximizing one's own well-being.

4. Not surprisingly, the stable returns of highly prized "fee-based businesses" (e.g., asset management companies) are the product of cumulative customer confidence.

5. Running a company by the financials is akin to playing baseball by watching the scoreboard—guaranteed not to achieve positive results.

6. *It's a Wonderful Life*. Copyright RKO Radio Pictures, 1946.

7. In recent years, these have primarily been confined to the S&L crisis of the early 1980s.

8. September 1994 was a watershed month for such events: Derivatives investments forced the first closure of a money market, fund, one of the nation's largest securities firms transferred management of its government securities mutual fund to an outside money manager after the portfolio value collapsed; as sophisticated an investor as Jacob Rothschild was shocked to learn that one of his own portfolios suffered a $700 million loss when the fund manager levered his position more than anyone suspected.

9. See extensive coverage in The *Wall Street Journal* and *New York Times*, 1992–1993.

10. *Wall Street Journal*, September 27, 1991.

11. Quoted in Tim W. Ferguson, "Long View Sees Global Gain, No Surge in Wall Street Graft," *Wall Street Journal*, September 24, 1991, p. A19.

12. The firm should attempt to serve a client's best interests: if, for example, debt financing serves a particular customer better than equity financing, the firm should steer the customer toward debt, even though the customer may have been originally solicited by the equity group.

13. It wasn't listening to customers who said that PCs and LANs had become the preferred products.

14. "Blue Period: Gerstner is Struggling As He Tries to Change Ingrained IBM Culture," *Wall Street Journal*, May 13, 1994, p. 1.

15. Ibid.

16. Louis V. Gerstner, IBM's new chief executive, ran two consumer products companies, American Express Travel Services and RJR, prior to joining IBM.

17. Robert A. Hendrickson, *The Rise and Fall of Alexander Hamilton* (New York: Van Nostrand Reinhold, 1981).

18. "You Can Bank on It: Without Glass-Steagall, History Will Repeat," by Benjamin J. Stein, *Barron's*, February 4, 1991, p. 16.

19. Ibid.

20. Prohibited by the Investment Company Act of 1940; Goldman and Continental are addressed here.

21. Prohibited by Glass-Steagall, but legal "separation" has been eroded by certain changes in the regulation.

22. Largely covered by Glass-Steagall and the Act of 1940, but was an issue in the S&L crisis.

23. In one recent case, a portfolio manager bought stock in a tiny company that had just hired his son.

24. Firms erect "chinese walls" to address this potential conflict.

25. This is also referred to as the "60 Minutes" or "Mike Wallace" test.

26. The view of John Templeton as discussed in Ferguson (see note 11).

Index

About the Editors and Contributors

HARRY W. BRITT is manager of operational audit and government compliance at Bath Iron Works.

DANIEL BRUGMAN is with the Department of Developmental Psychology at Utrecht University, The Netherlands.

MARK CHEFFERS is Financial Consultant and Investigator, Rhode Island Depositor's Economic Protection Corporation.

RABBI GORDON M. COHN is a lecturer in the Department of Accounting at Baruch College.

RONALD F. DUSKA is professor of philosophy at Rosemont College and Executive Director of the Society for Business Ethics.

CHRISTOPHER S. EKLUND is Vice President of Strategic Business Evaluation at Merrill Lynch & Co., Inc.

GERALD R. FERRERA is research fellow at the Center for Business Ethics and a professor of law at Bentley College.

ROBERT E. FREDERICK is research scholar at the Center for Business Ethics and associate professor of philosophy at Bentley College. He is the co-author, with Dr. Hoffman, Dr. Kamm, and Dr. Petry, of the Quorum book *Emerging Global Business Ethics* (1994), and with Dr. Hoffman and Dr. Petry of the Quorum books *Business, Ethics, and the Environment*

(1990), *The Corporation, Ethics, and the Environment* (1990), and *The Ethics of Organizational Transformation* (1989).

W. MICHAEL HOFFMAN is director of the Center for Business Ethics and professor of philosophy at Bentley College. He is the co-author, with Dr. Frederick, Dr. Petry, and Dr. Kamm of the Quorum book *Emerging Global Business Ethics* (1994), and with Dr. Petry and Dr. Frederick of the Quorum books *Business, Ethics, and the Environment* (1990), *The Corporation, Ethics, and the Environment* (1990), and *The Ethics of Organizational Transformation* (1989).

P. B. JUBB is with the Australian National University, Department of Commerce, at Canberra.

JUDITH BROWN KAMM is program director at the Center for Business Ethics and professor of management at Bentley College. She is co-author with Dr. Frederick, Dr. Hoffman, and Dr. Petry of the Quorum book *Emerging Global Business Ethics* (1994).

NANCY M. KANE is with the Department of Health Policy and Management at the Harvard School of Public Health.

JAY C. LACKE is assistant professor of management of the University of Maine at Augusta.

DAVID MOSSO is Assistant Director of Research and Technical Activities with the Financial Accounting Standards Board.

RICHARD N. OTTAWAY is the Chair of Management at Fairleigh Dickinson University.

NIKOS PASSAS is assistant professor of criminal justice at Temple University.

EDWARD S. PETRY is senior research associate at the Center for Business Ethics and associate professor of philosophy at Bentley College. He is the co-author, with Dr. Hoffman, Dr. Kamm, and Dr. Frederick, of the Quorum book *Emerging Global Business Ethics* (1994), and with Dr. Hoffman and Dr. Frederick of the Quorum books *Business, Ethics, and the Environment* (1990), *The Corporation, Ethics, and the Environment* (1990), and *The Ethics of Organizational Transformation* (1989).

FRANKLYN P. SALIMBENE is research fellow at the Center for Business Ethics and adjunct assistant professor of law at Bentley College.

ELAINE STERNBERG is a consultant, writer, and lecturer, London, England.

GARY L. TIDWELL is professor of legal studies at the School of Business and Economics, College of Charleston.

H. J. L. VAN LUIJK is director of the European Institute for Accounting and Auditing Research and professor of business ethics at Nijenrode University, The Netherlands.

CURTIS C. VERSCHOOR is senior research fellow, School of Accountancy, DePaul University.

MARCELLE E. W. WEISFELT is with the Limperg Institute, Interuniversity Institute for Accounting and Auditing Research, The Netherlands.

PATRICIA H. WERHANE is Ruffin Chair in business ethics at Darden School, University of Virginia and editor of the *Business Ethics Quarterly*.

ISBN 0-89930-997-6

HARDCOVER BAR CODE